PELICAN BOOKS
A228
BUDDHISM

Christmas Humphreys, born in London in 1901, is the
descendant of a line of lawyers. He was called to the
Bar on leaving Cambridge, and in due course became
Senior Prosecuting Counsel at the Old Bailey, like his
father before him. He is now a Commissioner of the
Central Criminal Court. He sits as Recorder of
Guildford and Deputy Chairman of Kent Quarter
Sessions.

Interested in Buddhism at an early age, in 1924 he
founded the Buddhist Society, London, which is now
the oldest and largest Buddhist organization in Europe.
As publisher to the Society, he has been responsible for
its wide range of publications, including six of his own.
His interest is in world Buddhism as distinct from any
of its various Schools, and he believes that only in a
combination of all Schools can the full grandeur of
Buddhist thought be found. In 1945 he expressed the
consensus of such doctrines in the now famous
'Twelve Principles of Buddhism' which, already
translated into fourteen languages, are in process of
being accepted as the basis of world Buddhism. In
1962 he was made Vice-President of the Tibet Society,
and Joint Vice-Chairman of the Royal India, Pakistan
and Ceylon Society.

BUDDHISM

CHRISTMAS HUMPHREYS

PENGUIN BOOKS

BALTIMORE · MARYLAND

Penguin Books Ltd, Harmondsworth, Middlesex, England
Penguin Books Inc., 7110 Ambassador Road, Baltimore, Maryland 21207, U.S.A.
Penguin Books Australia Ltd, Ringwood, Victoria, Australia

—

First published 1951
Reprinted 1952, 1954
Second Edition 1955
Reprinted 1958
Third edition 1962
Reprinted 1964, 1967 (twice), 1969

—

Copyright © Christmas Humphreys, 1951

—

Made and printed in Great Britain
by Cox & Wyman Ltd,
London, Reading and Fakenham
Collogravure plates by Harrison and Sons Ltd
Set in Monotype Times

TO
THE BUDDHIST SOCIETY, LONDON
ON THE OCCASION OF ITS
SILVER JUBILEE
19 NOVEMBER
1949

Contents

List of Plates

Preface

THE ideal author of this work would have a considerable knowledge of each part of the subject, be impartial in respect of all of them, and be able to see and to present the vast system as an integrated whole. No such person exists. There are experts in Theravada or Southern Buddhism; in the Mahayana or Northern Buddhism; in Tibetan Buddhism; on Buddhist Art and on Zen. But these are scholars working for the most part each in a limited sphere, and few if any of them know the condition of Buddhism in the world to-day. To compress the essence of all these subjects, in their due proportion, into a volume of this size is a bold ideal and a consummation easy to be missed.

My own qualifications are few. I have no knowledge of oriental languages, and therefore rely upon translations, yet as I belong to no one School of Buddhism I can study the whole dispassionately, and have done so for some thirty years. Of Buddhism in the world to-day I know more than most, and of Buddhism in the West as much as any man, having been the active President of the Buddhist Society, London, from its foundation in 1924.

Of these qualifications the practical experience is paramount. Any writer who studied the books in the Bibliography could tell of the bones of Buddhism; only a Buddhist can reveal its life. As Dr J. B. Pratt says in his Preface to *The Pilgrimage of Buddhism*: 'To give the feeling of an alien religion it is necessary to do more than expound its concepts and describe its history. One must catch its emotional undertone, enter sympathetically into its sentiments, feel one's way into its symbols, its cult, its art, and then seek to impart these things not merely by scientific exposition but in all sorts of indirect ways.' This is true, and a book on Buddhism should be subject to this test. Not that Buddhism is an emotional religion. Indeed, by the usual tests, it is not a religion so much as a spiritual philosophy whose attitude to life is as cool and objective as that of the modern scientist. But it lives, it lives tremendously, and is not, as the West is apt to regard it as, a museum specimen. To the hundreds of millions who are joyously treading to-day the Eightfold Way to Enlightenment it is the essence of life itself, and only by living it

can its truths be known. He who writes of it, therefore, should
have studied its principles and have loved and lived them too.

No attempt has been made to place Buddhism in the field
of comparative religion, for if all comparisons are odious
those between religions cause the greatest odium. Here is
Buddhism; let those who wish to compare it with anything
else make their own comparison.

I am grateful to those who have helped me so generously.
To Miss I. B. Horner, Hon. Secretary of the Pali Text Society,
who has read the chapters on the Theravada and made innumerable suggestions; to Dr E. J. Thomas of Cambridge,
who has done the same for the chapters on the Mahayana;
to the Bhikkhu U Thittila who checked what I had to say on
the Sangha, and as Librarian of the Buddhist Society, London, helped me to make the best use of its Library; to Dr
Reginald Le May who checked my chapter on Buddhist Art;
to Mr R. E. W. Iggleden for help with the Mahayana Canon,
and to Mr R. J. Jackson, who became a practising Buddhist
in 1905, for checking my account of the Buddhist movement
in England. Yet, though I have the approval of these and
other scholars for most of my facts, the responsibility for
their collation and my views upon them is entirely my own.

The illustrations were difficult to choose, and have been collected from all over the world. Many of the photographs are
my own; others were taken by Mr Frederick Page of objects or
photographs in my own or in the Buddhist Society's collection.
For the Chinese Kwan-Yin I must thank Sir Geoffrey and Lady
Burton. Mr C. Jinarajadasa, President of the Theosophical
Society, sent me the photograph of Colonel Olcott; Miss
Constant Lounsbery and Mme David-Neel provided their own
at my request, and the snapshot of the Bhikkhu U Thittila and
myself was taken in my London garden by Mr Colin Wyatt.

Some of these chapters have appeared in whole or in part
in various periodicals, and I am grateful to the Editors of the
Aquarian Path, the *Aryan Path*, the *Hibbert Journal*, *Rider's
Review* and the *Theosophist* for permission to reproduce the
parts already published.

Finally, I am deeply grateful to Miss Amy Bedwell and Miss
Angela Clare for their patient typing, and to my wife for her
magnificent support of an author attempting the impossible.

St John's Wood, 19 November 1949   T. C. H.

Introduction

WHAT IS BUDDHISM? In one sense it is man's understanding of the Teaching of Gautama, the Buddha; in another it is the religion-philosophy which has grown about that Teaching. To describe it is as difficult as describing London. Is it Mayfair, Bloomsbury, or the Old Kent Road? Or is it the lowest common multiple of all these parts, or all of them and something more? In the *Udana*, one of the Scriptures of the Theravada or Hinayana School of Buddhism, is recorded the parable of the Elephant. A number of wandering philosophers living near the Buddha had become noisy about their several views, and some of the Buddhist Bhikkhus, or members of the Order, described their behaviour to the All-Enlightened One. He listened and then gave them the parable. In former times a Raja sent for all the blind men in his capital and placed an elephant in their midst. One man felt the head of the elephant, another an ear, another a tusk, another the tuft of its tail. Asked to describe the elephant, one said that an elephant was a large pot, others that it was a winnowing fan, a ploughshare, or a besom. Thus each described the elephant as the part which he first touched, and the Raja was consumed with merriment. 'Thus', said the Buddha, 'are those wanderers who, blind, unseeing, knowing not the truth, yet each maintain that it is thus and thus.'

Buddhism is in fact a family of religions and philosophies, but which of its parts is 'right' or 'original' is opinion added to objective fact. The Buddha himself wrote nothing, and none of his Teaching was written down for at least four hundred years after his death. We therefore do not know what the Buddha taught, any more than we know what Jesus taught; and to-day at least four Schools, with sub-divisions in each, proclaim their own view as to what is Buddhism. The oldest and probably nearest to the original teaching is the Theravada (the Doctrine of the Elders), and this to-day is the religion of Ceylon, Burma, Siam, and Cambodia. The Mahayana (large Vehicle) includes the rest of the Buddhist world. But the peculiarities of Tibetan Buddhism, which covers Tibet and its neighbours, Bhutan, Sikkim and Nepal, are so marked that though it is part of the Mahayana it may be considered a School on its own, and the same applies to the Zen School of Japan, which is utterly different from any other School of Buddhism or from any other religion-philosophy.

The range of Buddhism is enormous. In time it covers 2,500 years; in space it covers the Theravada countries already described, the Mahayana countries of Tibet and its neighbours, and Mongolia, China, Korea and Japan, though China is not, in the sense that the others are, a Buddhist country. Buddhism is therefore to be found to the North, East and South of its parent country, India, while in the West its influence, first felt in Roman times, is growing rapidly to-day.

Its range of subject is no less vast, and it is in fact the most comprehensive and profound school of spiritual achievement known to history. Those who consider it simple, or to be expressed in a few brief words, have never studied it. In its earliest form it included the finest moral philosophy then known to man, with a range of mind-development and pioneer psychology second to none. In its developed form it includes religion, advanced philosophy, mysticism, metaphysics, psychology, magic and ritual; the triple Yoga of India – intellectual, devotional, and the way of action – and its own unique contribution to human achievement, Zen. In every country it raised the indigenous culture, and in China and Japan produced the greatest art of each country. Indeed, the art of the T'ang Dynasty of China, often described as the finest in the world, was largely Buddhist art, while throughout the East it has set such a standard of tolerance, gentleness, and a love of nature and the lower forms of life, that in religious history, where these virtues have not been prominent, it stands supreme.

The field of Buddhism may be considered in three concentric circles; the original Message, its development, and additions to it. Considering first the additions, all arise from the excess of tolerance which Buddhism displayed from the first. As it gently flowed into country after country, whether of a higher or lower culture than its own, it tended to adopt, or failed to contest the rival claims of, the indigenous beliefs, however crude. In this way the most divers and debased beliefs were added to the corpus of 'Buddhism', and embarrass the student to-day. Thus in Ceylon, Burma and Siam the worship of nature-spirits continues side by side with the later teaching, while in China and Japan the Confucian, Taoist and Shinto beliefs have modified the entering stream of Buddhism. Still more has the indigenous Bön religion of Tibet corrupted Tibetan Buddhism, itself already mixed with Hindu Tantric practices.

Several of the additions, however, came from internal weakness, and might be described as degenerations as distinct from developments. Thus the excessive worship of the written word, so striking a feature of Buddhism in Ceylon, as also the 'popular' form of Shin Buddhism in Japan, whereby the formal repetition of an act of faith suffices for personal redemption, are alike quite alien to the spirit of the earlier School.

A third type of addition comes from later grafting, such as the Tantric ingredients in the Mahayana Buddhism which entered Tibet in the seventh century, and the development of a priestcraft which claims to be essential to the layman's spiritual life.

It is far more difficult to distinguish between the Message and its development, for such a distinction implies a measure of certainty as to the Message. But what are the authorities by which to judge? The first, of course, is the Pali Canon of the Southern or Theravada School, but how much of this is in the form in which it was written down in the first century B.C., and how much of that was a fair rendering of the Master's words? These are matters on which no scholar would dare to dogmatize. Yet the pioneer work of the late Mrs Rhys Davids, who submitted the Pali Canon to a 'higher criticism', has made it clear that the Buddha's original message to mankind was cast in positive form. The positive Mandate recoverable in fragments from the somewhat emasculated and negative remainder shows, as common sense would expect, that his Teaching was a call to the More of life, not to the ending of it, and not to the running away from a relative and imperfect world. The ephemeral self must die, so much is clear; but what shall attain salvation, become enlightened, reach Nirvana, when this unreal, separative, misery-causing self is dead? The answer is man.

What else exists in the way of 'authority'? Some of the

Chinese Agamas are translations of Sanskrit works as old as
much of the Pali Canon, but the Sutras of the Mahayana
School, though put into the Buddha's mouth, are clearly the
work of minds which lived from three to seven hundred years
after his passing. There remains the esoteric tradition, none
the less potent, none the less reliable for the fact that it is
nowhere, in more than fragments, written down. The Theravada, the Southern School of the Pali Canon, ignores the
story in the *Samyutta Nikaya* of the simsapa leaves. Which
were the more numerous, the Buddha asked his disciples,
taking a handful of leaves from the forest floor, the leaves
in his hand or those in the forest about him? The reply being
given, he explained that such was the relation of the truths
which he had revealed to those which he knew but had not
revealed. Of all his knowledge he taught, he said, only those
things which conduced to the holy life, to peace of mind,
to the finding of Nirvana. Ignoring this, the Theravadins
cling to a single phrase in the *Mahaparinibbana Sutta*, to the
effect that the Buddha was not one who had the closed fist
of a teacher who kept some things back, an obvious reference to his major task on earth, to make available to all
mankind the principles of the Wisdom which the Brahmans
had hitherto preserved as their tight monopoly.

The Mahayana School has no such doubts or differences.
All its sects admit the distinction between truths available to
all and those power-producing secrets which are taught only
by word of mouth from *guru* to *chelas* as the latter prove, by
their moral character, worthy to be given them. The mathe-
matician who lectured a class of children on the Integral
Calculus would be a fool; in matters of spiritual knowledge
the last word lies with the *Tao Te Ching*: 'He who speaks
does not know; he who knows does not speak.'

In fact, the search for Buddhist authority is always vain.
'Do not go by hearsay', said the Buddha in his famous advice to the Kalamas, 'nor by what is handed down by others,
nor by what is stated on the authority of your traditional
teachings. Do not go by reasons, nor by inference, nor by
arguments as to method, nor by reflection on and approval of
an opinion, nor out of respect, thinking a recluse must be
deferred to . . .' What, then, is the test? The Sutta quoted,
like most of the Pali Canon, first gives the answer negatively.
'When these teachings, followed out and put into practice,

One, and do not delay with enquiries
rovenance, nor the name and tribe of
Now is the moment of salvation, of the
ffering. 'Sufficient unto the day is the
undoing.

build no house upon it; a river – cling
to either of them; a gymnasium – use it
d on the apparatus of circumstance; a
d walk on! The 'passing show' is to be
njoyed nor ignored, for behind the show
d-Only. There are some to whom the
id is frightening; their eyes are as yet
he road ahead and they cannot see the
eed to focus on infinity, and all men have
to gaze upon something, albeit a Mind-
ust so much ahead of them, and not too
ts of God and gods, of Saints and Saviours.
do not exist; they are thoughts within an
e-existing Mind. Hence *Amida*, for some
he abstract Essence of the All-Enlightened
lt which calls upon his Name; hence the
ee Bodies of the Buddha, by which on the
s of matter the One is manifest. And yet, 'Be
that I am God.' The Void is a Plenum-
is already full. It is filled with Tao or Zen or
These names are noises, man-made noises for
he Light is within thee', said the Egyptian
let the Light shine.'

n

dhist all forms of life, being manifestations of
interrelated in a complex web beyond our full
he 'Pairs of Opposites' are modes of the ulti-
sis of Being and not-Being and are infinite in
the parts and the whole are related in the utter-
iffusion' of Jijimuge. The Mahayana stands, it
n the twin pillars of Wisdom (*Prajña*) and Com-
aruna), of Law which manifests as justice, and
proves as mercy. Yet 'Love is the fulfilling of the
like the light and darkness, male and female, life
the two are ultimately and, if the truth were
mediately One.

conduce to loss and suffering – then reject them.'[1] Or, in
modern parlance, see if they work; if so, accept them.

In the absence of authority there are three ways to decide
what is Buddhism. The first is eclectic, whereby the individual selects those portions of the Teaching which suit his
immediate needs and makes them his own. A second and
more satisfactory method is to find by elaborate study the
common ground between the multiple Schools and sects and
to express the result in general principles. A far more difficult method, and that which I have humbly attempted here,
is to take the whole field of Buddhism for study, and then to
distil, with the aid of intuitive thought and much meditation,
a picture, however incomplete, of *Buddhism*, as distinct from
any one School or part of it. This implies, it is true, a personal Buddhism, in the sense of a personal understanding of
Buddhism. Why not? Buddhism, like any other form of relative truth, must vary with the individual, and grow for him
with his individual growth. Only the Buddha fully understood 'Buddhism'!

Such study shows that Buddhism may be compared to a
net, a net of principles, life-tendencies, knots in the flow of
life, vortices of force called matter. For life is motion and
life is one. Pick up a knot of the net, therefore, and the rest
of the net comes with it. One's choice of eternal principles
for a brief yet sweeping survey of the field of Buddhism is a
choice among these 'ganglia'. When I essayed this method
seven Principles emerged. The first three, as I noticed, having
chosen them, were universal in scope. The second three applied to the individual man, and the seventh enclosed the six
in the circle of unity. In these, I believe, all Buddhism is
somewhere to be found, for a symbol, if it be true, can be
read on many planes – 'the casket of Truth has seven keys'.
Yet this is at best a tentative chart to the ocean of Buddhism;
only the study of many a book and profound meditation on
every part of it will provide the flavour of a single drop.

1. *The Buddha's Enlightenment*

The Buddha was the Buddha because he was *Buddha*,
Awakened, Enlightened, made Aware. *Bodhi*, Wisdom, acquired by the faculty of *Buddhi*, the intuition, the power of
direct dynamic spiritual awareness, has many names and

1. From Woodward, *Some Sayings of the Buddha*, p. 283.

many degrees of achievement. *Satori*, the spiritual experience of Zen Buddhism, and *Samadhi*, the last step on the Noble Eightfold Path, are steps on the way to it; Nirvana (Pali: *Nibbana*) is its human goal. Yet beyond lies Parinirvana, for Buddhism is a process of becoming, and admits no conceivable end.

The Buddha's Enlightenment is therefore the womb, the heart and *raison d'être* of Buddhism. It is the criterion of all Buddhist teaching that it conduces or does not conduce to the achievement of Enlightenment. Bodhi, the *Maha Bodhi* or supreme Wisdom, is the purpose of all study, of all morality, of all attempts at self-development. It is for this that the false and separative self is slain and the true Self steadily developed; it is the sole end of all progress on the Eightfold Path; it is the *Buddh* in Buddhism.

There are infinite degrees in this development, from a 'bright idea' when a faculty greater than reasoning breaks through into the cage of a concept-ridden mind, to Parinirvana – and Beyond. The Buddha achieved (and hence his title) supreme Enlightenment, yet his victory was not unique. Buddhas before him had opened the Thousand-petalled Lotus to its perfect flowering; there are Buddhas to come. In the end each living thing will achieve Enlightenment. It is therefore the hope and the promise of Buddhism, and all study and attempted practice which loses sight of this ultimate, supreme experience may be useful, but is not Buddhism.

2. *Mind-Only*

In the beginning is the One, and only the One *is*. From the One comes Two, the innumerable Pairs of Opposites. But there is no such thing as two, for no two things can be conceived without their relationship, and this makes Three, the basic Trinity of all manifestation. From the three (or its six permutations and integrating seventh) come the manifold things of 'usual life' which the Chinese call the Ten Thousand Things. These are unreal in a world of unreality, comparatively real in a world of comparative reality, Real in that each is part of an ultimate, unmanifest Reality. As Reality must be, if anything is, supremely Enlightened, this faculty of supreme Enlightenment informs all things, though none of them owns it. It alone is Real.

From the viewpoint of the centre all phenomena or things

are fa
ence
pure',
manifes
result o
Imagina
we make
thoughts;
thoughts.'

To the B
the mind,
stand aloof
we allow the
value and all

Anicca, ch
'soul', is *Ana*
separative ego,
duces the doct
things, when an
continuous form
Mind-Only, all t
ultimate content,
the finest of Budd
life apart from it;
without the least of
whole, not merged
while retaining the f
no less One for the
Such is the *Jijimuge* d
nese Buddhism. Under
The world of distinctio
crimination falls away.
finite apart from finite
There is neither here nor
is neither now nor then, f
nor that, still less a fusio
only This, in a here and n
alone is of supreme importa
conceptual belief is valuele

1. *The Sutra of Wei*
2. *The Dammapada,*
3. *The Sutra of Wei L*

arrow, said the Perfec
as to its length and
the man who shot it.
making an end of su
evil thereof', and its

Life is a bridge –
not to its banks nor
to develop the min
journey – take it, a
used, and neither e
is only mind, Min
thought of the V
short-focused on
Goal. It is hard in
at times preferred
projected Thing,
far. Hence though
They exist, and
ultimate and so
Buddhist minds
One, and the c
Trikaya, the thr
successive plane
still and know
Void; the Void
Life or Light.
the Infinite.
Hierophants;

3. *Interrelatio*
To the Bu
one life, are
conceiving.
mate antithe
number; all
most 'intere
is said, upo
passion (K
Love which
Law', and
and form,
known, in

The interrelation is absolute and intrinsic. Cause and effect are one, though we see the two sides of the coin in the relative illusion of time. For causation is only interrelation expanded into the 'past', 'present', and 'future' for convenience of our understanding, and is only one mode of interrelation. Yet for us it may be the most important. It has been said that the Buddha-Dhamma was well expressed in the mighty phrase which, offered at second-hand by the Bhikkhu Assaji to the Brahman Moggallana, opened in the latter 'the eye of the everlasting', and brought him in a flash to Enlightenment. 'Of all things springing from a cause, the Tathagata hath shown the cause, and also its ceasing.' Such is the formal plan of the Universe, an infinite interrelation of parts including but never limited by causation. There is no First Cause; no ultimate End. Manifestation, so long as it endures, is a Wheel of Becoming, and all 'selves' within it are bound upon that Wheel. We are what we are and are incomplete, unhappy, filled with suffering. The cause of that misery is desire; the cause of desire is ignorance, the old illusion of self, the belief that the part can pit its separate self against the will and welfare of the whole.

For the law of the Wheel is love. If life be one, compassion is the rule of it, a 'feeling with' all forms of it by the littlest part. 'Compassion is no mere attribute. It is the Law of laws – eternal Harmony, Alaya's SELF; a shoreless universal essence, the light of everlasting Right, and fitness of all things, the law of love eternal.'[1] All who love are healers of those in need of it. Hence the doctrine of the turning over of merit. There is no monopoly in the effects of a deed; it affects for good or ill all manifested things. Mind gave it birth; it ripples out to the margin of the universe, and then flows back to the mind which gave it birth; and this too is Mind-Only. Each must perfect himself, his own brief vortex in the flow of life; each is responsible for the changing complex of attributes called Self which grows only as the craving 'ego' dies. 'Work out your own salvation', said the Buddha, 'with diligence.' How? It is immaterial. All means (*upaya*) belong to the unreal world of duality; the mountain peak is indifferent to the path by which men climb. There is the soft way of Shin Buddhism, or *Bhakti* Yoga, of devotion to the Beloved Ideal which the mind, fearing as yet the Void,

1. *The Voice of the Silence.*

creates for its following; there is the harder road of the
Theravada, with its Right Understanding (*Jnana* Yoga) and
Right Action (*Karma* Yoga); there is the hardest because the
straightest road of Zen, the Yoga of the will, the direct road
up the mountain-side. Meanwhile, for the vast majority of
men there is no road at all, only the drift of suffering minds
which, blinded still by *Avidya* (Ignorance), meshed in their
own illusion-fed desires, have not yet faced the fact of
suffering, and its cause, and the Way which leads to the end
of it. Of such men it is said that they stand in their own light
and wonder why it is dark.

The implications of the doctrine of Karma (Cause-Effect)
are vast, and frightening to all but the strongest mind. If all
that we are is the result of what we have thought, all that
we shall be is the result of what we are thinking now. We are
building now our to-morrow, creating hour by hour our
heaven or hell. There is no such thing as luck or chance, or
coincidence, and no such thing as fate. Predestination and
freewill, the antitheses beloved of the school debating club,
are falsely imagined; we are predestined now by the previous exercise of our own freewill. The world of time and space
is newly seen as the workshop of an individual character, for
while the whole is greater than its parts, each part perfected
is needed for the perfect whole. Only by right action beyond
reaction will the individual purge his mind of the old illusion, self; not until the Self we now call 'I' has died past
resurrecting will the Self appear which knows itself as One.

4. Self

The Teaching of the Buddha on self is clear, yet a number
of western Buddhists and Theravadins ignore this clear tradition in favour of a doctrine of their own. The Atman of
the Upanishads is the absolute SELF, and is the property of
no man. But this by the Buddha's day had become debased
into an immortal entity within each mind of which it was
even possible to give the size. Against this view of the Atman
(Pali: *Atta*) the Buddha taught the doctrine of non-Atman
(Pali: *Anatta*) in which he analysed the thing called man and
proved it to contain no single permanent factor, nor anything resembling a changeless and immortal 'soul'. This,
however, has been narrowed by later Buddhists to a doctrine
of 'no soul' for which there is neither Scriptural authority

nor the support of sense. Examine the five ingredients of the man we know, said the Buddha, and you will find a body (*rupa*); sensation, in the sense of emotional reaction (*vedana*); the mind's reaction to sense stimuli (*sanna*); the mental processes based on predispositions (*sankharas*); and consciousness (*vinnana*). All these without exception are in a state of flux, and even the body, the grossest of them, is utterly changed each seven years. Where, then, is the 'immortal soul'? If the personality be called the self, it is perishing hour by hour; if the character, the individuality, be called the Self, the same applies, though far more slowly. What, then, of a SELF? If by this be meant the principle of Enlightenment, or Life itself, it is not the property of man or of any man. To the extent that it is part of man, one of his faculties, it is not immortal; to the extent that it is immortal it is not the property of any man. Yet if there be nothing which, within the illusion of manifestation, grows and moves towards Enlightenment, what of the Noble Eightfold Path to the Goal? Who treads it – what walks on? The answer is consciousness, the integrating factor or Self which, subject like all else to *anicca*, change, and *dukkha*, suffering, is unquestionably *anatta*, lacking a permanent immortal something which separates it from the Whole.

The Way from the unreal to the Real, from the existing fact of Enlightenment to its realization is long, and no one life on earth or a hundred of them will bring the pilgrim to that goal. Rebirth, not of a changeless soul, but of an ever-evolving, karma-created bundle of characteristics is accepted by the whole world east of Karachi, and only in the West must text-books of Buddhism give it space. The evolving consciousness achieves successive states of spiritual achievement until the last, to our mortal knowledge, is reached in Buddhahood. Only then is the self entirely dead, to rise no more, and the Self, released from the last of its Fetters, is merged as a dew-drop in the Shining Sea.

5. *The Middle Way*

The doctrine of causation applied to the individual character is expressed in the Four Noble Truths; the omnipresence of suffering; its cause, selfish desire; its cure, the elimination of that separative desire; and the way to this removal. This way is the Middle Way between extremes. For if manifestation is based on the 'pairs of opposites', the way to the Unity from which they sprang must be between them and above them and beyond.

The Noble Eightfold Path of Buddhism, acknowledged by all Schools, is the noblest course of spiritual training yet presented to man. It is far more than a code of morality. If the first five steps on the Way may be classed as ethics, the last three are concerned with Bhavana, the mind's development. 'Cease to do evil; learn to do good; cleanse your own heart; this is the teaching of the Buddhas.' There is here no word of faith, save that which a man has in a guide who tells him of a journey and a goal and a way to it; no word of a Saviour who will make that journey for him. Each must develop his own mind, first by creating the instrument with which to develop its inner powers, and then by using them. The East has always set great store on the inner powers of the mind, knowing that its resources are infinite, and there is no instrument yet invented which can do more than the mind of man can do when its powers are fully developed. And this is but common sense. If there is Mind-Only, there exists in Mind all the power and knowledge of the Universe, and the *Siddhis* (Pali: *Iddhis*), or supernormal faculties are only a foretaste of the powers to be unfolded by the man made perfect on a day as yet unborn.

6. *Direct seeing into the Heart of Man*

The purpose of Buddhism, let it be repeated, is to attain Enlightenment, for oneself and all creation. In the lower stages of this climb all means and devices are legitimate, to be discarded when their use is ended. A raft is useful for crossing a river; he is a fool who bears it on his back when the river is crossed. There comes a time, however, when all devices are seen as hindrances, and even the Scriptures are fetters about the awakening mind. Authority is a term which daily lessens in meaning, and the sole criterion of all value passes within. The faculty of *Buddhi* (intuition) slowly but steadily awakens, and the world of discrimination, which lives by the dreary comparison of opposites, is steadily left behind. Tolerance widens, compassion deepens, serenity becomes a constant companion which neither the passions nor the problems of the human mind disturb. Certainty comes with intuitive awareness, and though sorrow still be the

portion of the ever-returning night, joy as certainly comes
with the morning.

The developed will begins to take the hill straight. The
veils fall steadily and there comes an increasing awareness of
that which lies beyond all veils. The 'three fires' of greed,
anger and illusion begin to die for want of fuelling. The
scales turn over in 'conversion', a new birth. The stream is
entered, and all effort becomes increasingly 'right' effort. In
brief, the faculty of *Buddhi* is awakening, and the fact that
it dwells in all and needs but awakening is cardinal to Buddhism. 'So far as Buddha-nature is concerned, there is no
difference between an enlightened man and an ignorant one.
What makes the difference is that one realizes it while the
other is ignorant of it.'[1] Or, more briefly, in the words of
The Voice of the Silence, 'Seek in the impersonal for the
eternal man, and having sought him out, look inward – thou
art Buddha!'

7. *Man's Enlightenment*

The process of becoming is a circle; the process of becoming more, of growth, is a spiral, either up or down
according as the growth is towards or away from wholenesss.
Buddhism begins with the Buddha's Enlightenment and ends
with man's. And the final Goal? We know not, nor is it yet,
or likely to be for aeons to come, our immediate concern. The
faint of heart will ever seek some resting-place, some weak
finality; for the strong, the first and the last word is and ever
more will be – Walk On!

1. *The Sutra of Wei Lang* (Hui-neng), p. 27.

CHAPTER ONE

The Life of the Buddha

*

*Gotama, the Buddha – The Buddha's Task – The Birth of Gotama
– The Great Renunciation – The Enlightenment*

THERE are two points of view from which to regard the
Buddha and his Teachings. The first is objective and analytic,
the way of history. The other is subjective and direct, accept-
ing Gotama as in fact the Buddha, the Awakened One, the
new holder of the greatest office in the spiritual hierarchy of
mankind. The former is a critical examination of the body of
Buddhism; the latter is an intuitive perception of its life.
The first is the 'Doctrine of the Eye'; the other the 'Doctrine
of the Heart'.

Gotama the Buddha was the Buddha because he was
Buddha, the Enlightened One, and he who cannot accept this
premise will never know more than the shell of Buddhism.
Only in the light of this Enlightenment, or such reflection of
it as the perceiver in his highest moments is able to perceive,
can Buddhism, the Teaching of the Buddha, be understood.
The 'scientific' approach to the spiritual flame is blocked by
its own limitations. The Buddha's Teachings came from the
plane of consciousness which he, by countless lives of effort,
had achieved, and he who would understand it must climb
as near as he may to the same achievement.

This does not mean that critical analysis is vain. Such intellectual effort removes the false glamour of 'authority',
exposes the forced integration of heterogeneous parts into an
ill-fitting whole; gives dates and sequence to the development of doctrine. Yet in the end it only tears the flower in
pieces, and a beautiful legend written, as legends usually are,
in the shorthand of spiritual symbol, has far more life in it,
more power, than a dreary text-book of analysed facts. To
the extent that Buddhism is true it is, like the essence of
Christianity, beyond the accidents of time and place, of fact
or history. To the extent that it is untrue, it does not become

more true by being pinned to a set of words produced by a
certain man on such and such a day. Our lives are made, our
hearts' enlightenment attained, by stories, lives of example,
as all poets, all children not yet mired with analytic thought,
and the spiritual leaders of mankind have ever known. The
Life and Teaching of the Buddha, like those of Jesus, the
Christ, are beyond the accidents of history.

Gotama, the Buddha

Who, then, was Gotama, the Buddha? He was a man self-
perfected, one who had achieved the mind's Enlightenment.
He was the latest of a line of Buddhas, the fourth in the
series which guides and guards the cycle of evolution of mankind. By virtue of his office of *Samma Sambuddha* (Supreme
Buddha) he was and is the Patron of the Adepts, the apex
of the hierarchy of self-perfected men from whose ranks the
spiritual leaders of mankind are drawn.

He was a man, not a Solar Myth, as Coomaraswamy
suggests,[1] save that he was the incarnate Principle of Enlightenment in all men and in all forms of life, 'the Inner
Man of all beings',[2] and as such, in the technical sense of
the word, a myth, even as Jesus, who became Christos, the
Christ, was incarnate of the same Eternal Principle.

As *Tathagata*, 'the successor to his predecessors in office',
he had achieved the perfection of his spiritual powers, all
petals of the 'thousand-petalled lotus' of his super-personal
being having fully opened. 'Strange indeed are the Tathagatas, and endowed with strange powers. Marvellous indeed
are the Tathagatas, and endowed with marvellous powers',[3]
and 'Deep is the Tathagata, immeasurable, difficult to understand, even like the ocean.'[4]

In his life, therefore, he was, when using such powers, the
embodiment of his Teaching. 'As the Tathagata speaks, so
He does; as He does, so He speaks. Thus, since He does as
He says, and says as He does, therefore is He called Tathagata.'[5] Hence his explanation to his disciples when he lay
dying: 'It may be that in some of you the thought will arise,

1. *Hinduism and Buddhism*, p. 50.
2. *Ibid.*, p. 73.
3. F. L. Woodward, *Some Sayings of the Buddha*, p. 260.
4. Quoted in Pratt, *The Pilgrimage of Buddhism*, p. 13.
5. Woodward, *Some Sayings of the Buddha*, p. 291.

"The Word of the Master is ended; we have no Teacher more." But it is not thus that you should regard it. The Dhamma (Teaching) which I have given you, let that be your Teacher when I am gone.'[1] And even he could not attain Enlightenment for others. (Even) 'Buddhas do but point the way.'[2]

As a man he was 'friend Gotama' to his fellow seekers. Only when he attained supreme Enlightenment did he assume the title *Buddha*. Thereafter he was known as *Bhagavat* (Lord) and would refer to himself as *Tathagata*.

In this, his last incarnation on earth, his personal character was glorious. Of great physical beauty, his mind was of an equal beauty. His charm was magnetic. 'The venerable Gotama is well born on both sides, of pure descent, is handsome, inspiring trust, fair in colour, fine in presence, stately to behold.'[3]

Aristocrat by birth, he was at home with all men, high-caste Brahmans, kings and princes, philosophers, warriors, merchants, beggars and prostitutes. His compassion was absolute, and in one instance at least he expressed himself in terms which another Master of Compassion used later. When a man was sick unto death with dysentery, his fellows had neglected him as useless to the Order. 'Brethren,' said the Buddha to those about him, 'ye have no mother and father to take care of you. If ye will not take care of each other, who else, I ask, will do so? Brethren, he who would wait on me, let him wait on the sick.'[4]

His dignity was unshakeable, his humour invariable. He was infinitely patient as one who knows the illusion of time. When asked how long is an aeon, he answered, 'Just as if, brother, there were a mighty mountain crag four leagues in length, breadth and height, without a crack or cranny, not hollowed out, one solid mass of rock, and a man should come at the end of every century, and with a cloth of Benares, should once on each occasion stroke that rock: sooner, brother, would that mighty mountain crag be worn away by this method, sooner be used up, than the aeon.'[5]

1. From the *Mahaparinibbana Sutta*, chap. 6.
2. Woodward, *Some Sayings of the Buddha*, p. 300.
3. Pratt, *The Pilgrimage of Buddhism*, p. 9–10.
4. Woodward, *Some Sayings of the Buddha*, p. 127–8.
5. Woodward, *Some Sayings of the Buddha*, p. 185.

The Buddha's Task

His task was enormous, to reform the prevailing religion
of his time, which seems to have been an immature yet already corrupt form of Brahmanism, and at the same time to
add to the sum total of human wisdom from the boundless
store of his own. His teaching was not a break-away from
Brahmanism, as countless writers, such as E. E. Power,[1] have
stated; on the other hand, it was far more original than
Indian writers of to-day, such as Coomaraswamy,[2] declare.
Brahman terms were freely used, but given new meanings,
and much of the teaching was a purified restatement of
truths to be found in the Upanishads. Thus *Karma* and the
doctrine of Rebirth, the unity of life as distinct from its
forms, and the common goal of Liberation, were all to be
found in the Brahmanism of the Buddha's day, but, as in-
corporated into the Buddha Dhamma, received an original
setting.

The word 'Brahman' is used by the Buddha to indicate
not a member of the Brahman caste but that which a Brahman ought to be, and in places the word is used as meaning
excellent or perfect, which, in view of the average standard
of the day, borders on irony.

The Buddha's inner teaching probably differed little, if at
all, from that of the initiated Brahmans of his day. 'His
teachings, therefore, could not be different from their doctrines, for the whole Buddhist reform merely consisted of
giving out a portion of that which had been kept secret from
every man outside the "enchanted" circle of Temple-Initiates
and ascetics. Unable to teach *all* that had been imparted to
him – owing to his pledges – though he taught a philosophy
built upon the groundwork of the true esoteric knowledge,
the Buddha gave to the world its *outward* material body and
kept its *soul* for his Elect.'[3] This 'soul', the Doctrine of the
Heart, is to be found in fragments, usually mutilated, in all
the Scriptures of the world. It is the ancient Wisdom to
which all Arhats, Rishis and other perfect men achieve. It
has a thousand forms, yet is eternally one.

Did the Buddha reveal too much? This is the occult

1. *Path of the Elders*, p. xiii et seq.
2. *Hinduism and Buddhism*, p. 45.
3. H. P. Blavatsky, *The Secret Doctrine*, Vol. I, p. xxi, 1st edn.

tradition, and there are hints in the orthodox Scriptures to support it. Obviously no more than a fragment of the Wisdom can be broadcast to the stupid, selfish, material-minded bulk of humanity. Truth is a sacred trust, and he who reveals it to those unworthy of it bears the karma of his act and that of the evil, which flows from the wrong use of the truth revealed. 'I also, Brethren, have seen these things before, yet I did not reveal them. I might have revealed them, and others would not have believed them, and, if they had not believed me, it would have been to their loss and sorrow.'[1]

If the Buddha, in his zeal to make available to all men the Wisdom which the Brahmans held exclusively for their own emolument, revealed too much, he paid dearly for the excess of his compassion. The Brahmans were immediately hostile, and although thousands and tens of thousands supported his reforms and innovations, the hard core of the ravished priestcraft won in the end. Hinduism was vastly improved by Buddhism, but after a while, and 1,500 years is not long in the history of the world, the reformer's teaching as such was driven from India.

At the time of Gotama's birth in North-East India, the main power of the Brahmans lay in the North-West. In Kosala in North Bengal the Kshatriya, or warrior, caste was still dominant. Wandering ascetics vied for the ear of those who sought for Reality, and hermits were to be found in caves who taught, to such as accepted them as *Guru*, or teacher, their own spiritual experience. Animism, polytheism, dualism and even advanced monism, all competed for authority, and in a gentle land whose Indian climate, cooled with the high Himalayan air, lent itself to such speculation, the spiritual soil was ripe for new seed.

The Birth of Gotama

Such were the conditions which the Buddha-to-be chose for his final incarnation. He was born of the Aryan race in the Kshatriya caste of the Sakya clan, whose country lay along the south edge of Nepal. Its capital was Kapilavastu, and it was on a journey from it that his mother, Maya – a name so obviously symbolic that one might have expected it – gave birth to a son in the Lumbini Gardens which lie just over the modern border of the Nepal Terai. His father,

1. Woodward, *Some Sayings of the Buddha*, p. 7.

Suddhodana, was Raja of the Sakya clan, and if not a king, as often described, was a native prince of substance.

The child was called Siddhartha, the family name being Gotama. The dates of his life are still controversial, but it is probable that he was born in 563 B.C., left home when he was 29, attained enlightenment when he was 35 and passed away in 483 B.C., at the age of 80. But no biography was written for several hundred years after the Life had ended, and the available sources for such information are such a mixture of history and legend as to prove the despair of all historians. As many as four different versions are sometimes given of one event, and as others appear in widely different sequences, only by piecing together a score of passages from various parts of the existing Canon does a consistent story appear. If, in the form as given us by the English translations, it lacks the incomparable language in which the Gospels were first given to the English ear, it still displays the sweep and rhythm of a great symbolic story, and a nobility, serenity and deep compassion which places the central figure among the foremost spiritual leaders of mankind. For it is of course, symbolic. As the centuries rolled by, each version of the Life acquired an increasing garland of fabulous adventure, miracle and heavenly assistance. But legend is often a poetic form of history, and lifts the story to a plane above the accidents of time and place. The *Jatakas* (Birth-Stories), many of which reappear in Aesop's and La Fontaine's Fables, are a history of the evolution of consciousness upon this earth as recorded in what, for want of a better term, may be called the esoteric tradition. In the same way the '32 marks of the Great Man', from which the sage Asita was able to prophesy the glory which awaited the child Siddhartha; the seven steps to North, East, South and West which the baby took to proclaim to each his incomparable wisdom; his mother's death just seven days from his birth; the three palaces in which the growing boy lived; the intervention of Mara, the Tempter, at key points in his life, are all of obvious symbolic meaning, and are easily equated with the symbolic stories of earlier and later Saviours of mankind. Indeed the whole Life, like that of Jesus Christ, may be read as the mystery story of the evolution of man from birth to final attainment.

The boy, we are told, led the normal life of ease of his birth and calling. At sixteen he won in a contest of arms his wife, Yasodhara, and by her had a son, Rahula. But from earliest childhood he had been unusually self-possessed and never satisfied for long with sensuous delights. He was a man with a mission, and the new brain soon became aware of the destiny of the man now using it.

The Great Renunciation

The story tells how, in spite of his father's efforts to keep all knowledge of worldly woes from his eyes, the young prince, driving forth from the palace, saw an old man, then a sick man, then a dead man, and at the sight of each asked his charioteer the meaning of what he saw. 'This comes to all men', said the charioteer, and the Prince's mind was troubled that such was the effect of birth, the common cause. Then he saw a recluse with shaven head and a tattered yellow robe. 'What man is this?' he asked, and was told it was one who had gone forth into the homeless life. Then follows one of the loveliest passages in the Scriptures. He returned to the palace, deeply pondering, and, that night, while his pleasure girls lay sleeping in unbecoming postures at his feet, he revolted from sensual pleasures, and at the same time the flame of compassion awoke within him. Not for the first time, but now with overpowering effect, he felt the positive call to save not only himself but all mankind from birth in the world of suffering. He bade farewell to his sleeping wife and babe, and in the silence of the Indian night went forth with Channa, his charioteer, and Kanthaka, his stallion. At the edge of the forest he alighted, cut off his long black hair with his sword and sent it back to the palace by the hand of Channa. He exchanged his princely robes with those of a beggar, and went forth into the homeless life, alone.

The purpose of his search was clear, the extinguishing of craving, selfish craving, the cause of suffering in this life and of rebirth on the Wheel. It is said that he had recently heard a maiden singing when she fell in love with his beauty as he passed her by:

> Happy indeed is the Mother,
> Happy indeed is the Father,
> Happy indeed is the Wife,
> Who has such a Husband.

Well spoken, thought the Buddha-to-be. But what is it

which, extinguished, makes the heart eternally happy; for flesh will grow old and will die? He realized that it was lust and craving in all its forms, the extinguishing of which (*Nirvana*) was the end of suffering. He was then twenty-nine.

He visited first Alara Kalama, a noted sage, and studied with him, but he found no answer to his heart's imperious demand. So he went to Uddaka, another sage, and received the same reply. He passed through the country of Magadha to the town of Uruvela, and there settled down in a grove of trees to find Enlightenment. For six long years he meditated, practising the utmost physical austerities until he all but wasted away. He conquered fear; subdued all lusts of the flesh; he developed and controlled his mind, but still he did not find Enlightenment. Finally he realized that not in austerities could truth be found. He decided to eat again, and the five ascetics living with him departed in disgust. He accepted a bowl of curds from a maid, Sugata, and having eaten and bathed, seated himself in the lotus posture at the foot of a tree, determined to achieve without more delay the full fruits of Enlightenment. It was the night of the Full Moon of May, and he was thirty-five.

The Enlightenment

The hosts of Mara, the Evil One, approached and claimed the throne of grass which he had made for himself. The Bodhisattva, the Buddha-to-be, touched earth, calling the earth to witness that the throne was his by right, and the earth gave witness. Mara, his assaults by fire and darkness and all his violence having failed, withdrew. The moon rose and the Blessed One passed, as he had passed a thousand times before, into deep meditation.

Now victory was near, the goal of hundreds of lives of effort devoted to one end. He passed in review his former births, the cause of all rebirth and its consequent suffering, the spokes of the Wheel of Rebirth which rolls and rolls unceasingly. He rose in consciousness through the planes and sub-planes of material existence. He linked the various component parts of self to the Self which uses them, and the Self by the faculty of *Buddhi* (intuition) to the *Maha Bodhi* (utmost wisdom) of which, in his inmost being, he was a manifestation on earth. Finally he bound in one the Self which still is human, and the SELF of pure Enlightenment.

The journey was over, and a new Buddha, the fourth of his line, was born.

He broke into the famous Song of Victory:

> Many a house of life
> Hath held me – seeking ever him who wrought
> These prisons of the senses, sorrow-fraught;
> Sore was my ceaseless strife!
> But now,
> Thou builder of this Tabernacle – Thou!
> I know Thee! Never shalt thou build again
> These walls of pain,
> Nor raise the roof-tree of deceits, nor lay
> Fresh rafters on the clay;
> Broken Thy house is, and the ridge-pole split!
> Delusion fashioned it!
> Safe pass I thence – deliverance to obtain.[1]

The earth which he had called to witness his approach to Buddhahood knew of the victory, and the forces of nature and the gods of heaven rejoiced that another Buddha was born. For seven days he rested under the Bodhi-Tree whose sapling grows on the self-same spot to-day, and the Nagas (Serpent Kings) of the Earth, the symbolic name of the Initiates of Wisdom, approved that Gotama was now the Buddha, and made *puja* to him.

But the Buddha for the last time was assailed with doubts by Mara, the Evil One. He who had given up all to seek release for all, what was the use of his telling all men of the Path which leads to the end of suffering? Earth trembled and awaited his reply. Then the Buddha-Heart of compassion wakened to man's eternal need. Brahma himself pleaded for mankind.

'Lord, let the Blessed One preach the Dhamma! May the Perfect One preach the Dhamma! There are beings whose mental eyes are scarcely darkened by any dust; if they do not hear the Dhamma they will perish. There will be some who will understand.'

And the All-Enlightened One had pity on Mankind.

[For Bibliography see end of Chapter Two]

1. Sir Edwin Arnold, *The Light of Asia*.

The Ministry

*

The First Sermon – The First Missionaries – The First Retreat – The Return to the Palace – Women admitted to the Order – The Sutta of the Great Decease – The Passing – The Cremation and Relics

THE decision was made. The Buddha would preach the Dhamma to mankind. 'I will beat the drum of the Immortal in the darkness of the world.' But preach to whom? His earliest *gurus*, Alara Kalama and Uddaka, had passed away. He decided to teach the five ascetics who had left him when he parted from their austerities. He rose and slowly made his way to Benares. There, in the Deer Park of Isipatana, he found them and they called him 'Friend'. But the Buddha told them of his Enlightenment and they paid him the respect that was due to him.

The First Sermon

On the night of the Full Moon of July he preached to them his First Sermon of 'Setting in Motion the Wheel of Righteousness'. He spoke of the two extremes of sensuality and mortification, and of the Middle Way, the sweetly reasonable Middle Way which lies between; he taught the Four Noble Truths of suffering and its cause, desire or selfishness, of the removal of that cause, and of the Eightfold Path which leads to the end of suffering. And the leader of the ascetics, Kondanna, 'obtained the pure and spotless Dhamma-Eye' and was the first to be ordained a disciple of the Tathagata.

There in the Deer Park of Sarnath near Benares is the site where the Buddha proclaimed his Dhamma, 'glorious in the beginning, glorious in the middle, glorious in its end'. Soon, the other four ascetics perceived the Truth of the Dhamma and they, too, were ordained. And to them the Buddha preached his Second Sermon, setting forth the famous *Anatta* doctrine which many in the West, and many of the Southern

School of Buddhism in the East, so sadly misunderstand.
All the five aggregates of personal being, body, feeling, perception, predispositions of mind, and consciousness alike are
prone to suffering, are transient, without a permanent 'soul'.
Of the nature of the soul itself he said nothing.

The First Missionaries

The number of converts rapidly increased and, mindful of
his resolution to proclaim the Dhamma to all mankind, the
Buddha sent them forth into the world with the famous exhortation, 'Go ye forth, O Bhikkhus, on your journey, for
the profit of the many, for the bliss of the many, out of compassion for the world, for the welfare, the profit, the bliss, of
devas (Angel-gods – a parallel evolution to mankind) – and
mankind. Go not any two together. Proclaim, O Bhikkhus,
the Dhamma, goodly in its beginning, goodly in its middle,
goodly in its ending. In the spirit and in the letter make ye
known the perfect, utterly pure, righteous life. There are
beings with but little dust of passion on their eyes, who perish
through not hearing the Dhamma. There will be some who
will understand.'[1] Moreover, he gave these, his first missionaries, the power to ordain their converts in some simple
formula which, in its final form, is still repeated by millions
of his followers:

> I take my refuge in the Buddha,
> I take my refuge in the Dhamma (Teaching),
> I take my refuge in the Sangha (Order).

The Buddha himself returned to Uruvela to keep the rainy
season of *Vassa*. On the way he displayed that genius for an
apt and spontaneous parable which a later Teacher used in
Palestine. He passed a band of thirty young men who were
picnicking with their wives. One of them had no wife, and
had brought a woman with him who had stolen their belong-
ings and run away. The young man asked the Buddha
whether he had seen such a woman. 'What do you think,
young man,' asked the Buddha, 'which were better for you,
to seek for the woman or to seek for the Self?' This is the
first occasion on which the Self is mentioned as distinct from
the 'Not-Self' of the Anatta doctrine.

At Uruvela, he found a group of Fire-Worshippers, headed

1. Woodward, *Some Sayings of the Buddha*, p. 30.

by Kassapa, and to them he preached his famous Fire-Sermon. 'All things', said the Buddha, 'are on fire; the eye is on fire, forms are on fire, eye-consciousness is on fire; the impressions received by the eye are on fire, and whatever sensation originates in the impressions received by the eye is likewise on fire. And with what are these things on fire? With the fires of lust, anger, and illusion, with these are they on fire, and so with the other senses and so with the mind. Wherefore the wise man conceives disgust for the things of the senses, and being divested of desire for the things of the senses, he removes from his heart the cause of suffering.' By this sermon, Kassapa and all his followers became disciples of the Tathagata.

The First Retreat

The Buddha then proceeded to Rajagaha, whither his fame had preceded him. King Bimbisara came to him with a host of citizens and asked to be taught the Dhamma, and on hearing it he was converted. The Buddha accepted a meal at the palace and was given the park known as the Bamboo Grove for the use of the Order as a permanent retreat. While they were resting there a remarkable incident occurred. A newly ordained disciple, Assaji, met Sariputta, the disciple of another famous ascetic who dwelt near by. Sariputta had a friend Moggallana, and the two men had promised to tell one another when either of them 'attained the immortal'. Sariputta was deeply impressed by Assaji's dignity and self-possession as he moved about the city begging for alms, and asked him, as was customary for one ascetic to another, who was his teacher, and what his teaching might be. Assaji told him that his teacher was Sakyamuni (the Sage of the Sakyas), but being but newly ordained himself he could not preach the Dhamma in its entirety. 'Then tell me a little', said the eager Sariputta, and Assaji produced the following remarkable reply:

> Of all things which proceed from a cause
> The Tathagata has explained the cause,
> And also has explained their ceasing.
> This the great Adept has proclaimed.

Sariputta apparently took this to mean 'Whatsoever is a rising thing, that is a ceasing thing', and there arose in him 'the Spotless Eye of the Dhamma', that is, the awakening of the higher consciousness which leads to Enlightenment. Such was the immediate effect on him that his friend Moggallana, on seeing him, knew at once that he had 'attained the Immortal', and he too, being told the Dhamma in the same remarkable formula, attained arahantship. That these two men, later to become the chief disciples of the Tathagata, should achieve such attainment at second-hand, as it were, and by such a formula is difficult to accept unless it be, as the esoteric tradition tells, that a number of men of high attainment had earned the right to be on earth at the time of the Master's final incarnation, and were therefore 'ripe' for such an experience.

The Return to the Palace

By now, the Raja Suddhodana was longing to see his son again, and sent him repeated messages. Finally, when spring had come, the Buddha returned to Kapilavastu with a train of followers, and for the first time since the Enlightenment saw his father and wife and child. And the story tells how Rahula was sent by his mother to the glorious figure in the yellow robe, who stood with downcast eyes at the palace door. The boy asked for his inheritance and the Buddha, his father, turning to Sariputta, said, 'Receive him into the Order.' Thus did the heir to the throne of the Sakyas receive his spiritual inheritance.

The Master returned to Rajagaha, and to him came Anathapindika, a wealthy merchant of Savatthi. Being converted, he built a resting-place at every league of the way from Rajagaha to Savatthi, and there presented the Order with the Jetavana Grove as a third retreat, buying it from Prince Jeta with as much gold as would cover the ground. The Buddha thanked him by receiving him as a disciple, and the Monastery built in the Jetavana Grove became his headquarters for the rest of the Ministry.

About this time Visakha, the wife of a guild-master of Savatthi, who was converted to the Dhamma as a girl, gave to the Order her gorgeous jewelled headdress which, when sold, provided funds for yet another retreat. Thus householders of both sexes as well as kings and princes gave their best to the Order in exchange for the Dhamma which leads all men to the end of suffering.

The Buddha's fame as a Teacher and even as an arbitrator
quickly spread over North-East India. On one occasion he
averted a local war. In the Burmese life of the Buddha[1]
appears the following. Would that the modern leaders of men
were equally amenable to reason!

It is recorded that two princes were once about to engage in a
terrible battle in a quarrel that took place about a certain embank-
ment constructed to keep in water. Between these kings and their
assembled armies Buddha suddenly appeared and asked the cause
of the strife. When he was completely informed upon the subject
he put the following questions:
'Tell me, O kings! is earth of any intrinsic value?'
'Of no value whatever', was the reply.
'Is water of any intrinsic value?'
'Of no value whatever.'
'And the blood of kings, is that of any intrinsic value?'
'Its value is priceless.'
'Is it reasonable', asked the Tathagata, 'that that which is
priceless should be staked against that which has no value what-
ever?'
The incensed monarchs saw the wisdom of this reasoning and
abandoned their dispute.

Women admitted to the Order

It was not only men that came to him. Women claimed to
be admitted to a female branch of the Order, and the story
tells how Mahaprajapati, the Buddha's stepmother, on the
death of his father cut off her hair and, shaving her head,
appeared before him in the yellow robes of the Order. Again
and again the Buddha refused, and it was through the
insistence of Ananda that they finally gained admission. Even
then the female order of Bhikkhunis was founded only under
strict and humiliating rules, and the Buddha is reported to
have said that their admission would materially shorten the
life of the Buddhist religion. Whether he truly made such a
prophecy we do not know, but his attitude towards women
is clearly shown in a delicious example of his sense of humour.
Ananda, as the Buddha lay on his death-bed, asked:

'How are we to conduct ourselves, Lord, with regard to
women?'

1. Bigandet, *The Life or Legend of Gaudama*, p. 191.

'Do not see them, Ananda!'
'But if we should see them, what are we to do?'
'Abstain from speech.'
'But if they speak to us, Lord, what are we to do?'
'Keep wide awake, Ananda!'

Ananda and Devadatta were cousins of the Buddha, the former becoming his personal attendant for the last twenty-five years of his life, and the latter assuming, no doubt with the assistance of later legends, the rôle of Judas. Consumed with jealousy at his cousin's position, Devadatta managed to cause a split in the Sangha, and at one time created a serious dissension by winning Ajatasattu, the son of King Bimbisara, from allegiance to the Buddha. It is said that, having failed to acquire the power he craved, he plotted to kill the Buddha, and, after hired assassins had failed, attempted the appalling deed himself. The most famous of these attempts, often portrayed in Buddhist art, was the letting loose of a ferocious elephant on the road along which his cousin was to come. The Buddha was warned of the attempt but insisted upon proceeding. The elephant rushed at him, but the Buddha roused in him the quality of *Metta*, loving-kindness, and on reaching him the elephant knelt down in homage, while the Buddha passed upon his way.

Thereafter, Devadatta renewed his attempts to cause a schism in the Order, and actually persuaded a number of Bhikkhus to leave. Then Buddha sent Moggallana and Sari-putta to preach to them, and they returned to the fold. Later, it is said, Devadatta repented, was received into the Order again, and died.

So the Ministry continued, and for forty-five years the Master moved from place to place in North-East India, organizing the expansion of the Order, and preaching to all who came to him. None was refused. Ambapali, a noted and beautiful courtesan, was treated with the same respect as any of the kings who came to visit him, and having secured the Blessed One's consent to dine with him, she refused to sell the privilege for a large sum to the Licchavi Princes. They tried to woo the Buddha from his promise and, having failed, departed, not pleased at having been 'outdone by the Mango girl'. Ambapali presented the Order with her park and mansion for yet another retreat.

The Sutta of the Great Decease

The last three months of the Ministry are recorded in some detail in the *Maha-Parinibbana-Sutta*, which is the Pali name for 'the Sermon of the Great Passing'. As might be expected, the Buddha's utterances in the closing stages of his last life on earth are carefully preserved. In his last retreat he was taken ill. Ananda was alarmed, and expressed the hope that the Exalted One would not pass away until he had left instructions concerning the Order. But the Buddha announced that he had no such intention, saying, 'Surely, Ananda, should there be anyone who harbours the thought "It is I who will lead the Community", it is he who should lay down instructions concerning the Order!' He made it clear that he was about to pass away, and thereupon delivered one of the most famous speeches in religious history – 'Therefore, O Ananda, be ye islands unto yourselves. Take the Self as your refuge. Take yourself to no external refuge. Hold fast to the Dhamma as an island. Hold fast as a refuge to the truth. Look not for refuge to anyone besides yourselves ... And whosoever, Ananda, shall take the Self as an island, taking themselves to no external refuge, but holding fast to Truth as their refuge, it is they, Ananda, who shall reach the very topmost height – but they must be anxious to learn.'

The Master recovered from his illness. Later, when speaking to Ananda of his coming death, he consoled him for his obvious grief, and said, 'But now, Ananda, have I not formerly declared to you that it is in the very nature of all things near and dear to us to pass away? How, then, Ananda, seeing that whatever is brought into being contains within itself the inherent necessity of dissolution, how can it be that such a being (as the visible Gotama) should not be dissolved?' And he told Ananda that within three months he would pass away. Thereafter, he went with him to a meeting-place in the forest and announced to those assembled his intention of leaving them. 'Behold now, O Bhikkhus, I exhort you, saying, All component things must grow old. Work out your own salvation with diligence!'

The Passing

Thereafter the Buddha proceeded to Pava and halted at the Mango Grove of Cunda, the blacksmith. Cunda invited the

Master and his brethren to dine at his house on the following day. For this purpose, he prepared a special meal for him, and it is sometimes said that the Buddha died thereof. The word used for the principal ingredient of this dish means pig's flesh, or perhaps pig's food, such as truffles, and more than one writer has pointed out the absurdity of taking this literally. That a man such as Gotama, the Buddha, of perfect mental and physical purity and in full possession of his faculties, should die of indigestion through eating pork is absurd. But if the pork be taken as symbolic of Hindu doctrine, too much of which he had revealed, it does make sense.

Having eaten this meal, he went on his way to the Sala Grove of the Mallas, and having arrived there said, 'Spread for me my couch, Ananda' (for he had to eat and digest the products of his indiscretion). 'I am weary and would fain lie down.' 'Even so, Lord', said the venerable Ananda, and the Exalted One lay down on his right side and was mindful and self-possessed. The Bhikkhus assembled about him and the dying Gotama noticed that Ananda was not among them, but stood a way off, weeping because his Master was about to pass away and he had not attained Arhatship. The Master sent for him and comforted him, saying, 'For a long time, Ananda, you have been very near to me by acts of love. You have done well, Ananda. Be earnest in effort and you too shall be free from the cankers of sensuality, of becoming, of false views and ignorance.' And he sent to the nearby village of Kusinara to inform the Mallas that the Tathagata was about to pass away. The Mallas came to him and Ananda presented them to the Master, family by family, in the first watch of the night. And when men came to him to be received into the Order, he still accepted them and gladdened them with discourse on the Dhamma. The Buddha asked the Bhikkhus if there were any among them who had any doubt concerning the Dhamma and the Eightfold Path, and none replied. Then again the All-Enlightened One addressed the Brethren, saying, 'Decay is inherent in all component things! Work out your own salvation with diligence.' These were the last words of the Tathagata. Thereafter, he entered the first of the *Jhanas* or higher states of consciousness, and so the second, the third and the fourth; he passed still further into the realms of consciousness which none but a Buddha, an All-Enlightened One, may know.

Thereafter he descended to the fourth stage of consciousness and immediately passed away. Thus Gotama the Buddha ended his last incarnation and passed from the eyes of men.

The Cremation and Relics

Anuruddha, the Elder, exhorted the Brethren not to lament. 'If all that is born contains within itself the seeds of dissolution, how is it possible that this body, too, shall not be dissolved?' Ananda sent for the Mallas of Kusinara, who, after paying homage, seven days later cremated the remains. The ashes were divided, it is said, into ten parts, and given to the Rajas of the lands where the Buddha had lived and died. *Stupas* or *dagobas* (reliquary chambers) were erected over them, and all too soon the respect and worship of these relics grew into a cult. Even to-day the undoubted relics of Gotama the Buddha receive a respect which he, it would seem, would be the first to deplore. Only recently the relics of Sariputta and Moggallana, which had reposed in the Victoria and Albert Museum in London since being taken from the Sanchi Stupa in the middle of last century, were returned to India via Ceylon, to be re-interred with immense veneration in the Stupa whence they came. Of the ten Stupas said to have been erected over the ashes of Gotama, few have been identified with any certainty. A Stupa in Bhattibrolu, however, in the province of Madras, was found to contain a crystal phial, labelled as containing relics of the Buddha, and the Stupa itself is at least of the first or second century B.C.[1] The relics were presented by Lord Ronaldshay, then Viceroy of India, to the Maha Bodhi Society, and in due course a Vihara, or Temple Hall, was built in Calcutta at the headquarters of this famous Society to receive them.

Relics lead to pilgrimages, but of the four sites for Buddhist pilgrimage two only are easily found. The Lumbini Gardens, where Gotama was born, lie in the difficult Nepal Terai, and Kusinara, where the Buddha passed away, has little to show, but Buddha Gaya, the site of the Enlightenment, and the Deer Park at Sarnath, near Benares, the site of the Buddha's 'setting in motion the Wheel of the Law', are immensely popular, and pilgrims come from all parts of the Buddhist world to visit them.

1. Ronaldshay, *Lands of the Thunderbolt*, p. 87.

The beauty and peace of Buddha Gaya is marred by unfortunate influences, for the Temple is still, in spite of fifty years of Buddhist pleading, to a large extent Hindu-controlled, but Sarnath, now maintained by the Maha Bodhi Society, is one of the spiritual centres of Modern India, and there may be found some measure of the peace of heart which comes to those who follow in the footsteps of Gotama, the Buddha, the All-Enlightened One.

BIBLIOGRAPHY

FOR CHAPTERS ONE AND TWO

Arnold, Sir Edwin. *The Light of Asia.*

Brewster, E. H. *The Life of Gotama the Buddha.*

Bigandet. *The Life or Legend of Gaudama* (from the Burmese).

Cleather, Mrs A. L., and Crump, Basil. *Buddhism the Science of Life.*

Coomaraswamy, Ananda. *Buddha and the Gospel of Buddhism. Hinduism and Buddhism.*

Davids, Dr T. W. Rhys. *Buddhism* (S.P.C.K.).
Buddhism, Its History and Literature (Putnam).
Early Buddhism.

Davids, Mrs Rhys. *What was the Original Gospel in Buddhism?*

Grousset, René. *In the Footsteps of the Buddha.*

Hackmann, H. *Buddhism as a Religion.*

Lillie, Arthur. *The Popular Life of Buddha.*

Olcott, H. S. *The Buddhist Catechism.*

Pratt, J. B. *The Pilgrimage of Buddhism.*

Radhakrishnan, S. *Indian Philosophy*, Vol. I.

Reischauer, A. K. 'Buddhism' (in *The Great Religions of the World*, ed. Jurji).

Rockhill. *Life of the Buddha* (from the Tibetan).

Saunders, Kenneth. *Epochs in Buddhist History.*
A Pageant of Asia.

Singh, Iqbal. *Gotama Buddha.*

Smith, Vincent. *Asoka: The Buddhist Emperor of India.*

Thomas, E. J. *The Life of Buddha in Legend and History.*
The History of Buddhist Thought.

Valisinha, Devapriya. *Buddhist Shrines in India.*

[For Scriptures, see General Bibliography.]

CHAPTER THREE

The Rise of the Two Schools

*

*The Emperor Asoka – The Third Council – The
Origin of the Mahayana – Complementary Differences
– Nagasena and King Milinda – The Fourth Council –
Famous Mahayana Scriptures – The Prajña-Para-
mita – Amida and the Pure Land – The Transference of
Merit – Mind-Only – The Decline of Buddhism in India*

As soon as the 'lamp of wisdom had been blown out by the
wind of impermanence', a Council of the Sangha was convened at Rajagaha (Sanskrit: Rajagriha) to settle, if it were
possible, the contents of the three *Pitakas*, or Baskets, of the
Canon. The venerable Kassapa presided; Upali, the oldest
disciple, repeated the Rules of Discipline of the Order (the
Vinaya-pitaka); Ananda recited the *Sutta-pitaka* (the Basket
of Sermons), and Kassapa himself recited the *Abhidhamma*,
or the Pitaka of metaphysics, psychology and philosophy,
most of which, as it exists to-day, is a later commentary.

A second Council was held at Vesali about a hundred years
later. A section of the Sangha, considering the existing Rules
too irksome, demanded that a number of them be relaxed,
but, being defeated, this 'progressive' party, probably the
Mahasanghikas, seceded, leaving the Sthaviras, the fore-
bears of the Theravadins of to-day, in control.

The main doctrinal difference between the two parties
seems to have been the means of attaining Buddhahood, the
orthodox Elders maintaining that it was the fruit of strict
observance of the Rules, and the unorthodox minority holding, as the Mahayana holds to-day, that Buddhahood already
dwells within, and only needs developing. The defeated
minority held a Council of their own, and from this dichotomy
within the Sangha may be traced the manifold sects into
which the corpus of 'Buddhism' was split within a hundred
years or so of its foundation. The historicity of these two
Councils is impugned by certain scholars, but it is difficult

to see why such a host of detail should have been invented about matters which may quite easily have occurred.

The Emperor Asoka

Little is known of Buddhism for the next hundred years, but in 270 B.C. there came to the throne of India one of the greatest men in history, Asoka Maurya. Asoka was the grandson of Chandragupta, an army officer who, at the news of Alexander's death in Babylon, defeated the Greek forces left in India and founded an Indian Empire. Asoka, like his father, continued to expand these imperial conquests until, revolted by the horrors of war, he was converted to the Dhamma and became an *upasaka*, a lay adherent of the Order. Thereafter, as head of 'Church' and State, he rapidly converted Buddhism from a teaching popular in north-east India to a world religion.

The Buddhism which he taught was practical morality backed by his own example, and although he was later ordained a Bhikkhu he spoke as a layman speaking to laymen, leaving the niceties of doctrine to the more learned Brethren. The effect of his conversion was tremendous, and his dynamic mind was felt in every corner of the Empire. In the life of this greatest of India's kings, the friend of man and beast, we see what the Dhamma, bereft of its monastic limitations, can do for a nation. Converted by the horrors of war, Asoka became a man of peace, and called upon his subjects and upon neighbouring countries to accept this 'greatest of gifts', the Dhamma of filial piety, of brotherly kindness to all living things, of justice and truth, of tolerance and strenuous endeavour after the higher life. Setting a noble example in his own care for his people, he built for them hospitals, dug wells and reservoirs, and everywhere built glorious Stupas, commemorating not only the life of Sakyamuni but that of former Buddhas; and in their honour he stimulated India to produce an art unsurpassed in her history. By such means he united his people in the Dhamma, and Buddhism became the established religion of India.

Asoka was an ardent missionary. We know from one of the innumerable pillars which he erected throughout his vast dominion that he sent imperial messengers to all other parts of India, as well as to Syria, Egypt, Cyrene, Macedonia and Epirus. The most important of these missions, however, if such they may be called, was that to Ceylon, described in the next chapter. In his own country he set an example of benevolent dictatorship which has never since been equalled. His power was absolute, and exercised, it seems, entirely for good. He signed himself on his edicts as Piyadasi, 'The Humane', and by his kindliness to all men and to all living things, his tolerance for all points of view, and his powerful exhortations to all men to live the Buddha-life, he set an example which few, if any, of the rulers of history have even attempted to attain.

The Third Council

It is said that under his auspices a third Council was held at his capital, Pataliputra, under the chairmanship of Tissa, son of Moggali. Its purpose was partly to suppress a number of heresies whose exponents, probably Brahman pretenders, were causing dissensions in the Order by their loose teaching and even looser lives, and partly once more to revise and confirm the Canon. Whether such a Council was held under the patronage of Asoka, or, as some suggest, in his grandfather's reign, is uncertain. The Northern Schools make no mention of it; if it was held, it was probably a sectional Conference of the Theravada only, and a substantial split was already in existence. Meanwhile, the reactionary Brahman forces were gathering strength, and after Asoka's death his Empire was soon overthrown. Brahman teachings began to filter back into the religion from which they had for a time been ousted. Buddhism, from its outset fatally tolerant of all other teachings, even when antithetical to its own, made little effort to stem the process, and soon a number of sects were exhibiting Brahman doctrines which were unknown in the earlier Teaching.

This process was undoubtedly one of the formative influences in the rise of the Mahayana or Northern School of Buddhism. The nature and strength of the other causes will always be a matter for argument, and though contributory factors which led to the division can be examined separately, the interaction of the several streams of influence is impossible to define. Even the origin and meanings of the terms Mahayana and Hinayana is uncertain. *Yana* means literally career, with a secondary meaning of vehicle; *Maha* means 'great' as distinct from *Hina*, 'small'. The terms were invented by Mahayanists, who claimed that theirs was a career or course of life large enough to bear all mankind to salvation; the various sects of the Hinayana, of which the best known is the Theravada, the Doctrines of the Elders, claimed to teach the Buddha-way as pointed out by the Master.

The Origin of the Mahayana

The two extreme suggestions as to the origin of the Mahayana are, on the one hand, that it was the esoteric doctrine of the Buddha as taught to his Elect, and on the other, that it was a collection of deplorable heresies by which the pure teaching of the Master was all too soon defiled. There is truth in both. The Mahayana Canon contains a larger proportion of the esoteric Wisdom than any other religion, and has always adhered more closely to the 'Heart' as distinct from the 'Eye' doctrine, the eternal life rather than the changing form of the Message. On the other hand, much of the teaching to be found to-day in the Mahayana schools is, on the face of it, the exact antithesis of the Message as recorded in the Pali Canon.

Another, and perhaps more helpful, approach to the problem is the psychological. More than one writer had pointed out that the rise of the Mahayana as a revolt from the Hinayana was inevitable. The Indian mind, already heir to some of the noblest achievements of mystical reasoning, could never be long content with the moral philosophy of the Southern School. Low-lighted as it is with the Puritan lamp of self-suppression, and largely arid of the poetry, spiritual excitement and the sense of humour of many of the Mahayana schools, such 'a cold, passionless metaphysics devoid of religious teaching could not long inspire enthusiasm and joy. The Hinayana ignored the groping of the spirit of man after something higher, and wronged the spiritual side of man.'[1]

The negative philosophy of the Hinayana could never easily become a popular religion. When Buddhism became universal in spirit and embraced large masses, the Hinayana could no longer serve. A religion more catholic, a less ascetic ideal, was required.

Certainly within a hundred years of the death of Asoka the change was profound and all but complete. From a human being the Buddha had become a super-human Being,

1. Radhakrishnan, *Indian Philosophy*, Vol. I, p. 589-90.

and his spiritual Essence had entered a pantheon nearly as large as that of the Hinduism from which it derived.

The Arhat ideal, that of the human being who, by strenuous effort, acquires Enlightenment, gave way to that of the Bodhisattva, the Saviour of Mankind, and compassion (*Karuna*) received far greater emphasis. A moral philosophy for the few became a religion for all, and salvation by faith, the transference of 'merit' to the benefit of others, the practice of Bhakti Yoga, or devotion to a personified ideal, these and the other habitual accompaniments of religion filled the lives of men who claimed to be followers of one who would, it seems, have none of them. There was a profound turnover from the negative emphasis of the Theravada to a positive statement of eternal principles. History lost its importance, for the Mahayana had passed beyond the accidents of time and place. The science of first causes was openly studied, and a magnificent cathedral of metaphysics and philosophy lifted its head and heart to the sky.

Anicca-Anatta, the doctrine that all things are impermanent, even the 'soul', was developed until it reached the stage of absolute *Sunyata*, the Plenum-Void; the emphasis on *Dukkha*, suffering, was lowered, and the happiness of a Buddhist heaven held up to the lazy eyes of the multitude as easy to obtain. 'Work out your own salvation with diligence', said the Buddha, and until the founding of the Ch'an (Japanese: Zen) School in the sixth century in China, when the old virility reappeared, this clarion call to spiritual effort was replaced by the general plea: 'Have faith; express that faith repeatedly, and the Buddha Principle within will save you from the consequences of your sins.'

But, enormous though these changes were, the Mahayana claimed from the first that it never rejected the Theravada or any part of it. There are Schools to-day in China and Japan where the Pali Canon is still studied, for, as Dr McGovern says: 'While Hinayana regards Mahayana as a corruption of the original Buddhism, or at the best a false and decadent branch, Mahayana regards Hinayana not as false or contrary to true Buddhism, but simply as incomplete, or the superficial doctrine which Sakyamuni taught to those who were incapable of comprehending the more profound truths of Mahayana.'[1]

1. *Introduction to Mahayana Buddhism*, p. 123.

The Mahayanists have always claimed that Mahayana is the extension of Hinayana and not its replacement. As John Blofeld, in his Introduction to *The Huang-Po Doctrine of Universal Mind*, says of the relation of the two Schools, 'The Hinayana view is that Mahayana is a later development which constitutes a great departure from the real teaching of the Buddha. The Mahayana view is that the Buddha taught various aspects of truth at different stages in his life, specially adapted to the capabilities of people whose powers of understanding were at different levels.'

With the expansion of Theravada to Mahayana the tension for the individual slackened. 'Right Effort' came to imply very little effort. It is far easier to feel pleasantly benevolent to all creatures than to work for the eradication of hatred, lust, and illusion from one's own very human mind. The Bodhisattva ideal of world compassion may be more attractive to the sentimentalist; it is, in all but its higher levels, far easier than the slaying of one 'fond offence' and the desire which leads to it.

But all this development was dual, downwards to a popular religion, upwards to the noblest philosophy the world has known, and, from this point of view, the Theravada stands as a Middle Way between the two extremes. As a religion, Buddhism lost in depth what it gained in surface extension. On the other hand, if the *Tat tvam asi*, 'Thou art THAT', of Indian philosophy seems to be the pinnacle of human thought, the *Jijimuge* of the Kegon school of Japanese Buddhism, in which the part and the whole are utterly 'interfused', while yet the parts retain their individuality in a whole which ever remains the whole, is higher still, and thought can go no further.

It is easy to indulge in generalizations, but it is probably true to say that the cleavage between the two Schools falls into a recognizable pattern. The Mahayana refused to be inhibited; the Hinayana was bound by the Canon. The former was speculative, metaphysical; the latter rational and authoritarian. The Mahayana was fearless in its logic and its mystical flights; the Theravada was content to be the guardian of the Dhamma as handed down. The closed circle of intense self-development became a religion for all, and a formula of salvation branched out into a heterogeneous mixture of apparently opposed and incompatible teaching.

Complementary Differences

Such lines of cleavage, however, fundamental as they seem, are clearly psychological in character, and therefore deeper and more universal than any historical explanation would lead one to suppose. Certainly the fundamental distinction seems to be that between the emotions and the mind, of Bhakti Yoga as distinct from Jnana or Karma Yoga. From this in time flow the other complementary antitheses, men tending towards the more intellectual view, involving the austere philosophy and ethics from which the feminine temperament recoils; women preferring the devotional and more emotional approach, with the expansive mysticism which such implies. If this be true, and all my avenues of knowledge, including the study of Buddhism and psychology, and personal research into the Schools of various Buddhist countries, tend to confirm it, then all argument as to 'better' and 'worse' must cease. Men and women, day and night, inbreathing and outbreathing, the head and the heart, these are alternates, not alternatives, and argument on relative worth is no more than debate on the two sides of a coin. And just as male and female characteristics, physical and mental, are present in each human being in differing proportions, so all these pairs of qualities are present in each School.

These differences of doctrine were naturally enhanced by the nation developing them, and national variations are seen in the Buddhism of Tibet, China and Japan. The Theravada may be likened to the hub of a wheel, with the various schools of the Mahayana lying at the end of the spokes which radiate from it. If each displays a substantial difference in doctrine from that at the hub, those which have developed in an opposite though complementary way must be far indeed from each other. Only such an analogy can explain the differences existing in some of the Schools in Japan, where, for example, the 'Pure Land' Buddhism of salvation by grace and the Zen school of strenuous self-enlightenment, by 'seeing directly into the heart of man', exist in mutual tolerance side by side. And yet, as Dr Suzuki has written, 'There are not two Buddhisms; the Mahayana and the Hinayana are one, and the spirit of the founder of Buddhism prevails in both. Each has developed in its own way, according to the difference in environment in which each has thriven and grown, understanding by environment all those various factors of life that make up the peculiarities of an individual or nation.'[1]

Nagasena and King Milinda

To return to our brief outline of Buddhist history, little is known between the death of Asoka and the 'conversations' of Nagasena, some time in the second or first century B.C., with King Milinda, the Indian name for the Graeco-Bactrian King Menander. This *Milinda-Panha*, or *Questions of King Milinda*, which Dr Rhys Davids describes as 'the masterpiece of Indian prose', is an apologia by Nagasena for the main teachings of the orthodox schools, designed, it has been suggested, to win the wavering minds of the day from the new, unorthodox Buddhism. Yet herein are to be found the seeds of at least two important Mahayana doctrines, salvation by faith and the Bodhisattva ideal. Nagasena, a magnificent dialectician, reduces Buddhism to a negative dogmatism from which revolt was inevitable, thereby possibly hastening the process of development in the opposite direction.

The Fourth Council

Soon after the reign of Milinda the Kushans overran his kingdom in North-West India, but fortunately the greatest of the Kushan kings, Kanishka (78–103 A.D.), became an ardent Buddhist, and followed Asoka's example by holding a Council, which may reasonably be called the fourth. But whereas the Mahayanists make no mention of Asoka's Council, only the Sarvastivadins, a sect of the Hinayana, were present at Kanishka's Council, together with Tibetans and Chinese; the Hinayanists of Ceylon, Siam and Burma ignored its existence. The purpose of the Council was to attempt to harmonize the growing divergence of teaching in the two main Schools, but in this it seems to have been only partly successful. Dissentient views were already finding their way into writing, and the *Lalita-Vistara*, for example, an early Sanskrit work, while belonging to the orthodox School, bridges the gap between it and its rival.

1. 'The Development of Mahayana Buddhism', from *The Buddhist Review*, Vol. I, 1909.

Kanishka himself is the hero of two of the stories in the *Sutralamkara* of Ashvaghosha, who was certainly one of the greatest poets of India, and by reason of the strong Mahayanist tendencies of his accepted writings has been called by Ananda Coomaraswamy the 'Father of Mahayana Buddhism'. The *Sutralamkara*, like his earlier *Life of the Buddha*, was written in Sanskrit instead of Pali, a change which was contemporary with a slow removal of the centre of Buddhism from the north-east India of its birth to the north-west of its final Indian development. Here, in the kingdom of Gandhara, with its chief city of Purusapura and its university of Taxila, the rapidly developing religion came under the Hellenistic influence of Alexander's conquests and, far more important, that of a developed Brahmanism, with its cult of Yoga, its expansive mysticism and its highly metaphysical cast of thought. To this expansion the Hinayana Schools could only reply with a further extension of the Abhidhamma, or 'further Dhamma', the third portion of their Canon, and it is clear that its later portions were considerably influenced by Brahmanic thought.

Famous Mahayana Scriptures

A Scripture which bridged the two main Schools was the *Mahavastu*, compiled by the Mahasanghika, a sect of the Hinayana, from whom most scholars derive the birth of Mahayana. The whole tendency of the Mahayanists was to deny the reality of phenomena, and thus to rob history of its value. The Buddha became increasingly a spiritual Principle, but a different trend developed in the *Sukhavati-Vyuha* and still more famous *Saddharma-Pundarika*, which were probably written about this time. Of the former, Kenneth Saunders says: 'The luxuriance and enthusiasm with which the *Sukhavati-Vyuha* abounds are eloquent of the hunger of Buddhist hearts for a heavenly city ... In this apocalyptic heaven and in the cult of Maitri Buddha, which belongs to the same era, we may see that, the attainment of Arhatship having ceased, men were constrained to find satisfaction in contemplating either rebirth in a new era of enthusiasm, or in a Paradise beyond this vale of tears.'[1]

This cult of Amida and the Bodhisattva ideal are further developed in the *Saddharma-Pundarika*, 'The Lotus of the

1. *Epochs in Buddhist History*, p. 59–60.

Good Law', the principal Bodhisattva being Avalokitesh-vara. The Buddha, his temporal qualities shed, becomes eternal.

To the extent that it is possible to place the more important Mahayana Sutras in sequence, the next would be the *Avatamsaka*, the transcendental philosophy of which undoubtedly influenced Nagarjuna. But in this, as in most other works of the Mahayana School, there are signs of considerable development of thought in the Sutra itself, and the difficulty of either summarizing their contents or describing their influence upon each other is immense. This Sutra, however, was undoubtedly one of the basic 'studies' of the great University of Nalanda. From the second to the ninth century, Nalanda was one of the greatest universities in India, and received the unbounded admiration of those shrewd and critical observers, the Chinese pilgrims Hiuen-Tsiang and I-Tsing, who successively spent many years at the University in the seventh century. According to the former, the residents at any one time amounted to ten thousand men, of whom eight thousand five hundred were students and the rest teachers. Every then known line of thought and point of view was studied in an atmosphere of mutual tolerance. Students came from Japan, Korea, Mongolia, China and Tartary, as well as from the whole of India, and chose from the hundred lectures given every day whatever they required. The Library must have been one of the finest in the world, while the teachers at any one time included the finest brains in India.

The Prajña-Paramita

One of the greatest of these teachers was Nagarjuna, perhaps the greatest Buddhist philosopher. He formulated, or at least consolidated, the Madhyamika, or Middle Path School, which attempted to reconcile the doctrines of realism and nihilism, the vehicle for his teaching being the veritable library of works known as the Prajña-Paramita. In the very brief *Prajña-Paramita-Hridaya Sutra*, recited daily throughout the Far East in a thousand monasteries, the emptiness of all form is magnificently summarized. To this must be added the famous 'Eight Noes' from the *Madhyamika Sastra*, 'No production nor destruction; no annihilation nor persistence; no unity nor plurality; no coming in nor going out.' Reality lies between these negatives, but only the Zen school has described the way to reach it. Perhaps the best known work of the Prajña-Paramita group, however, is the *Vajracchedika* (*Diamond*) *Sutra*, the recital of which enabled Hui-Neng to achieve *Satori* or Enlightenment (see Chapter 14, on Zen Buddhism). These groups of Sutras developed the doctrine of Sunyata (Void) and its related doctrine of Tathata, or 'suchness', the seeds of which, as already explained, are to be found in the Hinayana. For Sunyata is Anicca carried to its logical conclusion, and the suchness of things is that quality by which they are one with the principle of Enlightenment. More important, in a way, as holding out a hand to the Hinayana, is the clear distinction to be made between abstract and relative truth, the former needing Enlightenment for its full possession, the latter advancing with the development of the individual.

Amida and the Pure Land

The cult of Amitabha (Jap.: Amida) and the Pure Land, or Sukhavati, to which all true believers would, with sufficient faith, be transferred at their physical passing, are two more doctrines which received considerable development. Amida is the spiritual Essence or Dhyani Buddha, who manifested on earth through the Bodhisattva Avalokiteshvara as Gotama the Buddha (see Chapter 15 on Tibetan Buddhism), and the *Amitayadhyana Sutra* is a development of the *Sukhavati-Vyuha* already mentioned. The larger and smaller *Sukhavati-Vyuha* and the later *Amitayadhyana Sutra* may well have expressed and moulded the devotional life of Nalanda, and in them we may trace the gradual development of the doctrine of faith at the expense of the older doctrine of merit. By now the Bodhisattva ideal had almost replaced the earlier Arhat ideal of the Theravada. The word Bodhisattva means one whose essence or being (*sattva*) is perfect Wisdom (*Bodhi*), but historically it meant one who has dedicated his life to the welfare of mankind, delaying thereby his entry into Nirvana, the reward of his own Enlightenment. To the extent that the Bodhisattva ideal replaced the Arhat ideal, self-development was subordinate to other-self salvation. The antithesis, of course, is ultimately false, for neither is possible without the other, and even if the development of compassion is apparently a great advance on the earlier concentration on self-development, it is easy to confuse a true compassion with laziness in self-development, and a preference for interference with other people's affairs.

The Transference of Merit

A natural development of the doctrine of compassion for all life is the transference or turning round of 'merit' (*parivarta*) from the actual earner to some particular or general beneficiary. The effect on the doctrine of Karma is profound. If life is one, it is logical to hold that the act of each part affects the whole, and all other parts of it, for good or evil. To this extent Karma is no longer merely particular but general. In the words of H. P. Blavatsky, 'It is an occult law that no man can rise superior to his individual failings without lifting, be it ever so little, the whole body of which he is an integral part. In the same way no man can sin, nor suffer the effects of sin, alone. In reality there is no such thing as "separateness". . . .'[1] But Karma does not cease thereby to be personal. If a stone is thrown into a pond the ripples flow out to the margin of the pond. They then return, to the point where the stone initiated the cause. Thus, even though 'merit', the result of good acts, may be offered to all, it returns in the first place, like the result of evil deeds, to the doer, and the doctrine of irresponsibility has no place in Buddhism.

Mind-Only

About this time the Buddhist doctrine of Mind-Only acquired its chief development. The purpose of the Yogachara (Teaching or Practice of Yoga) Schools, founded about the fourth century A.D. by two Brahmans named Asanga and Vasubandhu, was essentially mystical. The importance of Vijñanavada, the doctrine of Mind-Consciousness, is inherent in the Theravada Scriptures, but under the genius of these two brothers it achieved a magnificent presentation. This subjective idealism developed several of the principles now basic to the Mahayana School as a whole. All save consciousness is unreal, though in a world of appearances one acts as if appearances were real. Thus suffering (*dukkha*) belongs to the world of illusion, but a man should act as if the suffering were real and assist all sufferers accordingly. Consciousness is stored in a central Alayavijñana which contains

1. *The Key to Theosophy*, p. 127.

the suchness (*Tathata*) of all things; and individual consciousness is a partial manifestation of this whole. This interrelation is an advance on the *Lankavatara Sutra* composed about this time, for the sense of mystical union is now absolute. But the development of the central consciousness to the margin of its manifestations may be conceived in stages, and the doctrine of *Trikaya*, the appearance of the Absolute in three increasingly dense forms, was developed accordingly. In the same way man's approach to the central truth has three *lakshana*, or stages. First is the ordinary naïve realism. Later, we realize that things are not what they seem. We begin to understand the relativity of all things. From this in turn we pass to the final and perfect knowledge in which we know, beyond all doubting, that the world in which we live is only the appearance of the Essence of Pure Mind. In time this School adopted much of the esoteric use of *Mantras* (the magical use of sound) and *Mudras* (the magical use of gesture).

In the Yogachara School, the Alayavijñana was still to some extent a psychological term, but in *The Awakening of Faith in the Mahayana* it becomes metaphysical and cosmic, and is replaced by a still higher term, *Bhutatathata*, usually translated as 'Suchness'. This famous little treatise is often attributed to Ashvaghosha, but there were a number of writers of that name, and as it seems to be a development of the Yogachara School it may be as late as the fourth century A.D.

In the seventh century the Mahayana poet Santideva of Nalanda produced his 'Students' Compendium' (*Sikshasamuccaya*), a book of moral rules for the budding Bodhisattva, and this love of the Bodhisattva ideal is expanded in his still more famous *Bodhicaryavatara*, or 'Training for Enlightenment', which has been called the finest poem of Buddhism.

The Decline of Buddhism in India

By the seventh century the tide had turned for Buddhism in India. Though the patronage of the Emperor Harsha enabled the religion to recover somewhat from the attacks of the White Huns, who looted and destroyed many of the monastic cities, the respite was brief. The reports of the Chinese pilgrim, Hiuen-Tsiang, who travelled through India in the middle of the seventh century, compared with those of his predecessor, Fa-Hien, who travelled the same area about a hundred years earlier, show a noticeable decline in the number of monasteries occupied and the virility of thought within them. The two main Schools were still equally represented, but the North-west corner of India was already largely regained by the Brahmans, and when the Chinese pilgrim, I-Tsing, visited India towards the end of the seventh century he bemoans the dying religion which he loves.

There was a brief revival in Magadha under the Pala Dynasty, but by the year 1000 little was left of Buddhism in India for the invading Moslems to destroy. Early Buddhism depended largely upon its Sangha, and when the monastic life became corrupted by the return of Hindu practices, the Sangha fell in popular esteem, and the giving of alms by Buddhist laymen declined accordingly. Brahmanism influenced the growing Mahayana with its Shaivite and Tantric practices, and the Mahayana, while refusing to appease the human appetite which craves for sacrifice and escapist ritual, became less and less distinguishable from the religion of the people. Moreover, as it spread wide, it grew weaker in content, and much of its energy was dissipated in various states of mystical intoxication which sapped its virility.

The popular forms of Hinduism, as the compound of Indian religions based on the Vedas and Upanishads may be called, had been enormously improved by Buddhist moral philosophy, while Buddhism had in many respects been debased by its lazy tolerance of the forms of Hinduism. In the result, the distinctions between them were reduced in value, while to the extent that Mahayana was at variance with Theravada the Brahmans increasingly deprived them both of independent life.

Thereafter the two Schools severally began that pilgrimage which, while it made of Buddhism an exile from the land of its birth, led it to spiritual heights of understanding, a profundity of moral worth and a magnificent harvest of art and culture which raised it to the status of the largest, and, in many senses of the term, the greatest of the world's religions. For even if the two Schools had divided widely, their common ground still formed the greatest spiritual force on earth, deriving as it did and does to-day from the Supreme Enlightenment of 'the greatest of the sons of men', Gotama the Buddha.

BIBLIOGRAPHY

FOR CHAPTER THREE

Davids, Prof. T. W. Rhys. *Buddhism.*

Dutt, N. *Aspects of Mahayana Buddhism and its Relation to Hinayana.*

Coomaraswamy, Ananda. *Buddha and the Gospel of Buddhism.*

Hackmann, H. *Buddhism as a Religion.*

Kimura, R. *Hinayana and Mahayana and the Origin of Mahayana Buddhism.*

McGovern, W. M. *An Introduction to Mahayana Buddhism.*

Pratt, J. B. *The Pilgrimage in Buddhism.*

Radhakrishnan, S. *Indian Philosophy,* Vol. I.

Saunders, Kenneth. *Epochs in Buddhist History.*
  A Pageant of Asia.

Suzuki, D. T. *Outlines of Mahayana Buddhism,* 'The Development of Mahayana Buddhism' (from *The Buddhist Review,* Vol. I, pp. 103 *et seq.*).

Thomas, E. J. *The History of Buddhist Thought.*

CHAPTER FOUR

The Spread of Buddhism

*

Buddhism as a Missionary Religion – Buddhism in Ceylon – Buddhism in Burma – Buddhism in Siam – Buddhism in Cambodia – Buddhism in China – Buddhism in Korea – Buddhism in Japan – Fourteen 'Fundamental Buddhistic Beliefs' of Colonel Olcott – The 'Twelve Principles of Buddhism' of the Buddhist Society, London

BUDDHISM was from the first a missionary religion. Within a few days of the First Sermon the Buddha sent his handful of converts into the world with the famous exhortation, already quoted, 'Go ye forth, O Bhikkhus, for the gain of the many, for the welfare of the many, in compassion for the world. Proclaim the Doctrine glorious, preach ye a life of holiness, perfect and pure.' And the same command appears in the Mahayana work, *The Voice of the Silence*. 'Point out the Way – however dimly, and lost among the host – as does the evening star to those who tread their path in darkness. Give light and comfort to the toiling pilgrim, and seek out him who knows still less than thou, who in his wretched desolation sits starving for the bread of Wisdom – let him hear the Law.' For part of the Buddha's task was to make available to all men the universal principles of truth which the Brahmans of his day considered their monopoly, and Buddhism was from the first a Message for all mankind.

To proclaim a Teaching, however, is not to proselytize in the sense of forcing ideas upon an unwilling audience, much less to use pressure to obtain adherence to one's own point of view. A man's sole right, a right which to the Buddhist is also a duty, is to offer to all the knowledge of a path which the Buddha proclaimed as a way to Enlightenment, and which the speaker or writer, so far as he has trodden that Path, has found to be true. Some seed, of course, will fall on stony ground, but some will flourish abundantly, and 'the gift of the Dhamma is greater than all other gifts'.[1]

1. *Dhammapada*, v. 354.

Nor did the Buddha preach 'Buddhism' to his monks, although they in the course of centuries gradually codified in formulas what once was given as a living stream of spiritual experience. The Tathagata pointed out the nature of the manifested universe and the Path which leads from the world of appearances to ultimate Reality. He dealt with life, not with the changing forms of it, and life can never be locked away in glorious phrases. The Buddha's Teaching was a mode of living, a method of approach to life itself. Buddhism is man's attempt to create a cage for this experience, and to the extent that he succeeds he fails to inherit the Wisdom which the Master offered to mankind.

The method of teaching was by preaching and subsequent discussion. The India of the Buddha's way was full of men who were ever ready to listen to and apply new spiritual experience, and it was to such men that the Dhamma was first offered. All might attend the new teaching, but only the few, with minds self-educated by strenuous thought and meditation, would fully appreciate its value. Nothing was written down, but the principles discussed were memorized, and formed in turn the basis of discussion. The Bhikkhu-preacher made no claim to authority, being content to open his discourse with the phrase which still is in vogue, 'Thus have I heard'. Even 'Buddhas do but point the way', and the individual must sooner or later work out his own salvation with diligence. There was therefore no dogma, and in the absence of any God or gods with power to advance or hinder a man's approach to his own enlightenment, there was no question of sacrifice or sacrament, still less of prayer.

Such is and always has been the method of making known the Dhamma adopted by the Bhikkhus of the Theravada, and such was probably the method used by the Mahayana preachers when they first left India. Only when the vital impulse of the Teacher's presence had largely spent itself did the lazy habits of religion appear, that religion which, under the guise of a way to Reality, so easily becomes a shield to protect the devotee from the terrors of direct experience. The original Message was, 'Here is a Path which leads to the end of suffering by the elimination of personal and therefore separative desire. Tread it.' All too soon this became a mere, 'Have faith; believe in the Dhamma, and you will be saved.'

*

Buddhism in Ceylon

The earliest definite mission was to Ceylon. Asoka, who
sent his ambassadors to most of the known world, sent, at
the invitation of King Tissa, the Thera Mahendra (Pali:
Mahinda), who was either the son or the younger brother of
the Emperor. The mission was apparently a great success.
According to the *Dipavamsa* (fourth c.) and the *Mahavamsa*
(fifth c.), two famous Sinhalese records, the founding of
Buddhism in Ceylon was attended with most notable miracles, but, however, this may be, several of the Chinese pilgrims who visited the island centuries later confirmed that
the inhabitants of Lanka, the name for Ceylon which figures
largely in Indian history, accepted the new faith with avidity,
and in spite of Tamil invasions from South India and later
European aggression, it remains the proud stronghold of the
Theravada to this day.

Mahinda converted the King and his Court to Buddhism,
and was soon followed to Ceylon by his sister, Sanghamitta,
who brought with her a cutting of the 'Bo' (the *Bodhi*) Tree
of Buddha Gaya, which is growing to-day in the ruins of
Anuradhapura, the then capital. These pipal trees (*Ficus reli-
giosa*) grow to enormous age, and as local records speak of
the tree from time to time through the 2,200 years of history,
there is no reason to doubt that this venerated growth is the
oldest historical tree in existence.

In honour of the Bhikkhu Mahinda, who made his headquarters at Mahintale, a hill near Anuradhapura, and his
Bhikkhuni sister, King Tissa founded a monastery with a
grant of land. On it he built the Thuparama Dagoba (or
Stupa, a reliquary mound), to enshrine yet a further gift to
Ceylon, a collar-bone of the Buddha, and this Dagoba, newly
restored, is one of the loveliest sights of the ruined city to-
day. Anuradhapura at one time, large enough to house more
people than nowadays live in the whole of Ceylon, was the
brilliant capital of a Buddhist Court which, though it later
moved to Pollunaruwa and thence to Kandy before the advancing Tamil invasion, remained faithfully Buddhist until
its overthrow in the nineteenth century.

In the third century A.D. Ceylon was still further honoured
with a tooth of the Buddha, which has become a national
treasure. Immense reverence is paid to this relic at the Temple

of the Tooth at Kandy, and even if some historians claim that the original was burnt by the Catholic Portuguese, the Sinhalese reply that what was burnt was only a substitute.

Meanwhile the Sangha was engaged in more valuable enterprises than relic worship, for it is recorded that in the first century B.C. the memorized Canon was reduced to writing, a historic fact which excuses to some extent the excessive honour paid by the Sinhalese to-day to the written word. The fifth century produced the first Buddhist commentator in Buddhaghosa, a Brahman convert to Buddhism from Gaya, His *Visuddhi-magga* ('Path of Purity'), written in Pali, maintains the original Arhat ideal, and crystallizes, as it were, the Theravada view of the original Message of the Buddha.

In the eleventh century Ceylon was being hard pressed by the Cholas of South India, and it seems that the Dhamma, too, had fallen on hard times, for the king of Ceylon sent to the king of Burma for Bhikkhus to strengthen the native Sangha. A century later, however, there was a great revival of Buddhism under King Parakrama Bahu, and according to Dr Le May, 'from that time up to the sixteenth century Ceylon was regarded by its brother Buddhist countries, Siam, Burma and Cambodia, with almost as much veneration as the holy places of Buddhism in India, as the fountainhead of the pure Theravada doctrines'.[1]

Buddhism in Burma

The earliest history of Buddhism in Burma is obscure. Asoka sent his missionaries to 'Suvannabhumi' (The Golden Land), which apparently means Burma, and the Indian infiltration of influence by land and sea must have brought with it the prevailing forms of Indian Buddhism. Some Burmese claim Buddhaghosa as the source of their Buddhism, but the early chronicles of Ceylon make no such claim. The great man's influence, however, was enormous and may well have affected the mixture of Mahayana and Hinayana Buddhism and indigenous *nat* (a kind of nature-spirit) worship which satisfied Burma for the first 1,000 years A.D. Even to-day the Sanskrit terms in Burmese Buddhism are evidence of its Mahayana origin, and as Kenneth Saunders[2] says,

1. 'The Development of Buddhist Art in Burma', *Journal of Royal Society of Arts*, June, 1949.
2. *Epochs in Buddhist History*, p. 111–12.

'Burmese Buddhists have a vague, pantheistic philosophy of life which is more akin to the Mahayana than the Hinayana', and for reasons given he concludes that 'the Buddhism of the Burmese masses is somewhere between the Hinayana and the Mahayana'.

The worship of *nats*, akin to the worship of *devatas* in Ceylon, is incurable, as J. B. Pratt says, 'The Burman loves the Buddha but fears the nats. The Buddha he knows will never harm him, but the nats may!'[1] But it is well said that if you scratch a Burman you will find a Buddhist. Behind the façade of a gay and a frivolous people is an intense love of the Buddha, and no force, political or otherwise, will ever remove it from their lives.

The greatest figure in Burmese Buddhism is King Anawrahta of Pagan (A.D. 1044–1077), who, being converted to Theravada Buddhism by a Shin Arahan, a wandering Bhikkhu from the neighbouring kingdom of Thaton, sent for full instruction, and Burma officially became thereafter attached to the Theravada School. The king soon made his capital city one of the wonders of the world, and such temple building has seldom been seen. Hundreds of Gothic churches were then rising all over Europe, but thousands of pagodas rose in a few square miles in Pagan, while one of the greatest temples on earth was raised about a century later in Rangoon, to dominate the city, then as now, with its pinnacle of plated gold. Here, too, in the Shwe Dagon, are enshrined relics of the Buddha, and this curious blend of market and forum with a holy place of pilgrimage is undoubtedly one of the world centres of Buddhism.

In the thirteenth century, Kublai Khan attacked Pagan and sacked it, and not till the sixteenth century was Burma again united as a Buddhist kingdom. Then came the British who, as elsewhere, respected the Triple Gem of the Buddha, Dhamma and Sangha, and to-day the orange robe of the Order, like the yellow robe of Siam and Ceylon, still dominates the landscape. The Siamese claim that their Sangha leads in the Vinaya Pitaka, the Rules of the Order; the Sinhalese Sangha, which at present produces the leading minds of Theravada Buddhism, concentrates on the Sutta Pitaka, the teachings of the Buddha. The Burmese Sangha, as the visitor will be told a dozen times before he is a week in the

1. *India and its Faiths*, p. 347.

country, is master of the Abhidhamma, that complex mixture of metaphysics, psychology and mind-development which partly derives from Indian Yoga. This deliberate choice is a further evidence that Burma began its Buddhist life as part of the Mahayana, although it is to-day, and has been for the last 1,000 years, a stronghold, like Ceylon and Siam, of the Theravada School.

Buddhism in Siam

It is probable that the people now known as the Siamese (or Thai) contacted Buddhism before migrating South from their native China. To-day, the interrelation of the various races and cultures which fill this south-east corner of Asia is so complex that it is difficult to isolate any single factor. The Burmese, meaning a compound of Burmese, Karens, Shans, Talaings, and Arakanese, and the Cambodians (Khmers), Chams, Annamese, Laos and others, who have fought each other, ruled each other and affected each other in the last 2,000 years, acquired at some time first, apparently, Mahayana Buddhism and later the Theravada, but when and whence and how it is hard to say.

By A.D. 1200 the Siamese were settled in their present territory, and indeed in a much wider area until deprived of a large part of it by acquisitive Western 'Powers'. In the fourteenth century, the King of the day, inspired by whom we know not, sent to Ceylon for a Theravadin Bhikkhu, who was received with considerable honour at the then capital, Sukhotai, and was created Sangharaja, or Supreme Head of the Order. The King, following Asoka's example, entered the Order, and from this springs the close connexion between the royal house and the Sangha which is a noticeable feature of Siamese Buddhism to-day.

Thus the trinity of the Theravada, Ceylon, Burma and Siam, with all that matters in common, proudly maintains its joint tradition of preserving at least reasonably intact the essential Teaching of the All-Enlightened One.

Buddhism in Cambodia

South-east Asia is vaguely claimed by the Theravada, but much of it is so heavily influenced by China, and an earlier Hinduism, that is it difficult to substantiate such a claim for more than Cambodia. Until the fourteenth century the

T – C

religion of Cambodia was a blend of Hinduism and Mahayana
Buddhism; hence the complex history and art of the famous
temple of Angkor. Later, the Siamese influence became
paramount, and with it a Theravada ascendancy.

Buddhism in China

There is a strong tradition that Buddhism reached China
early in the Han dynasty (first century B.C.), but there is historic evidence that in A.D. 61 the Emperor Ming-ti, in consequence of a dream, sent messengers to India for Buddhist
books and teachers. Two monks returned to the Emperor's
capital of Lo-yang laden with images and scriptures of the
Mahayana School. One of their Indian companions translated the *Sutra of 42 Sections* into Chinese, and thus began
the tremendous task of making known the splendour of
Indian Buddhism to the Confucian and Taoist scholars of
the day. This Sutra is an anthology of precepts, largely
Theravada in spirit, but its influence was soon swamped
by later translations, and although the Pali Scriptures are
studied to this day in China and Japan it was the Mahayana
School whose doctrines the Chinese were asked to accept,
and which they accepted only after a modification so profound as all but to create a new form of Buddhism.

The new arrivals were not received with open arms. Their
doctrines were too subtle and metaphysical for the essentially
practical, not to say material, Chinese mind, and the disciples of Confucius objected to the habit of monkhood, then
unknown in China. It meant that men avoided their primary
task of parenthood, whereby they continued the line of filial
respect, and, what was nearly as objectionable, it taught
them to beg instead of working for their living. Moreover,
whereas in Ceylon and Burma and Siam the Indian culture
entered a land inferior in development, the Chinese culture
of the late Han Dynasty was second to none. Confucian and
Taoist ideals, almost exactly complementary, filled the minds
of the cultured levels of society and both, being indigenous,
combined to cold-shoulder the alien ideas from the West. It
is not surprising therefore, that it was only after three hundred years of effort that Buddhism joined the other two
philosophies to form the famous tripod of the Chinese
religion.

Success was largely due to the work of the translator

Kumarajiva (fourth and fifth centuries A.D.). His output was so enormous that a new wave of interest was created, which culminated in permission to the Buddhist laymen to become monks and to found a Chinese branch of the Sangha. Thereafter Chinese Buddhism, though continuing to receive support from India, was native and largely independent, and by the sixth century most of North-West China was Buddhist, though largely, it would seem of the Pure Land or, Amida School.

Up to this time, however, Indian Buddhism was still but an alien study, albeit a popular study, for the intelligentsia. It had not yet been translated into a native idiom. This was the work of Bodhidharma (Chinese: Tamo; Japanese: Daruma), an Indian Buddhist from Conjeeveram, near Madras, whose brilliant, ruthless mind made short work of the prevailing speculative thought and its companion, salvation by faith. Apparently without the least intention of doing so he founded the School which, within a few hundred years, was almost commensurate with Chinese Buddhism.

The purpose and technique of the School were early summarized:

> A special transmission outside the scriptures;
> No dependence upon words and letters;
> Direct pointing to the soul of man;
> Seeing into one's own nature.

In this famous summary Bodhidharma claimed to be returning to the spirit of the Buddha's teaching. This, he claimed, was *Dhyana*; hence his School was called, from the Chinese corruption of Dhyana, Ch'an, corrupted in turn by the Japanese into Zen. As such it passed in the twelfth century into Japan, and after fifteen hundred years is still one of the two main influences in the spiritual life of that country. It still represents such life as remains in Chinese Buddhism.

Buddhism reached its greatest strength in China in the T'ang Dynasty (620–907), when it combined with the Chinese native genius to produce some of the greatest art – some think the greatest art – which the world has known. Moreover, the steady stream of Buddhist scholars who came to China from India brought with them the science and medicine of the day, while it was the monks in China who originated printing by blocks, the first work to be so printed being the *Diamond Sutra*, still one of the most popular scriptures in China or Japan.

In China Buddhism suffered its first persecution, and for centuries its elevation or suppression turned upon whether the Emperor of the day was a Confucian or Buddhist devotee. But the double process of importation and assimilation went on steadily. The Chinese pilgrim monks, Fa-Hien, Hiuen-Tsiang, I-Tsing and others, from whom we learn so much of Buddhist history in India, continued to arrive with Sutras for translation, and strange and disturbing ideas. Of the various Schools of Buddhism, the Ch'an (Zen) School was, by the end of the Ming Dynasty (1368–1644), paramount. Yet even the virile Zen which, under the tremendous impetus of Hui-neng (Wei Lang), the sixth (Chinese) Patriarch, had filled the countryside with monasteries and centres of learning, began to fail under the rule of the Manchus. It is true that the greatest of the Manchu Emperors, K'ang-Hsi (1662–1723) and C'hien Lung (1736–1795) never suppressed the Buddhist religion, and even showed it favour, but under their rule Confucianism achieved its final ascendancy. The decline of Buddhism in China, however, was not produced by the failure of royal patronage, and was caused, as decline is usually caused, by its own debility.

Buddhism in Korea

As Sir Charles Eliot says, 'The Buddhism of Korea cannot be sharply distinguished from the Buddhism of China and Japan ... there is little originality in art: in literature and doctrine none at all.'[1] Buddhism, together with Chinese writing, reached Korea about A.D. 372, but though it flourished exceedingly for several centuries it was never entirely acclimatized, and when in the thirteenth century a wave of Confucian reaction arrived from China the Korean Court accepted its influence with avidity, and the Buddhist leaders of the day were unable to cope with the 'new' and popular teaching. Thereafter Buddhist influence began to decline, and what remains of it to-day is almost entirely the dynamic Zen.

The importance of Korea in the history of Buddhism is as a conduit pipe between China and Japan, and it is therefore important to note the type of Buddhism which was available

1. *Hinduism and Buddhism*, Vol. III, p. 336.

to cross the narrow seas. Kenneth Saunders, who spent some time in its beautifully sited mountain monasteries, says it is 'clearly a mixed Buddhism of the "accommodated" Mahayana, with Sakya Muni as a central figure, with meditation as the chief exercise, with the philosophy of the Void and the T'ien t'ai (Jap.: Tendai) classification tacitly assumed, and yet with some pietistic tendencies, as is evidenced by the place given to the Buddha of the Western Paradise'.[1] Even to-day the fierce technique of Chinese Zen is maintained, and R. H. Blyth, author of *Zen in English Literature*, who spent sixteen years in Korean monasteries, has described to the author the uncompromising severity of life and spiritual discipline which he found maintained. If, therefore, Korean Buddhism is failing in quantity, its quality survives.

Buddhism in Japan

Buddhism entered Japan from Korea in A.D. 552. There was mild resistance from certain quarters, but in the famous Regent Shotoku Taishi (593–622) the Buddhists found as their patron and leader one of the greatest men whom Japan has produced. A contemporary of Muhammad and St Augustine of Canterbury, Prince Shotoku's own influence was no less profound than theirs in his own country. He largely built the city of Nara, and in Horyuji, completed in A.D. 607, he built a monastic settlement which became the prototype of Japanese architecture to this day. Native craftsmen, taught by artist-craftsmen of all kinds imported from China and Korea, not only built the great shrines and temples, many of which survive to-day, but wrought great images of bronze and wood, painted the frescoes of Horyuji which ranked, until destroyed by fire in 1949, with the best of Ajanta, and founded standards of culture which the Japanese, always brilliant in adaptation, had within a few years made their own. Nor was the Prince content with patronage. He wrote himself a series of commentaries on the *Saddharma-Pundarika*, the *Vimalakirti Sutra* and the *Srimala Sutra*, and by this selection went far to formulate Japanese Buddhism.

But the Buddhism which entered Japan under his patronage was already divided into rival schools, and although they developed peacefully side by side in the thousand years which followed, and were added to by indigenous sects, there

1. *Epochs in Buddhist History*, p. 160.

was no attempt at co-ordination, and it was not until the time of the famous fourteen 'Fundamental Buddhistic Beliefs', as formulated by Colonel Olcott in 1891, and the present writer's 'Twelve Principles of Buddhism', approved by all Japanese Schools in 1946, that a common ground was found for Buddhism as distinct from the varying forms of it to be found in the different schools.

The history of Japanese Buddhism will be considered later in describing its principal sects; here it is enough to add that all these sects, with the exception of Nichiren and Shin, were Chinese importations. All were to some extent influenced on the one hand by the indigenous Shinto cult, and on the other by the Confucianism which entered Japan with Buddhism from China and combined with Shinto, though never formally, to form a neo-Confucianism which at one time actually gained Imperial favour.

In China Buddhism was always a religion without political affinities; in Japan it was early an 'established' cult under Court favour. Zen at least was a major factor in the development of Bushido, the equivalent of our medieval knighthood, and as such an active participant in the complex internecine struggles of the 'closed' period of Japanese history. For most of its life a protégé of the Shoguns, Japanese Buddhism therefore suffered a serious loss of revenue and prestige with the abolition of the Shogunate in 1868. With the usual adaptability of the Japanese character, however, it weathered the storm, and reorganized itself as a disestablished Church. Now that Shinto, too, has been 'disestablished', the field is clear for any and every religion to attract the Japanese mind, and if the Shin and Zen Schools of Buddhism between them rule the minds of the vast majority of Japanese, it is mainly because between them they satisfy all complementary needs of the human mind. Yet it is certainly true to say that to the extent that Ceylon, Siam and Burma are Buddhist countries of the Theravada School, Japan is a Buddhist country of the Mahayana, and as the Buddhism of China is rapidly dying, and that of Tibet is in a sense a School of its own, Japan is now the country in which the Mahayana in all its aspects can best be considered and described.

Buddhism in Tibet, and in its neighbouring countries of Bhutan, Sikkim and Nepal, is described in Chapter 15, while

the history and development of the Zen School is described
in Chapter 14.

*

Such is a brief survey of the rise of the two main Schools
of Buddhism, and their spread throughout the East. To re-
sort to the analogy of the wheel, it seems that some of the
sub-divisions of the Mahayana have wandered so far from
the hub of the wheel, the Theravada, and in such divergent
directions that little remains in common between them.
There is therefore an element of irony in the fact that it was
left for an American, Colonel H. S. Olcott, Founding President of the Theosophical Society, to attempt to formulate
and publish the common ground. The East is reputedly the
more synthetic, the West more analytic in outlook; here,
however, it was first an American, and later an Englishman,
who attempted to reunite, for the better understanding of
all of them, the scattered aspects of the Teaching of the
Enlightened One. In 1891 Colonel Olcott, whose immense
work in the field of Buddhism in the East I found to be
warmly remembered, prepared, in fourteen 'Fundamental
Buddhistic Beliefs', a common platform for all Buddhist
Schools. They were considered in various Buddhist countries, and at a Buddhist Congress held at Adyar, Madras,
the headquarters of the Theosophical Society, approved by
the accredited representatives of Japan, Burma, Ceylon and
Chittagong. Later, the Colonel received a message from the
'Chief Lamas of the great Mongolian Buddhist monasteries' approving the propositions as drafted. Here they are, as
published as an Appendix to his famous *Buddhist Catechism*.

FUNDAMENTAL BUDDHISTIC BELIEFS

1. Buddhists are taught to show the same tolerance, forbear-
ance, and brotherly love to all men, without distinction; and an
unswerving kindness towards the members of the animal kingdom.
2. The Universe was evolved, not created; and it functions
according to law, not according to the caprice of any God.
3. The truths upon which Buddhism is founded are natural.
They have, we believe, been taught in successive kalpas, or world
periods, by certain illuminated beings called *Buddhas*, the name
BUDDHA meaning 'Enlightened'.
4. The fourth Teacher in the present kalpa was Sakya Muni, or

Gautama Buddha, who was born in a royal family in India about 2,500 years ago. He is an historical personage and his name was Siddartha Gautama.

5. Sakya Muni taught that ignorance produces desire, unsatisfied desire is the cause of rebirth, and rebirth the cause of sorrow. To get rid of sorrow, therefore, it is necessary to escape rebirth; to escape rebirth, it is necessary to extinguish desire; and to extinguish desire, it is necessary to destroy ignorance.

6. Ignorance fosters the belief that rebirth is a necessary thing. When ignorance is destroyed the worthlessness of every such rebirth, considered as an end in itself, is perceived, as well as the paramount need of adopting a course of life by which the necessity for such repeated births can be abolished. Ignorance also begets the illusive and illogical idea that there is only one existence for man, and the other illusion that this one life is followed by states of unchangeable pleasure or torment.

7. The dispersion of all this ignorance can be attained by the persevering practice of an all-embracing altruism in conduct, development of intelligence, wisdom in thought, and destruction of desire for the lower personal pleasures.

8. The desire to live being the cause of rebirth, when that is extinguished rebirths cease and the perfected individual attains by meditation that highest state of peace called *Nirvana*.

9. Sakya Muni taught that ignorance can be dispelled and sorrow removed by the knowledge of the four Noble Truths, viz:

1. The miseries of existence;
2. The cause productive of misery, which is the desire ever renewed of satisfying oneself without being able ever to secure that end;
3. The destruction of that desire, or the estranging of oneself from it;
4. The means of obtaining this destruction of desire. The means which he pointed out is called the noble eight-fold Path, viz: Right Belief; Right Thought; Right Speech; Right Action; Right Means of Livelihood; Right Exertion; Right Remembrance; Right Meditation.

10. Right Meditation leads to spiritual enlightenment, or the development of that Buddha-like faculty which is latent in every man.

11. The essence of Buddhism as summed up by the Tathagata (Buddha) himself is:

> To cease from all sin,
> To get virtue,
> To purify the heart.

12. The universe is subject to a natural causation known as 'Karma'. The merits and demerits of a being in past existences determine his condition in the present one. Each man, therefore, has prepared the causes of the effects which he now experiences.

13. The obstacles to the attainment of good karma may be removed by the observance of the following precepts, which are embraced in the moral code of Buddhism, viz: (1) Kill not; (2) Steal not; (3) Indulge in no forbidden sexual pleasure; (4) Lie not; (5) Take no intoxicating or stupefying drug or liquor. Five other precepts, which need not here be enumerated, should be observed by those who would attain more quickly than the average layman the release from misery and rebirth.

14. Buddhism discourages superstitious credulity. Gautama Buddha taught it to be the duty of a parent to have his child educated in science and literature. He also taught that no one should believe what is spoken by any sage, written in any book, or affirmed by a tradition, unless it accord with reason.

Drafted as a common platform upon which all Buddhists can agree.

H. S. OLCOTT, P.T.S.

In 1945 the Buddhist Society, London, felt the need of a brief summary of Buddhism which could be included in a leaflet for free distribution at meetings, The matter had to be confined to 3½ pages of an 8vo leaflet, and was therefore for convenience written in numbered 'propositions'. In drafting the leaflet at the request of the Council, however, I did not refer to Colonel Olcott's 'Buddhistic Beliefs', although I had read them some twenty years previously, and a comparison between the two sets, each attempting to express the common ground of all the Schools, is therefore interesting. While in Japan, I offered the Twelve Principles to a convention of seventeen of the principal Buddhist Sects, realizing that my greatest difficulty would be to secure the adherence of the Shin, or Pure Land Sect, to the proposition that every man must, in the end, 'work out his own salvation – with diligence'. But with the aid of the scholarly mind of the Prince-Abbot of the Nishi-Hongwanji Temple in Kyoto, joint Head of the Shin Sect, I secured even their allegiance, and thus for the first time, as described in greater detail in my *Via Tokyo*, produced a Japanese Buddhism, for the Shin School is notably missing from the list of Japanese Sects which approved Colonel Olcott's 'Beliefs'.

The Twelve Principles were approved by Japan, and later, after consultation with a specially convened Council of the Siamese Sangha, by the Supreme Patriarch of Siam. They have been approved by leading Buddhists in China, Burma, and Ceylon, by the late President of the Theosophical Society, Mr C. Jinarajadasa, himself a Sinhalese Buddhist, and by representatives of the Buddhists in Tibet. They therefore form a second step towards the formulation in simple terms of a World Buddhism. Here they are:

TWELVE PRINCIPLES OF BUDDHISM

1. Self-salvation is for any man the immediate task. If a man lay wounded by a poisoned arrow he would not delay extraction by demanding details of the man who shot it, or the length and make of the arrow. There will be time for ever-increasing understanding of the Teaching during the treading of the Way. Meanwhile, begin now by facing life, as it is, learning always by direct and personal experience.

2. The first fact of existence is the law of change or impermanence. All that exists, from a mole to a mountain, from a thought to an empire, passes through the same cycle of existence – i.e. birth, growth, decay and death. Life alone is continuous, ever seeking self-expression in new forms. 'Life is a bridge; therefore build no house on it.' Life is a process of flow, and he who clings to any form, however splendid, will suffer by resisting the flow.

3. The law of change applies equally to the 'soul'. There is no principle in an individual which is immortal and unchanging. Only the 'Namelessness', the ultimate Reality, is beyond change, and all forms of life, including man, are manifestations of this Reality. No one owns the life which flows in him any more than the electric light bulb owns the current which gives it light.

4. The universe is the expression of law. All effects have causes, and man's soul or character is the sum total of his previous thoughts and acts. Karma, meaning action-reaction, governs all existence, and man is the sole creator of his circumstances and his reaction to them, his future condition, and his final destiny. By right thought and action he can gradually purify his inner nature, and so by self-realization attain in time liberation from rebirth. The process covers great periods of time, involving life after life on earth, but ultimately every form of life will reach Enlightenment.

5. Life is one and indivisible, though its ever-changing forms are innumerable and perishable. There is, in truth, no death, though every form must die. From an understanding of life's

unity arises compassion, a sense of identity with the life in other forms. Compassion is described as 'the Law of laws – eternal harmony', and he who breaks this harmony of life will suffer accordingly and delay his own Enlightenment.

6. Life being One, the interests of the part should be those of the whole. In his ignorance man thinks he can successfully strive for his own interests, and this wrongly-directed energy of selfishness produces suffering. He learns from his suffering to reduce and finally eliminate its cause. The Buddha taught four Noble Truths: (a) The omnipresence of suffering; (b) its cause, wrongly directed desire; (c) its cure, the removal of the cause; and (d) the Noble Eightfold Path of self-development which leads to the end of suffering.

7. The Eightfold Path consists in Right (or perfect) Views or preliminary understanding, Right Aims or Motive, Right Speech, Right Acts, Right Livelihood, Right Effort, Right Concentration or mind-development, and, finally, Right *Samadhi*, leading to full Enlightenment. As Buddhism is a way of living, not merely a theory of life, the treading of this Path is essential to self-deliverance. 'Cease to do evil, learn to do good, cleanse your own heart: this is the Teaching of the Buddhas.'

8. Reality is indescribable, and a God with attributes is not the final Reality. But the Buddha, a human being, became the All-Enlightened One, and the purpose of life is the attainment of Enlightenment. This state of Consciousness, Nirvana, the extinction of the limitations of self-hood, is attainable on earth. All men and all other forms of life contain the potentiality of Enlightenment, and the process therefore consists in becoming what you are. 'Look within: thou *art* Buddha.'

9. From potential to actual Enlightenment there lies the Middle Way, the Eightfold Path 'from desire to peace', a process of self-development between the 'opposites', avoiding all extremes. The Buddha trod this Way to the end, and the only faith required in Buddhism is the reasonable belief that where a Guide has trodden it is worth our while to tread. The Way must be trodden by the whole man, not merely the best of him, and heart and mind must be developed equally. The Buddha was the All-Compassionate as well as the All-Enlightened One.

10. Buddhism lays great stress on the need of inward concentration and meditation, which leads in time to the development of the inner spiritual faculties. The subjective life is as important as the daily round, and periods of quietude for inner activity are essential for a balanced life. The Buddhist should at all times be 'mindful and self-possessed', refraining from mental and emotional attachment to 'the passing show'. This increasingly watchful attitude to circumstances, which he knows to be his own creation, helps him to keep his reaction to it always under control.

11. The Buddha said: 'Work out your own salvation with diligence'. Buddhism knows no authority for truth save the intuition of the individual, and that is authority for himself alone. Each man suffers the consequences of his own acts, and learns thereby, while helping his fellow men to the same deliverance; nor will prayer to the Buddha or to any God prevent an effect from following its cause. Buddhist monks are teachers and exemplars, and in no sense intermediates between Reality and the individual. The utmost tolerance is practised towards all other religions and philosophies, for no man has the right to interfere in his neighbour's journey to the Goal.

12. Buddhism is neither pessimistic nor 'escapist', nor does it deny the existence of God or soul, though it places its own meaning on these terms. It is, on the contrary, a system of thought, a religion, a spiritual science and a way of life, which is reasonable, practical and all-embracing. For over two thousand years it has satisfied the spiritual needs of nearly one-third of mankind. It appeals to the West because it has no dogmas, satisfies the reason and the heart alike, insists on self-reliance coupled with tolerance for other points of view, embraces science, religion, philosophy, psychology, ethics and art, and points to man alone as the creator of his present life and sole designer of his destiny.

BIBLIOGRAPHY

FOR CHAPTER FOUR

Alabaster. *The Wheel of the Law* (Siam).
Bigandet, Bishop. *The Life or Legend of Gaudama*.
Brodrick, A. H. *Little China*.
　Little Vehicle.
Copleston, R. S. *Buddhism in Magadha and in Ceylon*.
Edkins, J. *Chinese Buddhism*.
Grousset, R. *In the Footsteps of the Buddha*.
Hackmann, H. *Buddhism as a Religion*.
Pratt, J. B. *The Pilgrimage of Buddhism*.
Radhakrishnan, S. *Indian Philosophy*, Vol. I.
Reischauer, A. K., 'Buddhism' (in *The Great Religions of the World*, ed. Jurji).
Saunders, Kenneth. *Epochs in Buddhist History*.
Smith, Vincent. *Asoka*.
Thomas, E. J. *The History of Buddhist Thought*.
　The Life of Buddha in Legend and History.
Young, E. *The Kingdom of the Yellow Robe*.

CHAPTER FIVE

Theravada Buddhism
I. The Three Signs of Being

*

'No God, No Soul' – The Three Signs of Being – All is
Suffering – Happiness – The Nature of Pleasure –
All is Anatta – The Nature of Self

THE Buddha's first disciples became the founding members of the Sangha, and most of the teaching recorded in the Pali Canon was given to men, and later women, who had abandoned the life of home and family. Clad in the robes made of rags taken from the refuse heap, owning nothing but a few essentials, with shaven heads they passed their days, 'mindful and self-possessed', entirely devoted to the practice of the Dhamma. The Canon as we have it to-day is therefore a monkish compilation, and the Message appears through the eyes of men who had forsworn the world. It is therefore essentially for the few, difficult, hard to master, for the strong of heart and mind and will.

It is largely cast in negative form. The stress is always on *a-himsa*, non-harming, *an-atta*, no 'soul' as then understood; on *dukkha*, suffering, rather than on *sukha*, its opposite, and even the Goal, Nirvana, is negatively worded. The dying out, the waning out, the ceasing to be of the not-Self is the Goal, while the instinct of the human mind moves out to more, not less, to growth, not a fading away. Yet there is value in this contempt for the earth life, for only so does the all but smothered flame of the inner Light appear. As the Maha Chohan wrote, speaking of the 'struggle for Life', – 'Why has that struggle become the almost universal scheme of the universe? We answer, because no religion, with the exception of Buddhism, has hitherto taught a practical contempt for the earthly life, while each of them, always with that one solitary exception, has through its hells and damnations inculcated the greatest dread of death. Teach the people to see that life on this earth, even the happiest, is but a burden and delusion, that it is but our own Karma, the cause producing the effect, that is our own judge, our saviour in future lives, and the great struggle for life will soon lose its intensity.'[1]

As it stands to-day, although 'edited', negative and 'escapist' in form, the teaching of the Theravada School is still the finest moral philosophy extant. It is reasonable, making no appeal to dogmatic assumption; it is objective, and will stand the criticism of logic and science. It is self-reliant, claiming assistance from neither God nor gods, saviours or priestly men; it is the most tolerant creed on earth and expresses compassion not only for all men, but for all animals and the least living thing. By the ignorant it is described as pessimistic. If this were true, and it is quite untrue, it is strange that its adherents to-day, the Sinhalese, Burmese, Siamese and Cambodians, are among the merriest, happiest people on earth.

In terms of Western philosophy, it is derivable from inductive reasoning, that is, by logical inference from an observed first premise. The Buddha based his Teaching on no assumptions, least of all on the two which dominate the Western mind from earliest childhood, an absolute yet personal God, and an immortal soul which must be 'saved', and can only be saved with the assistance of this God.

'No God, No Soul'

As between the theist and atheist positions, Buddhism is atheist, but it would be more correct to say that it analyses the complex of conflicting ideas comprised in the term God with the same dispassionate care as it analyses the so-called soul. Such analysis, which all are pressed to make for themselves, proves, say Buddhists, that the Western ideas are inaccurate and inadequate. The Buddhist teaching on God, in the sense of an ultimate Reality, is neither agnostic, as is sometimes claimed, nor vague, but clear and logical. Whatever Reality may be, it is beyond the conception of the finite intellect; it follows that attempts at description are misleading, unprofitable, and waste of time. For these good reasons the Buddha maintained about Reality 'a noble silence'. If there *is* a Causeless Cause of all Causes, an Ultimate Reality, a Boundless Light, an Eternal Noumenon behind phenomena, it must clearly be infinite, unlimited,

1. *Letters from the Masters of the Wisdom*, ed. C. Jinarajadasa, p. 8–9.

unconditioned and without attributes. We, on the other hand, are clearly finite, and limited and conditioned by, and in a sense composed of, innumerable attributes. It follows that we can neither define, describe, nor usefully discuss the nature of THAT which is beyond the comprehension of our finite consciousness. It may be indicated by negatives and described indirectly by analogy and symbols, but otherwise it must ever remain in its truest sense unknown and unexpressed, as being to us in our present state unknowable. 'The Tao that can be expressed is not the eternal Tao.'[1]

In the same way, as already explained in the Introduction, Buddhism denies the existence in man of an immortal soul. The Enlightenment which dwells in life does not belong to one form of life. All that is man's is changing and mortal; the Immortal is not any man's.

The Three Signs of Being

The Buddha examined phenomenal life objectively. Studying effects, and tracing their causes, he produced a science of living which ranks with any other science known to man. Having analysed form, he described the life which uses it, and showed it to be one and indivisible. Man, he declared, can become Buddha, Enlightened, by the principle of Enlightenment within. The process, therefore, is to become what you are, to develop to the full the innate Buddha-Mind by destroying the ignorance-produced, desire-maintained illusion of self which binds us from life to life on the Wheel of Becoming. All forms of life, said the Buddha, can be shown to have three characteristics in common; impermanence, suffering, and an absence of permanent soul which separates each from the other forms of life. He pointed out how no 'thing' is the same at this moment as it was one moment ago. Even the 'everlasting hills' are slowly being worn away, and every particle of the human body, even the hardest, is replaced every seven years. There is no finality or rest within this universe, only a ceaseless becoming and a never-ending change. As Shelley says: 'Naught may endure but Mutability.' Like all other natural processes *anicca* is cyclic. It is an ever-rolling Wheel with four spokes – Birth, Growth, Decay and Death. Every form that comes into being goes through each stage in turn, and nought can stay the

1. *Tao Te Ching*, v. 1.

hand of time. The law of change applies to all compounded things, including man-made objects, ideas and institutions. From a granite cathedral to a china vase, from a code of laws to an empire, all things rise to their zenith, and then, however slowly, decay towards the inevitable end.

> The cloud-capp'd towers, the gorgeous palaces,
> The solemn temples, the great globe itself,
> Yea, all which it inherit, shall dissolve,
> And, like this insubstantial pageant faded,
> Leave not a rack behind.

And the same applies to man himself.

> We are such stuff
> As dreams are made on, and our little life
> Is rounded with a sleep.[1]

All is Suffering

Sabbe sankhāra dukkha. 'All compounded things are *dukkha.*' This statement of fact is cardinal to Buddhism. 'One thing I teach,' said the Buddha, '*dukkha* and the ending of *dukkha.*' For, as he pointed out, 'Birth is suffering, decay is suffering, disease is suffering, death is suffering, association with the unpleasing is suffering, separation from the pleasing is suffering, not to get what one wants is suffering.' But 'suffering' is only one translation of the Pali *dukkha,* which covers all that we understand by pain, ill, disease – physical and mental – including such minor forms as disharmony, discomfort, irritation or friction, or, in a philosophic sense, the awareness of incompleteness or insufficiency. It is dissatisfaction and discontent, the opposite of all that we mentally embrace in the terms well-being, perfection, wholeness, bliss.

To illustrate the omnipresence of *dukkha,* the Buddha told the story of Kisagotami and the mustard seed.

Once a distracted mother came to the All-Compassionate One with her dead babe in her arms, and besought him that it might be restored to life. He listened to her pleading; then sent her to fetch a grain of mustard seed from a house where

1. *The Tempest,* Act IV, Scene 1.

none had died. She sought for long, in vain, and then returned, and told him of her failure.

'My sister; thou hast found', the Master said,
'Searching for what none finds – that bitter balm
I had to give thee. He thou lovedst slept
Dead on thy bosom yesterday: to-day
Thou know'st the whole wide world weeps with thy woe:
The grief which all hearts share grows less for one.'[1]

Dukkha, then, is a fact, and either a man, on quiet consideration of life as he knows it, realizes for himself its omnipresence, or he does not. In the latter event, if he prefers to consider things as different from what they are, his lesson has yet to be learnt. Sooner or later time will teach it him.

But some there are whose lives are sufficiently unhappy, or who have sufficiently withdrawn themselves from the appearance of happiness in their own or in their neighbours' lives to be able to hear, in the stillness of the night or above the turmoil of the day, the ceaseless cry of anguish which rises from a blindly groping, sorrow-laden world. To such it is all too clear that, as phenomena in a phenomenal world, we are impermanent in all our parts and circumstances, and therefore are enmeshed in suffering.

Happiness

To the Buddhist, therefore, happiness, the goal of most human endeavour, is a low ideal, soon to be transcended. True, the word has many meanings, but in its usual sense it is but a gilded snare. Life as we know it is expressed through millions of units, large and small, each striving towards its own ideal. But whether the end in view be good or bad, the interaction of such ideals, ranging as they do from the purest altruism to the lowest form of selfishness, must inevitably cause friction and disharmony. Again, all effort, towards base or noble ends, involves a striving to become something different, something more, and this ceaseless 'becoming-something-else' is in itself productive of disharmony and discontent. Therefore, though an individual may at a given moment consider himself happy, each of the factors which compose that state of contentment is in process of change;

1. Edwin Arnold, *The Light of Asia*

hence, the moment a change in any one of them disturbs the harmony of the whole, his 'happiness' is ended. But suppose any one unit of life succeeds in achieving 'happiness', can all the millions of the earth's inhabitants achieve it simultaneously? Yet life is one, and though the forms may vary, the life within that suffers is the same in each. Hence the suffering of one is the suffering of all, even as the joy of one is the joy of all. That being so, how can any one rest content while his brother's life is filled with suffering? The happiness, therefore, which most men seek is a fool's paradise, a condition of self-induced illusion, a halting by the wayside to pluck the poisoned fruits of self, for it can only be obtained by ignoring the misery of our fellow men. Our very efforts to find happiness for ourselves prevent us finding it. Selfish happiness is at the best temporary, and its exclusive, separative nature reacts in time as pain. True happiness, as pointed out by all the great Teachers, and as may be proved by all who care to test it for themselves, is only to be found in ceaseless effort on behalf of suffering mankind. As Shelley wrote:

> For when the power of imparting joy
> Is equal to the will, the human soul
> Requires no other heaven.[1]

The Nature of Pleasure

Pleasure is equally transient, and usually selfish. All experience is obviously unpleasant or apparently pleasant. But wherein lies the difference? Is pleasure pleasure, or is pleasure gilded pain? As Drummond wrote, 'Earth's sweetest joy is but disguiséd pain', and Shelley refers to 'that unrest which men miscall delight'. Yet Buddhism is in no sense pessimistic. Whether or not we dislike the face of truth, the truth remains the same. Buddhism is neither pessimistic nor optimistic; both are extremes, and in all things the Buddha proclaimed the Middle Way. As Professor Bosanquet says: 'I believe in optimism, but I add that no optimism is worth its salt that does not go all the way with pessimism and arrive at a point beyond it.'[2] And again: 'It is a perfectly natural trait in human nature that we should run away from the disagreeable and thrust it out of sight. It is far more

1. *Queen Mab.*
2. *Social and International Ideals*, p. 43.

pleasant to dwell in a fool's paradise than in a wise man's purgatory. But the truly wise man seeks to see life as it is, and to see it *whole*.'[1]

Before we can escape from suffering we must face its existence and analyse its cause – desire. Such are the first two of the four Noble Truths of Buddhism, and if they stood alone they might be described as pessimistic. But if the omnipresence of *dukkha* and the nature of its cause, desire, be pessimistic, the teaching of the Way to liberation from Samsara, the Wheel of Rebirth, and the clear pronouncement that all may tread that Way to the self-same Goal is the noblest optimism yet proclaimed to man. There is here no patronizing and invidious choice by an extra-human power, whereby the individual 'soul' is 'saved' or 'damned'; only the pointing out of the age-long road by which each man may attain to freedom from the Wheel.

If Buddhism, therefore, seems to advocate a supreme contempt for this life, about whose beauty and glory the poets of the world have sung, it is only with a view to achieving a true perspective. For poets, who are men of vision, praise not the things of sense for themselves but for the beauty of the life within them. Indeed, as Mrs Rhys Davids has said: 'Buddhism enhances, perhaps more than any other creed, the value of life, when life is taken not in breadth and length', but for some 'special quality', that of depth, an inner realization of the transitory nature of phenomena, and of our oneness with that Noumenon compared with which this life is of the substance of a dream. It is not life which is evil, but a foolish cleaving to life, a binding of oneself more tightly on the Wheel. Buddhism is, therefore, to some extent a philosophy of suffering. If life is filled with suffering, and if suffering is the means by which we learn to put an end to suffering, is it not foolish to attempt to run away from school? Rather should we suffer willingly the consequences of our thoughts and acts in order that we may be free. If the doctrine of suffering is stressed in Buddhism, there is good reason for this emphasis. Although the doctrine is, taken by itself, an extreme view, it provided, when considered in conjunction with the complementary doctrine of deliverance, a philosophy all-sufficient for the immediate needs of men.

1. J. E. Ellam, *The Buddhist Review*, Vol. XI, p. 181.

All is Anatta

The third of the 'Signs of Being' is *an-atta*, which is not-*Atta* (Skt: *Atman*), the doctrine that nothing in existence has within it a permanent 'soul' or imperishable entity which distinguishes it from other forms of life.

The Anatta doctrine is basic to Buddhism, and must, therefore, be understood. It is, however, being at the very heart of the living man, a problem to be transcended rather than solved, a doctrine to be experienced rather than described. The difficulties in its understanding are inherent, for it is the Self which is striving to understand itself, and they are not made the easier by the persistent attempts of members of the Theravada School, in the West as well as the East, to substitute a cold and dreary doctrine of their own which is unknown to the Pali Canon.

Anatta is the opposite of the doctrine of Atman, or Atta, as generally understood by the Brahmans of the Buddha's day, for this Atta doctrine was of two kinds, the original and the degraded forms. The philosophy of the Upanishads, on which the Brahman philosophy is based, proclaims that life is one. At the heart of the Universe is the One Reality of which the universe as we know it is but a periodic manifestation. This is the only Supreme Deity known to Indian thought, for the Upanishadic philosophy, like Buddhism, 'revolts against the deistic conception of God'.[1]

But as the finite can never return to the Infinite unless it is in essence one with Infinity, so there is behind rather than in each man and all that lives 'the divine element which we call the beatific consciousness, the *ananda* state, by which at rare moments it enters into immediate relations with the Absolute'.[2]

This element is called the Atman or Atta, and the quintessence of Indian thought may be summed up by saying that the Atman of man and the Atman of the universe are one.

But this doctrine, which, under different terminology, is that of the Mahayana School of Buddhism, was gradually degraded into the belief in an 'immortal soul' as that part of man which distinguished and separated him from all other forms of life; whereas in truth this Atman is not the 'soul'

1. Radhakrishnan, *Philosophy of the Upanishads*, p. 79.
2. *Ibid.*, p. 80.

at all, though often loosely described as such, for it is no
'human' but the universal *absolute* principle which is common to and unifies man and the Universe.

This Atman, therefore, so far from being that which distinguishes man from man, is actually the 'common denominator' of all forms of life, and is hence the philosophic basis
of the brotherhood of man. The degradation of this noble
idea is paralleled in Christianity, in which the self-same
teaching of St Paul has been caricatured in the conception
of an 'eternal soul' which distinguishes each man from his
neighbour, and which will be either 'saved' or 'damned' at
death according as the preponderance of his deeds in one
short life has been good or bad.

Now the Buddha nowhere denies the Atman doctrine as
originally taught, but only in the degraded form of an 'immortal soul' which separates man from man. It is true that
in his *Buddhism in Translations* Mr Warren has collected a
series of extracts from the Pali Canon, and headed them,
'There is no ego', but the ego or self is not the soul. The
point of the argument in each case is that none of the factors
which collectively form what we know as man, consisting of
body, sensation, perceptions, etc., is in itself permanent, nor
are they so collectively, but each and all are in a constant
state of flux. Said the Buddha to his son, 'Whatsoever the
form, Rahula, be it past, present or future, inward or outward, gross or subtle, high or low, far or near, every form
must be regarded thus, as it really is, by perfect insight:
"This is not mine: not this am I: this is not the Self of me".'
Thus, not only is there no denial of the Atman, but there is
no denial of the soul of man as something 'capable of
growth, as of deterioration, changing according to the nature
of its deeds for better or worse', as Plato described it. Nowhere in the Scriptures does the Buddha deny the soul, but
any attempt to explain such a complex problem to those
whose fault was their love of metaphysical detail would have
been of no help to them in attaining liberation from the
Wheel. Hence, beyond denying that those who said, 'There
is a Self', were any more correct than those who said, 'There
is no Self', the Buddha, as always on such subjects, 'maintained a noble silence'.

To put the matter another way, 'That which is called the
ego, which says, "I am", is merely an aggregate of *skandhas*,

a complex of sensations, ideas, thoughts, emotions and voli-
tions. It is not an eternal immutable entity behind these. The
word "I" remains the same, but its significance continually
changes.'[1] Or, as Dr McGovern puts it, 'Buddhism insists
that the soul is not a rigid, unchanging, self-constituted
entity, but a living, complex, changing, evolving organism'.[2]
The maxim holds: 'Impermanent are *all* compounded things'.
In a universe in which there is clearly but one life, the fact
that each form of life is clothed in the temporary garments
of matter does not make those garments or any of them
separate the part from the whole. Hence Anatta may be described as the doctrine of 'non-independence', and the
Buddhist recognition of man's brotherhood as an existing
fact in nature and not merely as a beautiful idea. As Dr Suzuki
says of this doctrine in its developed (Mahayana) form, 'In
Buddhism each soul is not only related as such to the highest
reality, but also to one another in the most perfect network
of infinite mutual relationship.'[3]

It is through non-recognition of the Buddhist standpoint
of Anatta that man experiences greater suffering than is involved in the mere fact of existence. 'Sorrow is in fact the
result of the effort which an individual has to make to keep
separate from the rest of existence.'[4] And again, 'Life's long
enduring suffering has arisen out of the blind Nescience of
itself as One, out of the non-recognition by Life of its underlying unity of purpose and of aim.'[5] In brief, 'Such states of
mind as co-exist with the consciousness of individuality, with
the sense of separate existence, are states of suffering.'[6]

The Nature of Self

On the subject of Self, therefore, there are three 'selves'
to be considered, which may be equated, with reservations,
with the 'body, soul and spirit' of St Paul.

(1) *Spirit or Atman*, which is the 'common denominator'
of all forms of life, and is the monopoly of none. This alone
is eternal, but it is not an immortal entity, for 'there is no
abiding principle in man'.

1. Lakshmi Narasu, *The Essence of Buddhism*, p. 32.
2. *Introduction to Mahayana Buddhism*, p. 123.
3. *The Eastern Buddhist*, Vol. IV, p. 77.
4. Rhys Davids, *Buddhism* (American Lectures), p. 124.
5. Ananda Metteya, *The Wisdom of the Aryas*, p. xxi.
6. Rhys Davids, *Buddhism* (S.P.C.K.), p. 48.

(2) *Soul*, in the sense of a growing, evolving bundle of attributes or characteristics, forming 'character'. This is it which passes, by a process of causal impulse, from life to life on the long road to perfection.

(3) *Body*, here used in the sense of 'personality', composed of the lower attributes or *skandhas*. The point to be made clear is that there is nothing in man which entitles him to say, 'I am this and you are that', through all eternity. It is this 'Heresy of Separateness' which causes the rival hatreds of the West, for once established that 'I' am utterly different, separate from 'You', and fratricidal wars in trade, politics, and in the open field will follow as a matter of course. Above the clamour of competitive strife the self-same Teaching of the Christ remains unheard.

Unfortunately, in disclaiming the existence of a separate, immortal soul, some scholars of the Theravada have gone too far, and presume to interpret the Buddha's silence concerning the self as denying the whole of the Atta doctrine in its original form, and with it the evolving character. There are no grounds for such teaching, for if the five *skandhas* are the whole of man's heritage, what is the meaning of such phrases in the Scriptures as 'Self is the Lord of Self', which clearly imply the existence of a higher and lower self? 'Let a Bhikkhu reprove himself by the Self, and examine himself by the Self, so that he will live happily.'[1] 'Self is the Lord of Self and the goal of self. What other Lord can there be?'[2] 'It is of the Self', says Dr Coomaraswamy, 'and not of himself that the Buddha is speaking when he says, "I have taken refuge in the Self" (*Digha Nikaya*, ii, 120), and similarly when he asks others to "seek for the Self" (*Vinaya Pitaka*, i, 23), and "to make the Self your refuge and your lamp" (*Digha Nikaya*, ii, 100).'[3] And the same applies to the mastery of the self, which is given as one of the three masteries to be attained. Mastery of the self by what, if not by the higher Self which moves to Enlightenment in proportion as it gains such mastery? Yet all this talk of mastery and the like is nonsense in the absence of someone or something to control and ultimately crush the will of the separative self which causes, by its very existence, most of our suffering. But if the

1. *Dhammapada*, v. 160.
2. *Dhammapada*, v. 379–80.
3. Ananda Coomaraswamy and I. B. Horner, *Gotama the Buddha*, p. 27.

evolving 'soul' be taken as the reservoir of character brought
over from life to life, or, which is the same thing, as the resultant of the effects of past causes, we have an entity, growing, changing, and therefore impermanent as a separated
self, but none the less for the time being a thing, which
gradually learns to control the lower self, and its components
or vehicles, the *skandhas*. This is the Self which, having by a
long process of self-purification won to freedom, 'knows that
it is free', and, casting aside the last of the Ten Fetters which
bound it to the Wheel of Rebirth, enters Nirvana.

Such are the Three Signs of Being, and they are not un-
related aspects of the flow which men call life. 'Material shape
is impermanent. What is impermanent, that is suffering. What
is suffering, that is not the Self. What is not Self, that is not
mine, that am I not, that is not my Self.'[1] In brief, all is impermanent, including the soul. What is only partial, incomplete,
and separated from the wholeness of things by *avidya*, ignorance, knows suffering. Only when the three fires of attachment,
hatred, and illusion die is the Self freed from the bondage of
the self. Meanwhile Self must suffer the consequences of the
acts of the self. As Ananda Coomaraswamy put it, 'the
individual is, indeed, responsible for and will inherit the
consequences of his actions for so long as he thinks of
"himself" as the agent.'[2] For ultimately there is no 'I'
which acts or receives the effects of action. There is only a
long continuum which Enlightenment, by shattering the
house of self, will end.

[For Bibliography, see end of Chapter Nine]

1. Translated from the *Samyutta Nikaya*, *ibid.*, p. 156.
2. *Ibid.*, p. 15.

CHAPTER SIX

Theravada Buddhism
II. The Four Noble Truths

*

*Desire – The Noble Eightfold Path – Self-Reliance –
The Nature of Self – The Will*

To the extent that Theravada Buddhism can be expressed in a formula, it is to be found in the 'Four Noble Truths'. The first is one of the three Signs of Being, the omnipresence of Dukkha. 'Which, O Bhikkhus, think you is the greater: the tears which you have poured out, wailing and lamenting on this long pilgrimage, joined to the unloved, separated from the loved; or the waters of the Four Great Seas?'

Such is the disease which needs a Buddha's curing. The diagnosis of the Enlightened One proclaimed its cause to be desire, the never-ending craving of the senses, the selfish grasping of the lower self, indifferent to the needs and claims of others; the thirst for sentient existence. But a cure for the disease has been discovered and a prescription given by the Buddha. If the first two truths be pessimistic, the third and fourth are as trumpet calls to those who 'travail and are heavy laden', for they proclaim the end of suffering by the elimination of its cause, desire, and this is accomplished by the treading of the Noble Eightfold Path. Such is the ultimate minimum of truth which each must understand. Even if a man knows nothing of the Self or of the universe, or of what it is that is reborn, it is no great matter, for of these things the Buddha said: 'This question is not conducive to profit, to perfect calm, to supernormal wisdom, to Nirvana.' But let a man realize to the full these four great propositions and he will need no more, for whereas human knowledge is, at the best, composed of fragments of the truth, the Noble Eightfold Path is a way to Truth itself. The sooner these truths are learnt, the sooner will the sufferer be free, for it is 'through not understanding, through not penetrating the Four Aryan Truths, O Bhikkhus, that we have wandered on this long, long journey, you and I'.

Desire

Just as suffering is but a partial and somewhat misleading translation of *dukkha*, so 'desire', unless explained, is hardly an accurate translation of the Pali term *tanha* (Skt: *trishna*), for desire appears in many forms, ranging from ungovernable lust to the purest yearning for the helping of mankind.

Tanha means in the first place the craving which supplies the binding force to hold men on the Wheel of Rebirth, its nearest Western equivalent being Nietzsche's 'Will to Live'.

'Verily it is this thirst or craving, causing the renewal of existence, accompanied by sensual delight, seeking satisfaction now here, now there – the craving for the gratification of the passions, for continued existence in the worlds of sense.' Or, as Professor Rhys Davids points out in his comment on the above, 'the lust of the flesh, the lust of life, and the love of this present world.'

For the passional element of this desire, the word *kama* is generally used, and in this latter sense desire is associated with temptation, as is shown by a Chinese version of this second Noble Truth, which is 'the assembling of temptation.'

In brief, desire means those inclinations which tend to continue or increase separateness, the separate existence of the subject of desire; in fact, all forms of selfishness, the essence of which is desire for self at the expense, if necessary, of all other forms of life. Life being one, all that tends to separate one aspect from another must needs cause suffering to the unit which even unconsciously works against the Law. Man's duty to his brothers is to understand them as extensions, other aspects of himself, as being fellow facets of the same Reality.

It is, therefore, not desire itself which is the cause of suffering, but 'wrong', because 'personal', desire. 'It is the desire for what belongs to the unreal self that generates suffering, for it is impermanent, changeable, perishable, and that, in the object of desire, causes disappointment, disillusionment, and other forms of suffering to him who desires. Desire in itself is not evil. It is desire to affirm the lower self, to live in it, cling to it, identify oneself with it, instead of with the Universal self, that is evil.'[1] Ultimately when all that lives has reached the silence of Nirvana, desire itself will die. Meanwhile *tanha*, and especially that aspect of it known as *kama*, called by Mrs Rhys Davids 'natural, unregenerate desire', must be sublimated into higher forms, giving way to aspirations and ideals for which a better term would be good will rather than good desire.

The Third Truth states that the elimination of desire will remove the cause of man-made suffering, for Tanha is the force which keeps us in the realms of Samsara, over which alone Dukkha holds sway. If there were no way out of this whirlpool of desire, Buddhism would indeed be a doctrine of despair.

> If ye lay bound upon the wheel of change,
> And no way were of breaking from the chain,
> The Heart of Boundless Being is a curse,
> The Soul of Things fell Pain. Ye are not bound![2]

For one description of Nirvana is the dying out of the three fires of *lobha*, *dosa*, and *moha*; greed, hatred and illusion.

The Noble Eightfold Path

The Fourth Truth, the noble Eightfold Path, is a Way which is found in all philosophies and faiths which offer liberation from life's sufferings. As the Bhikkhu Silacara says,[3] 'The man who obeys the behests of morality, to whatever form of faith he belongs, is on the Path, whether he himself is aware of it or not. To that extent at least he may be called a Buddhist, for Buddhism is no mere creed. It is the Dhamma – the expression of the law of all the worlds – the statement of the Norm of all Existence, high and low; other than in compliance wherewith is felicity for none.' Viewed in the restricted sense of a moral code, it is the Path of strict morality taught by Confucius and Zoroaster; it is the Way of Taoism and the teaching of the Upanishads; it is the clear commandment of Christ. 'It is neither the habitual practice of sensuality, a low, unworthy way, nor the habitual

---

1. Edmond Holmes, *The Creed of Buddha*, p. 68 (abridged).
2. Edwin Arnold, *The Light of Asia*.
3. *Lotus Blossoms*, 19.

practice of asceticism. There is a middle path, O Bhikkus, avoiding these two extremes – a Path which bestows vision, which leads to peace of mind, to the higher wisdom, to awakening, to Nirvana. It is Right Views, Right Attitude of Mind, or Motive, Right Speech, Right Conduct, Right Means of Livelihood, Right Effort, Right Mind Control and Right Meditation or Serenity.'[1]

It is the mean between the 'pairs of opposites'. 'That all is existent is one extreme; that all is non-existent is another extreme. The Tathagata, avoiding the two extremes, preaches his truth, which is the Middle Way.'

The Path is a means and never an end, and may be regarded from the positive or negative point of view. Negatively, it brings about dispassion by the slow elimination of the thirst for sensuous pleasure; positively, it leads to pure compassion by the cultivation of a selfless love for all that lives. In the combination of the two lies liberation from the Wheel. From the mystic's point of view, each pilgrim must become the Way. As is said in *The Voice of the Silence*, 'Thou canst not travel on the Path before thou hast become that Path itself.' As Christ proclaimed, 'I am the Way, the Truth and the Life.' From another point of view the Path is that which leads from selfishness to altruism, from the unreal to the Real.

Self-Reliance

In spite of help which each may give to each, in the final stages of the Path we walk alone. The Buddhist attitude is summed up in one of the most famous of its Scriptures, the *Maha-Parinibbana-Sutta*. 'Therefore, O Ananda, take the Self as a lamp; take the Self as a refuge. Betake yourselves to no external refuge. Hold fast as a refuge to the truth. Look not for refuge to anyone besides yourselves. Work out your own salvation with diligence.' No louder clarion call to self-reliance has ever been given than is contained in these few words. Throughout the ages men have sought for some vicarious method of salvation from their own misdeeds, by cruel sacrifice or ardent prayer, or by the intervention of an all-powerful God who could divert at will the law of cause and effect. But, 'Be not deceived, God is not mocked; for whatsoever a man soweth, that shall he also reap.' Or, in the

1. *The Dhammacakka-ppavattana Sutta.*

older words of the *Dhammapada* (v. 165): 'By oneself evil
is done, by oneself one suffers; by oneself evil is left undone,
by oneself one is purified.'

The Nature of Self

As shown when considering the Anatta doctrine, self is at
least twofold, a Self and a self which is not-Self. The Buddha
proved the distinction by analysing the thing which men
habitually mean whenever they say 'I'.

In the Buddhist Scriptures man is described as being composed of five 'groups' of qualities or attributes, called *skandhas* (Pali: *khandha*). The first is *Rupa*, form, shape or body; in
this sense the physical body, as including the organs of
sense. The second is *Vedana*, which includes the feelings or
sensations, whether pleasant, unpleasant or neutral. The
third is *Sanna*, comprising all perception or recognition,
whether sensuous or mental. It is reaction to sense stimuli,
described as 'awareness with recognition' or the idea which
arises from such reaction. The fourth bundle, the *Sankharas*,
includes all tendencies, mental and physical, the elements or
factors in consciousness, all moral and immoral volitional
activity, and the mental processes of discrimination and
comparison between the ideas so brought into being.

Of all these bundles of attributes, so classified according
to the function each performs, it can be said that this is not
the Self, for it is changing every moment, and having come
into being must ultimately be dissolved. 'Impermanent are
all compounded things.'

The fifth of the Skandhas, *Vinnana*, is as perishable and
fleeting as the others. It is variously translated as consciousness, mind, and mental powers, including the 'mental, moral
and physical predispositions'. It is never the same for two
moments together, being in a constant state of flux. It is the
centre of conscious existence in its ever-changing forms, and
is 'like the current of a river, which still maintains one constant form, one seeming identity, though not one single drop
remains to-day of all the volume which composed that river
yesterday.'[1]

As one of the Skandhas, *Vinnana* appears to be equivalent
to self-consciousness, the perception by the individual that
he is at the moment different from his neighbour, the belief

1. S. Z. Aung, Intro. to *Compendium of Philosophy*, p. 8.

that 'I am I, not you'. As such it is one of the Fetters which have to be broken before the aspirant attains Nirvana, and is known as *Sakkayaditthi*, the heresy of separateness, of separate individual existence, the belief that the separated 'personality' is the real man. But though *Vinnana* is necessarily impermanent, it is, during the long pilgrimage towards perfection, a fact which must be recognized. To this extent only it is the soul of man, always remembering that it is impermanent and changing every moment of the day. It is a process of immense complexity, born of the creative thinking of previous lives beyond all reckoning. It is the descendant of the forces generated in the past, a composite of millions of existences. Its force is cumulative; it becomes deepened and enriched with each successive experience.

The Will

The will, or volition, is usually given as one of the Sankharas, or factors of consciousness, presumably because, while it functions on all planes, it is most noticeable as a quality of the mind. This close relationship, which brings about the dynamic power of thought, is well expressed in the opening words of the *Dhammapada*, which may be paraphrased, 'All that we are is the result of what we have thought: it is founded on our thoughts, it is made up of our thoughts.' Will is, therefore, the chief element in the bundle of Sankharas, and is, in fact, 'the most dominant aspect of consciousness, the basal element of human life'.[1] Will, however, as with all else in the universe, is sevenfold in outward form, and may appear as abstract energy or animal desire according to the plane or level of consciousness on which it is made manifest. As such, it clearly cannot be regarded as the Self. Yet he who strengthens and develops his will is more self-reliant than his weak-willed neighbour. But will is colourless. It is the motive with which it is used which makes it good or bad. It is a potent instrument to be used for good or evil at its user's choice. To the extent that he dedicates 'his' will to purposes in harmony with the Dhamma, his power for good will increase accordingly, but if he strives to turn 'his' will against the whole, he will meet with ever greater suffering, until, like a swimmer worn out

1. Radhakrishnan, *Indian Philosophy*, Vol. I, p. 404, where this complicated subject is discussed in its relation to other terms in Buddhist psychology.

with his efforts to overcome the current, he decides to swim with it. If this analysis be correct, and each may make it for himself, there is in man no changeless element, which he may call his own. The SELF, whatever that may be, is infinite and bound by none of its forms. It IS, and is *ex hypothesi* beyond the reach of thought. It is THAT of which the universe is a manifestation, and upon such matters the Buddha, for the reason that all such speculation is futile, maintained a 'noble silence'.

[For Bibliography, see end of Chapter Nine]

CHAPTER SEVEN

Theravada Buddhism
III. Karma and Rebirth

*

The Twelve Nidanas – Karma, or Cause-Effect –
Rebirth – The Nature of Death – What is Reborn?

THE law by which the part progresses towards Enlightenment or reunion with the Whole is Karma, literally action,
in the sense of cause-effect and their intimate relationship.
But this law is but a part of a larger law of causation. The
basis of existence is, in Buddhist teaching, an intricate network or interrelation of events and actions on all planes.
This vast conception is presented in the symbol of an ever-
turning Wheel, the Wheel of Life (*Samsara*), which has
twelve spokes, the twelve *Nidanas* or component factors in
its ceaseless turning.

The Twelve Nidanas

The spokes are usually enumerated as follows: Old Age
and Death and all the suffering which life entails are caused
by *Jati* – Birth. The cause of *Jati* is Becoming, coming into
being, *Bhava*, which as the karmic agent of rebirth, is caused
in turn by powerful attachment, or *Upadana*, which is the
craving for and clinging to life. 'It typifies attachment to
worldly things which the human being ignorantly grasps at,
supposing they will quench this craving thirst which has
arisen from sensation.'[1] The cause of this attachment, then,
is craving, *Tanha* (Skt: *Trishna*), or desire for sentient
existence.

> That thirst which makes the living drink
> Deeper and deeper of the salt sea waves
> Whereon they float – pleasures, ambition, wealth,
> Praise, fame, or domination, conquest, love;
> Rich meats and robes, and fair abodes and pride
> Of ancient lines, and lust of days and strife
> To live, and sins that flow from strife . .[2]

1. Rhys Davids, *Buddhism* (American Lectures), p. 159.
2. *The Light of Asia.*

Desire is brought about by *Vedana*, or Feelings. This perception by the senses is in turn produced by *Phassa*, Contact, the connecting link between the organs of sense and the object they cognize, while the six organs of sense, *Salayatana*, are produced by *Nama-Rupa*, literally Name and Form. The Organs of Sense are the usual five, with the addition of the mind. *Nama-Rupa* is more difficult to describe. The old translation, 'Name and Form', is insufficient. Rather is it the form and its significance, or conversely, the meaning and the form through which it is expressed. J. E. Ellam says: 'The word Nama-rupa indicates the essential provision of Buddhist philosophy; that is to say, the physical and the psychical are not to be considered as separate and distinct, but only as two sides of one and the same thing.'[1]

But although a self-contained conception, it is usually considered in conjunction with its cause, *Vinnana*, consciousness in general, which, to become self-conscious, needs a form of vehicle through which to gain experience and be 'itself'. Even as a river is such only by virtue of the limitations of its banks, else would it be but a nameless, undivided portion of water, so must this abstract consciousness submit to limitation in order that it may express itself in terms of time and space. *Nama-Rupa*, then, becomes equivalent to personality, a symbol of the necessary 'body of illusion' which the abstract must indue before it can appear in concrete form. It is, therefore, the birth of egoism, of the sense of separateness possessed by each fragment of reality which imagines that *its* 'self' is separate from the Universal Self from which it came.

Vinnana, of course, has many 'vehicles'. We have seen how it precipitates *Nama-Rupa* in the same way as thought precipitates action on the physical plane, but *Vinnana* is in turn the outcome of the *Sankharas*, here equivalent to Karma in the three worlds of illusion, the mental, emotional and physical planes. But Karma, in this sense, is in turn the child of Ignorance, *Avidya*, which is the father of all human suffering, and the basis of causation regarded from whatever point of view.

Such are the Twelve *Nidanas*, which Dr Paul Carus[2] has

1. *The Religion of Tibet*, p. 116.
2. *The Gospel of Buddha*, p. 40 (slightly compressed).

helpfully though loosely paraphrased in the following way:
'In the beginning there is existence blind and without knowledge; and in this sea of ignorance there are stirrings formative and organizing. From this there arises awareness which
begets organisms that live as individual beings. These develop the six fields, that is, the five senses and the mind. The
six fields come in contact with things. Contact begets sensation which creates the thirst of individualized being. This
creates a cleaving to things which produces the growth and
continuation of selfhood. Selfhood continues in renewed
births. These renewed births of selfhood are the cause of
suffering, old age, sickness and death. They produce lamen-
tation, anxiety and despair.'

In the *Samyutta Nikaya* we have the twelve links analysed
in terms of time. Ignorance causes actions which in turn
produces fresh moments of awareness or percipient consciousness. So much for the past, but these produce the necessity
for another life on earth, the Present, when *Nama-Rupa*,
product of *Vinnana*, causes sense organs to appear which
lead to contact, then to feeling, craving and grasping. So
much for the present, but this grasping, *Tanha*, causes a fresh
life in the future, from which rebirth comes suffering, disease,
old age and death. '*That* being present, *this* becomes; *this*
being present, *that* becomes ... Such is the coming to *be* of
this entire mass of suffering.'

Thus, like the revolutions of a wheel, there is a regular
succession of death and birth, the moral cause of which is
the cleaving to existing objects, while the instrumental cause
is Karma.

To stop the turning of the Wheel we must therefore remove its cause, desire or cleaving to Illusion, and from this
point of view, the doctrine of causation covers the ground
of the second and third of the Four Noble Truths.

It must be noted that the 'spokes' of the wheel are not to
be considered only in the order given; they are rather the
interrelated factors in an endless whole. 'The Buddhist conception of causation is applied to any relation of interaction,
interdependence, correlation or co-ordination, founded on
an intrinsic necessity ... The Buddhist would not confine the
causal relation within the idea of *time* relation.'[1]

Note the dual aspect of the Wheel from the viewpoint of

1. Anesaki, *Nichiren the Buddhist Prophet*, p. 154.

the purpose for which its existence was taught. It is at once a way of explaining phenomena in general, and *Dukkha* in particular, and in its reversed form the method by which the causes of *Dukkha* may be destroyed.

The law of causation is co-extensive with the Universe in place, time and subject, for Buddhism applies the doctrine of causality and non-substantiality to the mind as well as to the body. Even Buddhas can but show a Way which leads to a state of consciousness beyond its power, the spiritual counterpart of the hub of the revolving Wheel, where in the midst of motion there is peace.

Karma or Cause-Effect

Karma (Pali: *Kamma*) is literally 'action', 'doing', 'deed'. It is at once cause, effect, and the law which equilibrates the two. It is Newton's third law of motion, that Action and Reaction are equal and opposite, applied to the moral and all other realms of sentient life. For two thousand years have Christians heard it proclaimed from their pulpits: 'Be not deceived: God is not mocked, for whatsoever a man soweth, that shall he also reap', and Christ is reported to have said upon the Mount: 'Judge not that ye be not judged, for with what judgement ye judge ye shall be judged, and with what measure ye mete, it shall be measured to you again.'

From the Buddhist viewpoint, Karma stresses the converse of the Christian presentation of this law. Whatsoever a man reaps, say the Buddhists, that has he also sown. Believing in the operation of natural justice, Buddhism would say in reply to the Biblical enquiry: 'Who did sin, this man or his parents, that he was born blind?', that it was this man who had 'sinned', that is, had so behaved in a previous life as to cause in the life in question the effect of blindness. As Mrs Rhys Davids says, 'Afflictions are for Buddhists so many forms, not of pre-payment, by which future compensation may be claimed, but of settlement of outstanding debts accruing from bad, that is to say from evil-bringing, unhappiness-promoting acts, done either in this life or in previous lives'.[1] In Karma is to be found, in conjunction with its commonsense corollary, Rebirth, a natural and therefore reasonable answer to the apparent injustice of the daily

1. *Buddhism*, p. 124.

round. Why should this man be born a beggar, this a prince? Why this a cripple, this a genius, that a fool? Why this a high-born Indian woman, that a low-born Englishman? These are effects. Do the causes lie in the hands of an irresponsible and finite God or, as the Buddhists say, within the lap of law? As it is man who suffers the effects, so it is man who generates the cause, and having done so he cannot flee the consequences. Says the *Dhammapada* (v. 165): 'By oneself evil is done; by oneself one suffers. By oneself evil is left undone; by oneself one is purified.' And, again, 'Not in the sky, not in the midst of the sea, nor anywhere else on earth is there a spot where a man may be freed from (the consequences of) an evil deed' (v. 127). Thus every man is the moulder and the sole creator of his life to come, and master of his destiny. 'Subsequents follow antecedents by a bond of inner consequence; no merely numerical sequence of arbitrary and isolated units, but a rational interconnexion.' So said the Emperor Marcus Aurelius, and, speaking of the abstract laws of the universe, Emerson said that they 'execute themselves ... In the soul of man there is a justice whose retributions are instant and entire. He who does a good deed is instantly ennobled. He who does a mean deed is by the action itself contracted.' (*Miscellanies.*) And again: 'Secret retributions are always restoring the level, when disturbed, of the divine justice. It is impossible to tilt the beam. Settles for evermore the ponderous equator to its line, and man and mote, and star and sun, must range to it, or be pulverized by the recoil.'[1]

It is the mind which moulds man's destiny, action being but precipitated thought. It follows that one's lightest thought has vast effects, not only on the thinker, but on all that lives. Hence the tremendous power of hatred and love, which man, in childlike ignorance, is pouring out upon the world by night and day. Yet such dynamic qualities, controlled and cultivated, can make a man just what he wills to be. Karma is thus the very antithesis of fatalism. That which is done can by the doer be in time, as it were, neutralized. That which is yet to be depends on the deeds now being done. There is here no cruel Nemesis; only the slow and perfect action of an all-embracing law.

Omar Khayyàm was a Buddhist when he wrote:

1. *Lectures and Biographical Studies.*

> The Moving Finger writes; and having writ,
> Moves on: nor all thy Piety nor Wit
> Shall lure it back to cancel half a line,
> Nor all thy Tears wash out a Word of it.

But though the record of a deed remains indelible, it is the sufferer whose finger wrote his destiny, and who had it in his power to choose whether the deed were good or bad. It is but just that he who disturbed should in the end restore the equilibrium.

An individual's karma, in the sense of the sum of un-expended causes generated by him in the past, the burden which he has to bear upon life's pilgrimage, is classified with great precision in the various Schools, but can be analysed by any student for himself. Karma is an ever-generating force. It may be as a thundercloud, so fully charged that nothing can delay its equally complete discharge; it may be as a snowball on the mountain-side, so small and slowly moving at first that a slight expenditure of effort will bring its growing power to rest. Other analogies may be found with ease, but it is more important to understand the nature of Karma than to analyse its complex functioning.

The Buddhist, then, replaces Nemesis and Providence, Kismet, Destiny and Fate, with a natural law, by his know-ledge of which he moulds his future hour by hour. In the words of an old jingle:

> Sow a thought, reap an act;
> Sow an act, reap a habit;
> Sow a habit, reap a character;
> Sow a character, reap a destiny.

But even as the causes generated by one man react upon that man, so the mass causation of a group, be it family society or nation, reacts upon that group as such, and upon all whose karma placed them at the time therein. Each man has, therefore, several 'karmas', racial, national, family, and personal, yet all quite properly *his*, else he would not have found himself subject to their sway.

An understanding of the law of Karma leads to self-reliance, for in proportion as we understand its operation we cease to complain of our circumstances, and cease from turning with the weakness of a child to a man-made God to save us from the natural consequences of our acts. Karma is no God, for the gods themselves are subject to its sway. Only the ignorant personify Karma, and attempt to bribe, petition or cajole it; wise men understand it and conform to it.

The universe itself is an effect; hence all the units in it, viewed as events, are at once both cause and effect within a vast effect. Each is at once the result of all that has preceded it and a contributing cause of all to come. Yet, as we saw when studying causation, Karma is not only cause and effect in time; rather is it the law which governs the interrelation and solidarity of the Universe in all its parts, and hence, in a way, the karma of one such unit is the karma of all. It is 'the interdependence of Humanity which is the cause of what is called *Distributive Karma*, and it is this law which affords the solution to the great question of collective suffering and relief. No man can rise superior to his individual failings without lifting, be it ever so little, the whole body of which he is an integral part. In the same way no one can sin, nor suffer the effects of sin, alone.'[1]

Rebirth

All action has its due result. A stone thrown into a pond causes wavelets to circle outwards to a distance proportionate to the initial disturbance; after which the initial state of equilibrium is restored. And since each disturbance must start from some particular point, it is clear that harmony can be restored only by the re-converging to that point of the forces set in motion. Thus the consequences of an act re-act, via all the universe, upon the doer with a force commensurate with his own.

Now Karma involves the element of time; and it is unreasonable to hold that all the causes generated in an average life will produce their full effect before the last day of that period. The oldest sage would admit that at the close of a life of study his wisdom was as a raindrop to the sea. Nor is the idea of rebirth new. Almost every country of the East accepts the doctrine as too obvious to need proof, and Western writers have traced its presence in the legends and indigenous ideas of nearly every country in the world. It is to be found in most of the greatest minds of Europe and America, from

1. H. P. Blavatsky, *The Key to Theosophy*, p. 203.

Plato to Origen, from Blake to Schopenhauer, from Goethe, Boehme, Kant, and Swedenborg to Browning, Emerson, Walt Whitman, and leading minds of the Western world to-day.[1]

It is clearly present in such fragments of Christ's teachings as are still extant. Consider, for example, the story of the man born blind, and the rumours that Christ was Jeremiah or Elias come again.[2] Even Herod seems to think that he was John the Baptist 'risen from the dead'.[3]

The truth of the doctrine cannot of course be 'proved', but it is at least immensely reasonable.

A life on earth is, to the Buddhist, as a wayside inn upon a road. At any moment there are many travellers therein, and even as we speak more enter through the doors of Birth, and others leave by one whose name is Death. Within the common meeting-rooms are men and women of every type whose relations to one another form that reaction to environment we call experience.

Such a belief affects all blood relationship. The child may be an older pilgrim than its parents, and is at least entitled to its point of view. In the West we say that the child of a musical father is musical (if it be so) because of heredity. In Buddhist lands it would be explained that the child was born into a musical family, because it (the child) had developed musical propensities in previous lives, and was attracted to an environment suitable for the expression of those 'gifts', a reversal of the Western view. The age of the body is thus no criterion of the age of the entity using it. In the same way, 'infant prodigies' are the outcome of a series of lives devoted to the development of a special faculty. The body alone is the product of its parents. So may a house be built by a landlord, but the tenant need not take it against his will. But even though the body be not the direct creation of that 'Self' which uses it, yet was it chosen as the intrument most suited to the needs of the informing consciousness. Karma is therefore, with Rebirth, a double key to unexplained phenomena. Life does not die at the body's death, nor do the consequences of a deed. Forms are created and

1. See my *Karma and Rebirth* (Wisdom of the East Series) for a long series of quotations from Western writers who accept the doctrines of Rebirth.
2. Matt. xvi, 13–16.
3. Mark vi, 14–16.

destroyed; they come into being, serve their purpose and then die; but the life within knows no such limitation.

> Nay, but as when one layeth
>   His worn-out robes away,
> And taking new ones, sayeth,
>   'These will I wear to-day!'
> So putteth by the spirit
>   Lightly its garb of flesh,
> And passeth to inherit
>   A residence afresh

So wrote Sir Edwin Arnold in his verse translation of the *Bhagavad-Gita*, and, subject to understanding what it is which passes from life to life, the Buddhist would agree.

The Nature of Death

Man alone, says the esoteric tradition, has an individual karma, but life is one, and passes unceasingly from form to form with intervals of rest between.

> Feathered birds, and fishes finned,
> And clouds and rain and calm and wind,
> And sun and moon and stars declare,
> All life is one life, everywhere;
>
> That nothing dies to die for good
> In clay or dust, in stone or wood,
> But only rests awhile to keep
> Life's ancient convenant with Sleep.[1]

Death is the death of the body and its invisible counterpart. The body came into being; it must therefore one day die. Hence the Buddhist saying, 'The cause of death is not disease, but birth.' To mourn for the inevitable dissolution of a temporary garment is foolishness, and all the more so when the man who has thus cast off his outer clothing will return to earth to meet again, maybe, the friends he knew before. Karma takes no reckoning of time. A bond of love or hate between two persons is a cause that will need those 'persons' for the working out of its inevitable effect, and Karma can wait, if need be, for ten thousand years. Death is usually a well-earned rest, when the experience, great or small, of one life is quietly digested, to appear in

1. From Charles Dalmon, *Elegy for Edward Thomas*.

later lives as faculty, ability, and innate tendency. It is but an incident of life, and viewed from the standpoint of a thousand lives, an incident of no more importance and finality than sleep.

What Chuang Tzŭ wrote of his Master, Lao Tzŭ, applies still more to us: 'When the Master came it was at the proper time; when he went away it was the simple sequence of his coming. Quiet acquiescence in what happens at its proper time and quietly submitting to its ceasing, afford no occasion for grief or joy.' Death, therefore, is the gateway to a different form of life, one which is strictly limited in duration by the thoughts and acts of the individual. How can the consequences of a finite life be infinite anything – Heaven or Hell? A man's hereafter is the aggregate effects of the causes generated by him in the past. The cause was limited; equally so will be the effects. The limited and finite cannot cause eternity. Each man, the Buddha taught, suffers in after life the hell or heaven which he was manufacturing every hour of his life on earth. The 'Day of Judgment' is at all times and for everyone – To-day.

It is often asked why we do not remember our past lives. The answer is clear. Because physical memory needs a physical brain, and the brain which remembers incidents of this life is different from that which registered the deeds of the one before. But in fact the bridge from life to life is often crossed. Students claim to have trained their memories to go back step by step until they arrive at an accurate memory of their previous life or lives. The subsequent verification of remembered scenery, surroundings, and events seems to prove the truth of the experimenters' claims, and the Buddhist Scriptures show examples of this interesting but unprofitable exercise.

What is Reborn?

The nature of that which is reborn is the subject of much futile argument, but the details are of no importance in the treading of the Eightfold Path. The body dies at death, but the individual's karma, the resultant of all the causes generated by him in the past, lives on. This complex 'soul', the product of ten thousand lives, is clothed, as we have seen, with divers attributes or qualities, called *skandhas*. This it is which, in the intervening and subjective worlds, digests the lessons of the previous life until such causes as can take effect subjectively have been transmuted into faculty and innate tendency. That which remains to incarnate afresh may be regarded as an individual, as in the Northern School of Buddhism, or as a nameless complex residuum of karma, as in the Southern School. The danger of the former viewpoint lies in the tendency to look upon this individual as a 'separated soul' eternally distinct from other forms of life. The Southern viewpoint, on the other hand, anxious to enforce the doctrine of *anatta* in its literal sense, keeps to the letter rather than to the spirit of the Buddha's metaphors. One candle lighted from another – is the light of the second the same light as the first? Such imagery has its dangers to a certain type of mind, and leads them into a logical absurdity. Yet is the simile beautiful when understood. Light one candle from another and the light is the same, yet different; the same in essence yet seeming, maybe, to the outward eye, to shine more brightly than before. Perhaps the wax which formed the second candle was more purified, the wick of finer texture and the whole created from a finer mould. To that extent the second differs from the first, yet the Light or Life was one and the same, more brightly shining in the second case because of the purer *skandhas* of its form.

[For Bibliography, see end of Chapter Nine]

Theravada Buddhism
IV. The Noble Eightfold Path

*

Right Motive in Morality – The Eight Steps – The Five Precepts – 'Acquiring Merit' – The Siddhis

THE Eightfold Path is the Buddhist Manual to Self-Enlightenment. Much of it may be found in other religions and philosophies, but in Buddhism tremendous emphasis is laid on practical morality. In the words of the *Dhammapada*, 'The man who talks much of the teaching but does not practise it himself is like a cowman counting another's cattle' (v. 19), or again, 'Like beautiful flowers, full of colour but without scent, are the well-spoken words of the man who does not act accordingly' (v. 51).

Right Motive in Morality

The sanction of Buddhist morality is three-fold. At its lowest it is purely selfish. An understanding of the law of Karma makes one realize that it 'pays' to be good. At this stage of evolution there is, as Mrs Rhys Davids points out, 'no other certain sanction of goodness beyond the driving forces of pain waiting on immoral living, and the pleasures rewarding moral living, now or in the long run.'[1] This, when all is said and done, is the sanction of all man-made laws, and the Buddhist knows that the moral laws of nature carry with them both the punishment of disobedience and the virtuous man's reward. In Buddhism a man is punished by his sins, not for them.

Later comes the rational basis of morality. If life be one, each unit of that life reacts in all it does for good or evil on each other unit of the whole. Hence to do evil is to harm one's fellow men, while the strict morality of one such unit raises the level of all humanity.

1. *Buddhism*, p. 121.

Finally comes the ideal stage of 'motiveless morality', a realization that the highest virtue is in truth its own reward. 'Virtue rewards itself,' says Edmond Holmes, 'by strengthening the will, by subduing unworthy desire, by generating knowledge of reality, by giving inward peace. Sin punishes itself by weakening the will, by inflaming unworthy desire, by generating delusions, by breeding fever and unrest. For sin to be "forgiven" is as impossible as for virtue to forgo its reward, for the Path is lit by the ever-deepening foreglow of its goal. To depart from the Path is its own punishment, for the steps must, at *whatever cost*, be retraced.'[1]

It is said in the *Digha Nikaya* that the motives of wrongdoing are always one of four: desire, hatred, delusion, or fear, and the practice of the Eightfold Path removes the power of these four. Henceforth the pilgrim lives the loftiest of ethics every hour because he has lost, by the unification of his consciousness with life, the very power to do otherwise. As Shakespeare says in *Hamlet*:

> This above all. To thine own self be true,
> And it must follow, as the night the day,
> Thou canst not then be false to any man.

The Path is both simple and profound, simple in the clarity of its principles, profound in that its precepts rest on no external force, of God or man, but on the bedrock of immutable and natural law. It follows that the breach of any one of them is ultimately punished as unerringly as disobedience to the laws of health. There is no question of the 'will of God'. The Path knows no authority save the law of which it is the manifested code, and even 'Buddhas do but point the Way.'

The Path is a system of self-development according to law, a graded process of moral evolution within the law of Karma. It is the Middle Way between the two extremes of unnatural asceticism and self-indulgence. No two scholars have translated the eight terms by the same English words, for each term represents a concept to be fully understood only by the 'ever open eye' of Buddhi, the faculty of spiritual perception; but they may be described as follows.

1. *The Creed of Buddha*, p. 94.

The Eight Steps

The Eightfold Path consists of Right Understanding, Right Thoughts or Motives, Right Speech, Right Action, Right Means of Livelihood, Right Effort, Right Concentration, and Right Meditation. The word Right is equivalent to the Latin *Summum* or highest, the quality in its most perfect form. The steps are to be taken together, although their perfection will be attained only *seriatim*, as will presently appear.

1. *Samma Ditthi*, or Right Views or Understanding, covers an intellectual grasp of the Teaching of the Dhamma, a realization of the Three Signs of Being, the Noble Truths, the nature of self and the law of Karma.

2. *Samma Sankappa*, or Right Attitude of Mind, covers motive, the use to which all subsequent development should be put – the helping of our fellow man. It is Right Desire, the path of altruism and the slaying of self. Every path and sub-division of the path has two aspects, its right hand and its left, the right hand leading to Nirvana, and the left through selfishness to spiritual death. The difference between the two is but the motive behind the acquisition of the powers therein obtained. 'It is he alone who has the love of humanity at heart, who is capable of grasping thoroughly the idea of a regenerating practical Brotherhood, who is entitled to the possession of our secrets. He alone will never misuse his powers, as there will be no fear that he would turn them to selfish ends.'[1] The combined action of these two steps having prepared the pilgrim's mind, the third, fourth and fifth direct how such mentality should be applied; for as we think, we act, and action is precipitated thought. As someone wittily remarked, 'We are not what we think we are, but what we think, we are. '

3. *Samma Vacha*, or Right Speech, needs little comment. Its essence is control, until our every word is courteous, considerate and true. All idle gossip and unprofitable talk must be stamped out. Silence should be so respected that the words which break it must leave the world the better for their birth.

4. *Samma Kammanta*, or Right Action, is the keynote of the Eightfold Path, for Buddhism is a religion of action, not

1. *The Mahatma Letters to A. P. Sinnett*, p. 252.

belief. Action is twofold; positive, or what we do; negative, or what we refrain from doing. The negative aspect is expressed in *Pancha Sila*,[1] the Five Precepts or vows to abstain from killing, stealing, sensuality, lying and intoxicating liquors or drugs. But the Buddha laid down in terms that these Precepts apply equally to the mind. Murder is none the less murder in that it never left the heart, and a slanderous thought is as harmful to its thinker and his enemies as any spoken word. Again, it is possible to get drunk on excitement; theft is no less theft because it wears the cloak of custom; and a lustful thought befouls its owner's purity.

The Five Precepts

These five rules or Precepts, says Mr Edmond Holmes, 'indicate five arterial directions in which the Buddhist self-control is to be exercised. Thus, the first rule calls upon him to control the passion of anger, the second, the desire for material possessions, the third, the lusts of the flesh, the fourth, cowardice and malevolence (the chief causes of untruthfulness), the fifth, the craving for unwholesome excitement.'[2]

The first of the five should be translated, 'I undertake the rule of training to refrain from injury to living things' (see Pansil on page 240), the promise being made to oneself, and not to some external being. As is said in the *Sutta Nipata*, 'As I am, so are these. As these are, so am I. Thus identifying himself with others the wise man neither kills nor causes to be killed.' And again, 'Whoso strives only for his own happiness, and in so doing hurts or kills living creatures which also seek for happiness, he shall find no happiness after death' (*Dhammapada*). And yet again, 'In this sense we are our brothers' keepers, that if we injure them we are responsible. Therefore our duty is, so vigilantly to control ourselves that we may injure none, and for this there is no substitute: all other duties take a lower place and are dependent on it.'[3]

This Precept is to be found in almost every code of ethics, and each must use his common sense in applying to it the needs of daily life. Clearly, killing for sport or for personal

1. See Appendix Two.
2. *The Creed of Buddha*, p. 73.
3. From the *Sayings of Tsiang Samdup* in Talbot Mundy's *Om*.

adornment can never be defended, but in the far more difficult problems of the extermination of vermin, of killing for food, and in self-defence, no dogmatic statements can be made. The law is plain, that life is sacred, be it that of a butterfly or man. Let each, then, cultivate within his heart a genuine compassion for all forms of life, based on a reverence for its source and the oneness which such source entails, and common-sense decisions will be made.

With regard to the killing of animals for food, it is obvious that the purer the food we eat the more fit will our bodies become for the functioning of our inner faculties, but once more common sense must be employed. A Buddhist's first requirement is a healthy body in which to work. He must therefore eat such food as long experience has shown to be, not the most pleasing to his palate, but most suited to his health. To make oneself ill by insufficient nutriment is a form of vanity. Diet is not a matter of religion, but of climate, occupation and individual temperament. Indeed, Narasu quotes the Buddha as saying: 'My disciples have permission to eat whatever food it is customary to eat in any place or country provided it is done without indulgence of the appetite, or evil desire. '[1]

The Second Precept runs, 'I undertake the rule of training to refrain from taking that which is not given.' This covers every form of theft by whatever euphemistic term it may be known, from mental covetousness to business methods which, though legal, violate the moral law. The principle is based on social 'give and take' for to steal is an offence against the community of which the thief is part. The Buddhist may acquire wealth honestly to any amount, but he should use it to altruistic ends. As the Buddha said to Anathapindika: 'It is not life and wealth and power that enslave a man, but the cleaving to them. He who possesses wealth and uses it rightly will be a blessing unto his fellow beings.'

The third of the Precepts calls for self-control in regard to the most powerful of human instincts, sex. 'Buddha said: "Of all the lusts and desires, there is none so powerful as sexual inclination".'[2]

Hence the Buddhist attitude to women: 'Is she old? Regard her as your mother. Is she honourable? Regard her

1. *The Essence of Buddhism*, p. 74.
2. Beal, *A Catena of Buddhist Scriptures*, p. 198.

as your sister. Is she of small account? Regard her as your younger sister. Is she a child? Treat her reverently and with politeness.' To the Buddhist the sex of the body is a matter of karmic effect, and sexual desire is a carnal appetite as natural in its proper sphere as the appetite for food. But woman, too, is a pilgrim, as much a pilgrim as man. The Buddhist therefore reminds himself of the impermanence of fleshly beauty, and concentrates his attention on the beauty of the informing mind. All visual attraction is the reaction of the lower self, the craving of unregenerate desires. Hence the Buddhist meditation on the vanity of fleshly charm, comparable to the one-time custom in the West of having a human skull grinning its message of impermanence from the midst of the passing glories of the feast. Once regard woman in this light, and sex, from its morbid prominence in Europe and America to-day, drops to the level of the well-controlled expression of a natural desire. Once again it is the mental element which matters, for this Precept is primarily aimed at the control and sublimation of desire. Mere physical control with foul thoughts in the mind is a greater defilement than a natural physical outlet with a wholesome, clean mentality behind. For as a man thinks, so he is. It is important to distinguish between control and suppression. Man can harness the fiercest mountain stream, but he cannot dam the humblest rivulet without providing an outlet for its energy. So it is with sex, a clean impersonal creative force, as natural as water in a river bed, as restless and tremendous as the sea. On the physical plane we call it sex; on the emotional plane it functions as artistic impulse, enthusiasm and emotional power, while in the realm of mind it is that 'creative urge' which is responsible for all that man has ever made, inclusive of himself. Herein lies the essence of sublimation, to choose the channel through which the force shall flow. It is but a gradual withdrawing of the creative force from purely physical to emotional or mental levels by the exercise of ceaseless vigilance and self-control.

The Fourth Precept may be translated as 'I undertake the rule of training to refrain from falsehood.' This too applies to thought as well as to word and deed, and admits of no exceptions. It is one thing to avoid giving an answer; quite another deliberately to lie. The first is but withholding the truth, the second breaking it, and how shall a man attain

enlightenment if he violates that Truth which he strives so
fiercely to attain? The minor forms of lying, such as
inaccuracy and exaggeration, are reprobated as being so many
steps on the downward road to the pure deliberate lie, while
slander is doubly evil, for it is but lying with the motive, in
however mild a form, of hate, and the suffering generated
day by day by spiteful gossip needs no stressing. Unless it is
our bounden duty to tell another of a neighbour's failings
let the maxim stand: 'Hear no evil, see no evil, speak no
evil.' So shall the third step on the Eightfold Path – Right
Speech – be rigidly applied.

The fifth of the Five Precepts, aimed at slothfulness caused
by drink or drugs, seems to be less important than the other
four. Indeed, there are passages in the Scriptures where it is
omitted, while for Arhats we read of an alternate fifth, 'To
spend one's stored-up wealth in worldly enjoyments.'[1]

However this may be, it needs no argument to prove the
evils caused by excessive indulgence in alcohol. While a meat
diet may be necessary for some people, no healthy person
needs the aid of alcohol in keeping fit. Being unnatural to the
body, any excess, however small, will cause proportionate
harm. The principle underlying the Precepts is the necessity
for perfect mental, moral and physical control, and any
stimulant when taken to excess will make control more difficult. Whether the drugs be taken in a powerful form or in
the milder guise of coffee, tea or nicotine, the tendency will
be the same. It is for each man, having understood the principle, to apply it constantly with sincerity and common
sense.

These Precepts, like most of the Jewish Ten Command-
ments, are negative, but, as already pointed out, the equivalent positive injunctions appear again and again in the
Canon: 'Cease to do evil; learn to do good; cleanse your
own heart; this is the teaching of the Buddhas.' The Five
Precepts cover the first command, but they do but prepare
the way for the second of the moral trinity, *Sila*, *Dana*,
Bhavana. After *Pancha Sila*, the Five Precepts, comes *Dana*,
charity, at once the 'love' and the 'good works' of St Paul,
a kindly helpful attitude to all that lives, essentially active,
positive, dynamic. It may be described as the practice of
brotherhood in thought, word and deed. But even as *Sila*

1. *The Dialogues of the Buddha*, Part 3, p. 225.

explains how to 'cease to do evil' and *Dana* is the comple-mentary doing good, so *Bhavana* covers the injunction to 'cleanse your own heart', or, in less poetic terminology, to discipline and purify the mind by its deliberate control and exercise. This will be considered with the last two steps of the Eightfold Path.

'*Acquiring Merit*'

By the practice of Right Action the Buddhist 'acquires merit', that is, ensures the pleasant consequences of his deeds. This doctrine of merit, which forms a large part of the life of the common people in Theravada countries, is a useful application of Karma to the daily round. All may store up merits or 'good karma' by daily acts of kindliness, knowing that in a day to come each act will bring its due reward.

The motive, however, is more important than the deed. The effects of a deed are manifold, depending on many factors. An act is the outward expression of a thought, which in turn is coloured by emotion, the latter two characteristics forming motive, good or bad. The thought and act are hence inseparable. Too often the mere outward show of charity has atrophied the kindliness of heart which, from the doer's viewpoint, is the dominating cause in moulding the result. A good deed done with a wrong motive may benefit others, but will in the end be harmful to the doer's mind, for the *mind* is the maker of karma, good or bad, and hence the intention of the mind at the time of action determines the incidence of the resultant merit. As all life is one, it follows that the merit of a deed will be proportionate to the extent to which all living things are helped thereby.

To return to the Noble Eightfold Path:

5. *Samma Ajiva*, or Right Livelihood, consists in follow-ing a trade or occupation compatible with the above.

6. *Samma Vayama*, or Right Effort, is a necessary step be-tween the level so far reached and the heights yet to be won. 'This declaration of strenuousness', says the Bhikkhu Silacara, 'as a vital, if not *the* most vital feature in the Buddhist scheme of salvation, may come as a surprise to those who have been brought up in the opinion current in the West that Buddhism is a religion producing a state of chronic apathy. None the less there is no room in Buddhism

for the idler in any shape or form, as indeed could not be otherwise in a faith which teaches men to rely for salvation upon their own individual effort, and denies them all help from any outside source except such as is to be found in the sympathy and kindly goodwill of fellow pilgrims upon the same journey. The prize is only for the striving – for none else. '[1]

The Efforts have been given as four. To prevent new evil entering one's mind; to remove all evil that is there; to develop such good as is in one's mind; to acquire still more unceasingly. Right Effort involves the right use of one's energies, so directing them as to secure the maximum results with the minimum expenditure of force. This involves the whole field of modern psychology, in the elimination of every 'complex' and mental inhibition which results in friction and consequent loss of power.

7. *Samma Sati*, or Right Concentration, is the beginning of the final stage. Having acquired some degree of moral and physical control the Buddhist approaches *Bhavana*, the control and evolution of the mind. So little is its need and nature understood in the West that the emphasis which every Eastern school of practical philosophy has laid upon it since the dawn of history may puzzle those to whom true culture is unknown. Yet even as a high standard of ethics should be a prerequisite to a grasp of pure philosophy, lest the power thereby obtained be abused, so mind-control in its widest sense is a vital factor in the treading of the Eightfold Path. 'Concentration or Yoga', says Patanjali, 'is the hindering of the modifications of the thinking principle', the overcoming of its natural tendency to diffuseness, by learning to apply it to a single point to the exclusion of all else. This is the birth of true understanding, for 'the mind which has been trained so that the ordinary modifications of its action are not present, but only those which occur upon the conscious taking up of an object for contemplation, is changed into the likeness of that which is pondered upon, and enters into full comprehension of the being thereof.'[2] The fact that this, which is the bedrock of all mind-control, is almost unknown to the West, shows how in its zeal to be master of matter the West has hardly entered upon the field of mind.

1. *Lotus Blossoms*, p. 36–7.
2. From the *Yoga Aphorisms of Patanjali*, trans. W. Q. Judge, p. 1 and 15.

In the West man is still the slave of his mind; in the East, he controls and uses it. Truly 'all that we are is the result of what we have thought; it is founded upon our thoughts, it is made by our thoughts'.[1] Hence the necessity for learning the art of concentration and control of thought before we approach the final stage.

8. *Samma Samadhi* is a state of mind in which the waves of confusion aroused by thought are stilled. It is far more than trance, or mere psychic ecstasy; it is awareness of 'the still centre of the turning world'. This eighth step, being mind-development carried to heights beyond our normal understanding, any further attempt to describe its nature would serve no useful purpose.

Yet Samadhi is far short of *Prajna*, Wisdom, which, with its twin, *Karuna*, Compassion, is known by the faculty of *Buddhi*, the intuition or direct cognition, by the use of which the evolving consciousness cognizes and knows its oneness with the All of which it is part. When Samadhi is merged with *Prajna/Karuna* the individual has earned the title 'free', free from the fetters of *Avidya*, Ignorance, free from the snares of self and being free he knows that he is free, and finds himself upon the threshold of Nirvana.

The Siddhis

In the higher stages of the Path, certain qualities or faculties as yet unknown to the average man are gradually developed. These occult powers are known as the *Iddhis* (Skt: *Siddhis*) and will appear when the neophyte has produced within himself the moral strength and purity which will make it impossible ever to use them for selfish ends. All psychic 'gifts' as practised and, for a consideration, taught by countless self-styled Yogis, Seers and other charlatans, are as far removed from genuine occult powers as brass is from gold. No true initiate will sell, or even display such a faculty, nor may he teach it save to those both morally and mentally prepared by years of strenuous training. Even then these powers are never used for display. 'An ordained disciple must not boast of any superhuman perfection, be it celestial visions or miracles. The disciple who boasts of a super-

1. *Dhammapada*, 1.

human perfection, be it celestial visions or miracles, is no
longer a disciple of the Buddha.'[1]

Such, then, are the factors in the Noble Eightfold Path.
They must be practised simultaneously, although their perfection will be acquired only in a gradually ascending scale.
No step can be left out, for knowledge must be acquired and
used with right motives, and applied to speech, action and
the means of livelihood. Yet these are of no avail unless
directed and controlled intelligently, after which the basis of
true mind-control will have been laid, to culminate in time
in Self-enlightenment.

[For Bibliography, see end of Chapter Nine]

1. *The Gospel of Buddha*, Carus, p. 121.

CHAPTER NINE

Theravada Buddhism
V. The Four Paths and the Goal

*

*The Stage of Sotapanna – The Stages of Sakadaga-
min and Anagamin – The Path to Arhatship – The
Pairs of Opposites – The Problem of Evil – Freewill
and 'Fate' – The Religion of Love – The Four Brahma
Viharas – Nirvana*

IN the later stages of the Path the neophyte will reach an
important crisis in his spiritual development. Hitherto he has
been treading a path of elementary understanding and morality. There comes a time, however, when, without necessarily
leaving the householder's life, he dedicates himself irrevo-
cably to the life of the Spirit. Thereafter his advance is
marked by four Stages of advancement, which represent a
successive expansion of consciousness.

The Stages are:

1. The stage of *Sotapanna*, 'He who has entered the
stream', which will carry him in time to the ocean of Nirvana. This marks a first vision of Nirvana and hence a
conversion from the ways of men to the 'divine' life
within. It is the culmination of years and lives of self-
preparation, in which a realization of the basic principles of
the Dhamma has finally borne fruit in the practice of the
holy life. At this state three of the Fetters, of which there
are ten in all, have been removed. These are the Delusion of
Self (*Sakkayaditthi*); Doubt regarding the truth of the
Dhamma; and Belief in the efficacy of Rites and Ceremonies.

The Delusion of Self. – This fetter, the false belief that the
individual self is real and self-existent, is rightly given enormous emphasis, 'for the clinging to individuality, the desire
to affirm the apparent or actual self instead of looking forward into its expansion into the real or universal Self, has
its ethical counterpart in *egoism*, and egoism is the beginning
and end of sin'.[1]

1. Holmes, *The Creed of Buddha*, p. 77.

Doubt. The removal of doubt does not necessitate a blind belief, but little progress can be made on the Path while the pilgrim is uncertain of the end to which it leads. Yet, as Lakshmi Narasu points out, 'Buddhism does not underestimate the value of doubt during the period of investigation.' Its doubt 'is of that sort whose whole aim is to conquer itself by high aspiration and incessant toil, not of the sort which, born of flippancy and ignorance, tries to perpetuate itself as an excuse for idleness and indifference.'[1]

Belief in the Efficacy of Rites and Ceremonies. 'The disciple must free himself, first from the general delusion that correct outward action will ensure a man's salvation, and then from the particular delusion that religious rites and ceremonies have intrinsic value' to the attendant devotee.[2]

Much might be written on this attitude to ritual, so directly at variance with Western orthodoxy, yet it is cardinal to Eastern schools of thought. Not by outward show or priestly ritual, by labels, dogmas, prayers and creeds is wisdom gained, but rather by deep meditation until the outward appearance is but a mirror to the mind within. In short, nothing will avail in substitution for *self*-liberation. Always the Buddha taught: 'Buddhas do but point the way – work out your salvation with diligence.'

Buddhism is above all others a religion of individual effort, wherein no being, man or God, is allowed to stand for good or evil between a cause and its effect. 'Absolution' and the 'forgiveness of sins', as understood by the average Christian, are to the Buddhist mind absurd in that they strive to separate a cause from its effect, and to make some person other than the doer suffer the consequences of the deed.

2 and 3. The stage of *Sakadagamin*: 'he who will return to earth only once more.' At this stage the aspirant has to wrestle with the Fetters of *Sensuality*, the lower sensuous desires, and *Unkindliness* in all its forms, which are fully overcome only in the third or *Anagamin* stage. Of these two Fetters little need be said. The 'lusts of the flesh' are man's most powerful though not most subtle enemy, and must be slain to rise no more before the wayfarer may reach the goal. The fifth Fetter embraces every form of animosity. 'The

1. *The Essence of Buddhism*, p. 107.
2. Holmes, *The Creed of Buddha*, p. 77.

disciple has to subdue all the feelings of anger, resentment, envy, jealousy, hatred and the like which spring from his sense of separateness from the rest of living things, and from his subsequent reluctance to identify himself with Universal Life.'[1]

Civilization is inseparable from competition, which produces and implies antagonism. Man against man, business firm against business firm, nation against nation and race against race, such is the ceaseless cry. Competition has its uses, but when its usefulness is past it becomes a fetter in the path of progress, and must give way in time to cooperation based on mutual understanding and respect. One of the greatest pronouncements ever made in the field of morality is contained in the Dhammapada: 'Hatred ceaseth not by hatred: hatred ceaseth but by love. This is the eternal law.'[2]

When sensuous desire has been transmuted into higher forms of energy and every trace of ill-will is removed, the final stage is entered.

4. On this, the Path to Arhatship, the seeker for perfection has to overcome the remaining five of the Hindrances, or Fetters.

Desire for (separate) life in the worlds of form (rupa).
Desire for (separate) life in the formless (arupa) *worlds*.

The former relates to the world as we know it, and to those realms beyond the grave in which, though freed from an earthly body, man is no less clothed in matter, though of a far more tenuous form. This, too, is life within the whirlpool of illusion, even though, compared with earth, it seems to some as Heaven. Beyond these lie the 'formless worlds', where man, though free from material form, is still subject to the limitations of existence. For desire for existence under any conditions will be in time fulfilled, whereas the Buddhist's aim is to free himself from all existence in Samsara, the whirlpool of becoming.

The eighth of the Fetters, *Spiritual Pride*, explains a vast percentage of man's foolishness. Perfect is the man who finally excludes it in its subtlest form.

Self-Righteousness. – Much might be written about the

1. Holmes, *The Creed of Buddha*, p. 78.
2. *Dhammapada*, v. 5.

placing of these common weaknesses so close to man's perfection. Ought not these Fetters to have been broken long ago? 'Perhaps they ought', said Edmond Holmes, 'but the Buddha knew that even in the last stage of the upward Path the shadow of egoism may fall on one's thought. The man who can say of himself: "It is I who have scaled these heights: it is I who have suppressed egoism; it is I who have won deliverance", is still the subject of delusions.'[1]

Avidya, Ignorance, is the final obstacle, and the father of all suffering, for had we perfect knowledge we should never err. Even as *Avidya* is the first of the Twelve Nidanas, so it is the Fetter whose removal leaves a man self-liberated from Samsara, perfected and free. 'It is for the sake of knowledge – real, final, absolute knowledge – that the Path has been followed. To know that the Universal Self is one's own real self – to know this truth, not as a theory, not as a conclusion, not as a poetic idea, not as a sudden revelation, but as the central fact of one's own inmost life – to know this truth in the most intimate sense of the word *know*, by living it, by being it – is the final end of all spiritual effort. The expansion of the Self carries with it the expansion of consciousness; and when consciousness has become all-embracing, the fetter of ignorance has been finally broken and the delusion of self is dead.'[2]

The Pairs of Opposites

Life as we know it, including the intellect which surveys it, is composed of an endless series of apparently opposing principles. 'Everything is; everything is not. The world is an ending thing; the world is not an ending thing.' These are classical examples; others more familiar to the West are 'spirit' and 'matter', male and female, strength and weakness, pleasure and pain, life and death, all of which are complementary aspects of a whole. The antitheses 'of cause and effect, substance and attribute, good and evil, truth and error, are due to the tendency of man to separate terms which are related. Fichte's puzzle of self and not-self, Kant's antinomies, Hume's opposition of facts and laws, can all be got over if we recognize that the opposing factors are mutually complementary elements based on one identity.'[3]

1. Holmes, *The Creed of Buddha*, p. 80.
2. *Ibid.*, p. 80.
3. Radhakrishnan, *Philosophy of the Upanishads*, p. 55.

In terms of philosophy the Path is a Middle Way, for it carefully avoids both the pitfalls of extreme asceticism and the sophistry of those who claim that self-indulgence will eliminate desire. It lies between the Pairs of Opposites whose equilibrium is peace.

The Problem of Evil

Yet nothing can be manifested in a finite world without its opposite. Light implies darkness, else it would not be known as light, and breathing could not be sustained unless we breathed both in and out. Like the double action of the human heart, the heartbeat of the universe implies duality, a cosmic pulse, an alternation of in-breathing and out-breathing, of manifestation and rest. To the Buddhist good and evil are relative and not absolute terms. The cause of evil is man's inordinate desires for self. All action directed to selfish, separative ends is evil; all which tends to union is good.

The finest qualities in man, strength of purpose, patience and unselfishness, have been gradually developed from the interplay between these forces. Hence suffering and evil form the soul's gymnasium in which to strengthen virtue until, like a raft which has borne its travellers to the farther shore, it can be left behind.

As already explained, man's will is a natural force, to be used for good or evil at its user's choice. If a man uses power for good, his gain will be proportionate; if for evil, the transgressor is pitting himself against the whole force of the universe. For a while he may seem to flourish in his selfishness, but ultimately, by the process of inexorable law, the karmic pendulum will bring him the *dukkha*, suffering, which his acts have caused.

Freewill and 'Fate'

The Buddhist fails to see any conflict between the hypotheses of freewill and predestination, for karma and freewill are two facets of the same spiritual truth. 'Buddhism', Ananda Coomaraswamy says, 'is fatalistic in the sense that the present is always determined by the past; but the future remains free. Every action we make depends on what we have come to be at the time, but what we are coming to be at any time depends on the direction of the will. The karmic law merely asserts that this direction cannot be altered suddenly by the forgiveness of sins, but must be changed by our own efforts.'[1] Hence every man is free within the limitations of his self-created karma, the resultant of past actions of body, speech and thought.

A man may stand in a room before two doors, and leave the room by either. His will is free and he may choose. But suppose against one of the doors he should pile a mass of furniture and subsequently fall asleep. When he awakes he will find that he has no choice of exit, for one door will be barred. If he remembers nothing of his previous acts he will loudly complain that he has no choice of exit. Yet it was he who barred the second door, and every barrier which stands between him and his chosen end can be in time by him removed. Thus does the doctrine of Karma and Rebirth remove the excuse so constantly put forward for evil doing, that 'I could not help it, for my hands were tied.'

The Religion of Love

Such are the opposites and the Way which lies between them. So far, however, it may be said that the Dhamma itself is one-sided and unbalanced in that it is too rational and intellectual, too 'cold'. To this objection there are two answers: first, that the Buddhist is concerned with truth as it is, not as he would like it to be, and secondly, that the criticism is in fact untrue.

Buddhism is as much a religion of love as any on earth. As is written of the would-be Buddhist in the *Metta Sutta*, 'As a mother, even at the risk of her own life, protects her son, her only son, so let him cultivate love without measure towards all beings. Let him cultivate toward the whole world, above, below, around and everywhere, a heart unmixed with enmity. Let a man maintain this mindfulness for all his waking hours, whether he be standing, walking, sitting or lying down.' Is this a 'cold' religion? or again, as is written in the *Itivuttaka*, 'All the means that can be used as bases for right action are not worth the sixteenth part of the emancipation of the heart through love. This takes all others up into itself, outshining them in glory. Just as whatsoever stars there be, their radiance avails not the sixteenth part of the radiance of the moon, just as the sun, mounting up into

1. *Buddha and the Gospel of Buddhism*, p. 233.

a clear and cloudless sky, overwhelms all darkness in the realms of space, ... so all means towards right action avail not the sixteenth part of the emancipation of the heart through love.'[1]

In Buddhism love is a virtue to be deliberately developed and offered to the service of mankind. It is the first of the so-called *Brahma Viharas*, or Sublime States of Consciousness, which the Bhikkhu and layman are alike encouraged to develop and practise constantly. For before the quality of Loving-kindness, for example, can be 'broadcast' through the universe, it must be built in as a quality of the thinker's mind, for only then will it become an habitual attitude. This habit of sharing his spiritual treasures with his fellow-men becomes instinctive to the Buddhist; hence the phrase repeated on occasions of every kind: 'May all be happy!' The power of such an attitude of mind as a solvent of all egotism, hatred and unbrotherliness must be experienced before it can be understood.

The Four Brahma Viharas

The four are usually given as Love, Compassion, Joy and Equanimity. Of *Metta*, Loving-kindness as an active force, little need be said save that in Buddhism it is 'no mere matter of pretty speech, for strong was the conviction that "thoughts are things", that psychical action, emotional or intellectual, is capable of working like a force among forces. Europe may yet come round further to this Indian attitude.'[1] Its method of use in meditation is beautifully expressed in the *Tevijja Sutta*: and in many more. 'And he lets his mind pervade one quarter of the world with thoughts of love, and so the second, and so the third, and so the fourth. And thus the whole world, above, below, around and everywhere does he continue to pervade with heart of Love, far-reaching and beyond measure', for he who realizes to the full the oneness of his life with all its other forms will find his consciousness expand proportionately, and as he understands, so will he love, until his heartbeat is the heartbeat of the universe, his consciousness coincident with all that lives. Love has, of course, as many forms as hearts that hold it, yet in the end must the personal give way to the impersonal, the selfish to

1. Mrs Rhys Davids, *Dialogues of the Buddha*, Part III, p. 185.

the altruistic, for *Metta* is not 'love aflame with all desire, but love at peace'.

So is *Karuna* born. '"As I am, so are these. As these are, so am I. Thus identifying himself with others," the Buddhist can put himself in the place of the lowest, most degraded, most hopelessly "lost" of his fellow human beings, for the Buddhist *understands*.'[1] Compassion is the basis of morality, for 'we feel with and for each other because we are really one with each other. In the valuation of deeds Compassion is the touchstone which divides them into good and evil. It is no local, temporary, human code; it is the voice of the Cosmos heard in the ear.'[2]

The third of the four, *Mudita*, is translated as Sympathetic Joy, even as Karuna might be translated as Sympathetic Sorrow. 'Just as if, on seeing some person who is dear and agreeable, he should be glad on his account, even so he suffuses all beings with such gladness. The salient characteristic of sympathetic joy is gladness, its essential property the opposite of envy, its manifestation the abolition of disaffection, its proximate cause the sight of the success of others. To one who is in ecstasy of joy, contemplating the consciousness of beings who for some joyous reason are rejoicing, his heart becomes stored with and possessed by that consciousness. (Thus) sympathetic joy refers either to a state of joy in others, or in oneself, or just to the feeling impersonally considered.'[3]

The fourth of the Brahma Viharas is *Upekkha*, Even-mindedness or Equanimity, and it is the outcome of the other three. After sharing the emotions of others in every form the Buddhist returns to a calm detachment from all excitement, a restoration of the mind's impersonal serenity. 'The salient characteristic of Equanimity is evolving a central position towards others, its function is seeing others impartially, its manifestation is the quenching of both aversion and sycophancy, its proximate cause is seeing how each belongs to the continuity of his own karma.'[4] But every virtue has its corresponding vice, and equanimity is not to be confused with selfish indifference to the welfare of others, which is the outcome of *Avidya*, Ignorance.

1. J. E. Ellam in *The Buddhist Review*, Vol. XI, p. 182.
2. Loftus Hare, *Mysticism of East and West*, p. 83.
3. From the *Visuddhi Magga* of Buddhaghosa, chap. 9.
4. *On the Divine States*, Mrs Rhys Davids, p. 23.

Nirvana

The Goal of Buddhism is the condition of the Arhat, and the Arhat is one who has reached Nirvana (Pali: *Nibbana*). 'To have realized the Truths, and traversed the Path; to have broken the Bonds, put an end to the Intoxications, got rid of the Hindrances, mastered the craving for metaphysical speculation, was to have attained the ideal, the Fruit, as it is called, of Arahatship.'[1]

The existence of Nirvana is a logical necessity. 'There is, Brethren, an un-born, a not-become, a not-made, a not-compounded. If there were not, Brethren, that which is not-born, not-become, not-made, not-compounded, there could be no escape for the born, become, made and compounded. But since, Brethren, there is this unborn ... there is made known an escape for the born, become, made and compounded.'[2]

What, then, is Nirvana? 'There is, Brethren, a condition where there is neither "earth", nor "water", nor "fire", nor "air", nor the sphere of infinite space, nor the sphere of infinite consciousness, nor the sphere of the void, nor the sphere of neither perception nor non-perception ... that condition, Brethren, do I call neither a coming nor a going nor a standing still, nor a falling away nor a rising up; but it is without fixity, without mobility, without basis. It is the end of woe.'[3]

It is logically inexpressible. 'The Tao that can be expressed is not the eternal Tao', and all that is said about it is necessarily untrue.

> If any teach Nirvana is to cease,
>   Say unto such they lie.
> If any teach Nirvana is to live
>   Say unto such they err .. .[4]

Nor did the Buddha attempt to explain the Goal which he had himself attained. As Professor Radhakrishnan says, 'He felt that his mission was not so much to unveil the secrets of blessedness as to win men to its realization.'[5] Only a negative is possible, for we can conceive the Infinite only as the not-

1. Rhys Davids, *Early Buddhism*, p. 72.
2. *Udana*, chap. VIII.
3. *Ibid.*
4. *The Light of Asia.*
5. *Indian Philosophy*, I, p. 447.

finite, as the word implies. All positive description is adding predicates to the All, which is either absurd for redundancy or, by exclusion, a limitation of the All.

But it is not, as early translators of the Sutras thought, extinction, and such a belief is expressly described by the Buddha as heresy. The word literally means 'going out', as a fire dies out for want of fuelling. It is the cessation of becoming, a stopping of the Wheel of Rebirth because the motive power of its revolutions, desire for sentient life, has stopped. It is the end of separateness.

Nirvana is the extinction of the not-Self in the completion of the Self. It is, therefore, to the limited extent that we can understand it, a concept of psychology, a state of consciousness. As such it is, as Professor Radhakrishnan points out, 'the goal of perfection and not the abyss of annihilation. Through the destruction of all that is individual in us, we enter into communion with the whole universe, and become an integral part of the great purpose. Perfection is then the sense of oneness with all that is, has ever been and can ever be. The horizon of being is extended to the limits of reality.'[1] It is therefore not correct to say that the dewdrop slips into the Shining Sea; it is nearer to the truth to speak of the Shining Sea invading the dewdrop. There is here no sense of loss but of infinite expansion when, 'Foregoing self, the Universe grows I.'

The first and the last word on Nirvana may be given in one phrase: 'Nirvana is!' for no discussion with the finite mind will enable one to cognize the Infinite. It cannot be conceived; it can only be experienced. Yet the foothills of this final peak are described in much of the world's literature, and some account of these experiences is given in the chapter on Satori, the goal of Zen, in my *Zen Buddhism*.[2] Enlightenment is perceived as such as it progressively appears, for the practising Buddhist knows that it may be attained both here and now and not in a far-off heaven. As for Parinirvana, that which lies beyond, such an Absolute must be 'an Omnipresent, Eternal, Boundless and Immutable Principle on which all speculation is impossible, since it transcends the power of human conception and could only

1. *Indian Philosophy*, I, p. 448.
2. *Zen Buddhism*. An Enquiry from the Western Point of View. (Allen and Unwin, 1961.)

1. Standing Buddha of red sandstone. Mathura, India. 5th c. A.D.
By courtesy of Royal Academy of Arts.

2. Buddha Head of grey sandstone. Khmer (Cambodian). 10th c. A.D.
Victoria and Albert Museum. Crown Copyright.

3. Kwan-Yin, the Chinese 'Goddess of Mercy'. Wood. Early Sung Dynasty of China. (11th c. A.D.) By courtesy of Sir Geoffrey and Lady Burton.

4. The Daibutsu ('Great Buddha') or Amida Buddha at Kamakura, Japan. Bronze. 1252 A.D. Ht. 52 ft. Author's photograph.

5. Seated Buddha. Burmese gold-lacquered wood, 18th–19th c.
In the Shrine of the Buddhist Society, London.

6. Bodhidharma. The founder of Zen Buddhism in 6th c. A.D.
Japanese Ivory (19th c.)

7. The Buddhist Temple at Buddha Gaya, North India, where the Buddha attained Enlightenment. Author's photograph from *Via Tokyo*.

8. Todai-Ji, Nara, Japan. Headquarters of the Kegon Sect. The largest wooden building in the world. Author's photograph from *Via Tokyo*.

9. The Shwe Dagon Pagoda, Rangoon. The central spire is plated in pure gold. Author's photograph from *Via Tokyo*.

10. The Temple of the Tooth, Kandy, Ceylon. Author's photograph from *Via Tokyo*.

11. The Potala, Lhasa, Tibet. The palace of the Dalai Lama. From a water-colour brought from Lhasa for the Buddhist Society, London.

12. (LEFT) Professor D. T. Suzuki, the world authority on Zen
Buddhism. (RIGHT) the Abbot Daiko Yamasaki of Shokoku-ji,
Kyoto. (STANDING) the Abbot Ogata of Chotoko-In, one of the
smaller temples in Shokoku-Ji. Note on the Abbots the Robe of
the Rinzai sect of Zen Buddhism.

13a. Colonel H. S. Olcott, Founding President of the Theosophical Society and Author of the fourteen 'Fundamental Buddhistic Beliefs'.

13b. The Anagarika Dharmapala of Ceylon, Founder of the Maha Bodhi Society in 1891.

14a. The Bhikkhu Ananda Metteya, born as Allan Bennett, Leader of the first Buddhist Mission to the West.

14b. The Ven. Tai-Hsü of China, whose Mission to Europe in 1928–9 promoted the foundation of 'Les Amis du Bouddhisme' in Paris.

15a. Miss Constant Lounsbery, the American-born Founding President of 'Les Amis du Bouddhisme' in Paris.

15b. Mme David-Neel, the great French authority on Tibetan Buddhism who spent many years in Tibet.

16. The Bhikkhu U Thittila of Burma with the Author, Founding
President of the Buddhist Society, London, 1924. The Bhikkhu
wears the orange Robe of Theravada Buddhism. In Ceylon and
Siam it is yellow.

be dwarfed by any human expression of similitude. It is beyond the range and reach of thought . . .'[1]

Summary

Such is the Theravada, the Doctrine of the Elders. It is a strictly limited teaching and was so given. To a long list of what Rhys Davids calls the 'Indeterminates'[2] the Buddha refused to give an answer, on the ground that reply to such questions would not assist in the treading of the Path, whereon, but much, much farther on, the final answers lay. But that which is given is enough and more than enough for any man to apply. Within its largely negative form is a vital, positive way of life, a call to strenuous endeavour in the greatest fight of all.

'Warriors, warriors, Lord, we call ourselves. In what way are we warriors?'
'We wage war, Brethren; therefore are we called warriors.'
'Wherefore, Lord, do we wage war?'
'For lofty virtue, for high endeavour, for sublime wisdom – for these things do we wage war. Therefore we are called warriors.'[3]

Meanwhile the house of the self is on fire, and the wise man concentrates on leaving it. The emphasis is all the time on here and now, and the Buddha praised those followers who 'seized their moment', and blamed those others who let it pass them by. Buddhism is a religion without a God (in Zen terminology, 'All is God, and there is no God'). It therefore knows not prayer. It is mysticism in the sense that it strives for intuitive realization of the oneness of the universe, yet its feet are firmly based on a cold, dispassionate reasoning from observed first premises. It has no Pope, and submits to no earthly, still less a heavenly, authority. 'Work out your own salvation', said he who had done so, and each must in the end obey. 'Blind faith' is unknown to Buddhism; it does but accept a reasonable belief for the purpose of testing it, and the Buddha himself is only a guide who has pointed a Way. Faith is of value as a prelude to experience 'You say this in faith', said the Buddha to Ananda. 'I know it from experience.'

1. H. P. Blavatsky, *The Secret Doctrine*, Vol. I, p. 14.
2. *Early Buddhism*, p. 69.
3. *Anguttara Nikaya*.

It admits no caste, no sex or race superiority. Unlike the religion from which it sprang, its inmost shrines are open to all. As J. B. Pratt wrote, on coming from India to Burma, 'In place of the closed temple with its mysterious inner shrine, its *lingam* and Ganesh, and its fat priest keeping out all but Hindus and extorting unwilling money from poor pilgrims – instead of this one finds the white or golden pagoda, open on all sides to the sky, accessible to everyone (with or without shoes), and guarded by no priest . . .'[1]

It is utterly tolerant, and seeks no converts. The Buddhist proclaims the Dhamma to mankind. Those who wish may accept and apply it; those who do not wish to do so pass with a blessing upon their way. It is all the same to the speaker, for 'a Buddhist is as Buddhist does', and there is no salvation by formula. The Goal is conceivable and worthy; the Road lies clear ahead. Why, then, tarry in the house of suffering?

For 'Better than sovereignty over the earth, better than the heaven state; better than dominion over all the worlds is the first step on the Path to holiness.'[2]

1. J. B. Pratt, *India and its Faiths*, p. 343.
2. *Dhammapada*, v. 178.

BIBLIOGRAPHY

FOR CHAPTERS FIVE TO NINE

Note – This Section has been based upon the equivalent sections in *What is Buddhism?* first published by the Buddhist Society, London, in 1928, and now out of print.

Conze, Edward. *Buddhism, its Essence and Development.*
Coomaraswamy, Ananda. *Buddha and the Gospel of Buddhism.*
  Hinduism and Buddhism.
Coomaraswamy, Ananda, and Horner, I. B. *Gotama Buddha.*
Davids, T. Rhys. *Buddhism.*
  Early Buddhism.
Davids, Mrs Rhys. *A Manual of Buddhism.*
  Sakya, or Buddhist Origins.
  What was the Original Gospel in Buddhism?
Dahlke, Paul. *Buddhism, and its Place in the Mental Life of Mankind.*
David-Neel, Alexandra. *Buddhism, Its Doctrines and Methods.*
Evola, J. *The Doctrine of Awakening.*
Fussell, Ronald. *The Buddha and his Path to Self-Enlightenment.*
Hare, Loftus. *The Buddhist Religion.*
Holmes, Edmond. *The Creed of Buddha.*
Humphreys, Christmas. *Karma and Rebirth.*
  Studies in the Middle Way.
  Thus Have I Heard.
  Concentration and Meditation.
Lounsbery, Miss C. *Buddhist Meditation in the Southern School.*
Metteya, Ananda. *The Wisdom of the Aryas.*
Narasu, Lakshmi. *The Essence of Buddhism.*
Nyanaponika, Thera. *The Heart of Buddhist Meditation.*
Pratt, J. B. *The Pilgrimage of Buddhism.*
Radhakrishnan, S. *Indian Philosophy*, Vol. I.
  Gautama the Buddha.
Olcott, H. S. *The Buddhist Catechism.*
Power, E. E. *The Path of the Elders.*
Rost, Ernest. *The Nature of Consciousness.*
Silacara, The Bhikkhu. *Lotus Blossoms.*
  The Four Noble Truths.
  Pancha Sila.
  The Noble Eightfold Path.
Szekely, Edmond. *The Teaching of Buddha.*
Subhadra, The Bhikshu. *The Message of Buddhism.*

The Sangha

*

IN many religions the Order is founded after the Founder's death; in Buddhism the Triratna (Three Jewels) were from the first inseparable. For thousands of years teachers have gathered disciples about them to hear their teaching, and when this band of followers grows to a certain size it needs to be organized. The Buddha's Ministry was long, some forty-five years, and by the time of his passing his followers must have numbered many thousands, apart from the huge congregation of lay men and women who accepted the Dhamma and attempted to tread the Way. But the organization of the Sangha in the Buddha's lifetime was not, it would seem, the mere child of necessity. The Triratna was clearly conceived as a unit, for the Buddha said in terms that after his passing the Dhamma was to be the disciples' Teacher, and the Sangha was founded as a missionary enterprise within a few weeks of the Enlightenment.

Nor was the conception of the Triratna original to Buddhism. The Teacher, the Teaching and those who followed it is as old a trinity as spiritual teaching, and Christ declared that the Christos, or Buddhic Principle, was at once the Life, the Truth and the Way. The place of the Sangha in Buddhism, however, was always essential, and Sir Charles Eliot may be right when he says, 'The great practical achievement of the Buddha was to found a religious order which has lasted to the present day. It is chiefly to this institution that the permanence of his religion is due.'[1]

It is sometimes argued that such an organization, where men retire from worldly life, earn nothing, beg their food from the common people, and bear no children, is against the welfare of the community. The answer is manifold.

1. *Hinduism and Buddhism*, Vol. I, p. 237.

What is the purpose of life? If it be to achieve Enlightenment, it is 'a positive social and moral advantage to the
community that a certain number of its finest minds, leading
a life that may be called sheltered, should remain unattached
to social activities and unbound by social ties.'[1] Such men
have from the dawn of history set an example of the ascetic
life unfettered by worldly desire, and have proved themselves by their superior self-control and development the
counsellors of kings, the teachers of the people, and the
exemplars of all.

The function of the Buddhist Sangha is twofold, to provide the best possible conditions for individual development,
and to teach the Dhamma to mankind. As to the former, it
is an example of collective life arranged for the benefit of the
individuals composing it. As to the latter, the Buddha's
Sangha was an innovation, for whereas Indian teachers from
time immemorial would organize to some extent the body
of followers who were attempting to apply the Teaching
given, the function of such a body was usually negative and
introvert, to receive and apply. The Buddha's Sangha, however, was dynamically conceived. His first converts were his
first missionaries, and he at once infused into his followers
his own devotion to the service of all living things. The
Sangha, indeed, was the necessary means whereby he could
make known his Teaching. Where books were unknown, the
Bhikkhus became his walking library, and by them alone,
when he had passed away, could the Message be accurately
and widely spread.

While the Buddha lived he was Head of the Order. When
he died there was none to succeed him, and to this day there
is no Pope, nor even a special body of men with power to
declare what is and is not Buddhism. Each School, and later
each Monastery (*Vihara*) within each School, elected its own
head, who was, however, never more than first among equals,
for though each Bhikkhu (Skt: *Bhikshu*) obeyed the Rules as
to poverty and chastity, irrevocable vows were quite unknown, and there was never a vow or even a Rule as to
obedience. Each monastery had the same interior discipline,
and a monk would be expelled from the Order for one of
the four great offences. All lesser breaches of the Rules were
solemnly confessed, either by the Bhikkhus to each other or

1. Coomaraswamy, *Buddha and the Gospel of Buddhism*, p. 128.

in council, and a penalty might be imposed according to
their gravity. But not even the *Maha Nayaka*, or Abbot,
would presume to forgive, in the sense of remitting the consequences of an act, and absolution, in the Catholic sense,
has ever been unknown.

As the purpose of entering the Sangha was to destroy the
fetters of desire and thereby to attain Enlightenment, some
measure of self-imposed asceticism was necessary. In the
lovely words of a famous Scripture,

> A heart untouched by wordly things, a heart that is not
> swayed.
> By sorrow, a heart passionless, secure – that is the greatest
> blessing.[1]

To attain such a condition in one life needs tremendous
effort consistently applied, but it is useless to assuage the
fires of hatred, lust and illusion if the senses are ever providing more fuel for the flames. Hence the advisability of a
calm, sequestered life, avoiding, for example, contact with
women or with the erotic displays associated in the East
with 'song and dance', and likewise avoiding luxury of every
kind in appearance, dress, possessions, or mode of living.
Only when the Four Paths had been trodden to the end, and
the Arhat state attained, would it be safe to return to the life
of men. Meanwhile the Bhikkhu must be 'mindful and self-
possessed' in all that he does, and to the extent of his success
the people will appreciate his example and do him honour.
'While the layman may not be ready to forsake the world
himself he admires the man who has done so, and he feels
that some day, either in his old age or in some future rebirth
he, too, will take this important step. In the meantime it
behoves him to do the next best thing and loyally support
those who have taken the Buddha's teaching seriously ...'[2]

If the Bhikkhu dishonours the Robe it is the village folk
who will take it from him and drive him away. 'As long as
the monks act as monks should, they are held in great
honour; they are addressed by titles of great respect; they
are the glory of the village. But directly he breaks his laws
his holiness is gone. The villagers will hunt him out of the

1. *Sutta Nipata.*
2. Reischauer, from 'Buddhism', in *Great Religions of the Modern World*,
p. 118.

village, they will refuse him food, they will make him a by-word, a scorn.'[1]

Admission to the Order

Admission to the Order is, and always has been, open to all men over twenty who are healthy, solvent and free men. The new arrival is first a *Samanera*, or novice, and when he has thoroughly learnt the Dhamma and the Rules of the Order, he may apply for ordination. As a Samanera he shaves his head and takes the ten Precepts. These are the five taken by Buddhist laymen on all religious occasions, as set out in Appendix 2, though in a stricter form, and a further five, which are concerned with eating at forbidden times, that is, after noon, attending stage performances, using scents and garlands or a high (luxurious) bed, and handling money. All these are forbidden as savouring of luxury. At the *upasampada* ceremony the new Bhikkhu is given his Robes and a new name, but he takes no vows and may leave the Order upon notice when he will, either for a while or for ever. Some men join the Order late in life, when a house-holder's duties to his family are all performed, and a middle-aged man feels free to devote the remainder of his days to seeking the heart's release from suffering. In Burma, Siam and Cambodia every boy spends part of his childhood in a mon-astery, whether a few weeks or a period of years. He learns the Scriptures, something of discipline and humility towards his elders and betters, some sound morality and the virtues of the simple life. Such a custom makes for the practice of one's religion, and forges the links of love and respect for the San-gha which are deeply ingrained in the national character.

From *Samanera* to *Bhikkhu*; from *Bhikkhu* to *Thera* or Elder (Burmese: *Pongyi*; Siamese: *Phra*), from *Thera*, after twenty years as a Bhikkhu, to *Mahathera*, such is the hier-archy of attainment. Yet all alike, save the old and sick, go out at dawn with their begging bowls, taking whatever is given in silence. No thanks is offered for the gift, for it is the giver who profits by his generosity, and much merit is acquired thereby. Their food collected, the Bhikkhus and Samaneras return to the monastery to eat their meal, and spend the rest of the day in study, meditation, and teaching. They carry out their own monastic 'chores', but though the

1. Fielding Hall, *The Soul of a People*, 4th edn, p. 134.

diet is simple and the tenor of life ascetic, there is no undue
austerity, and all excess of behaviour, being a deviation
from the Middle Way, is forbidden. The Buddha ordained
that his followers should be simply dressed, and to this day
the Robe is of the cheapest cotton. Yet the orange Robe of
Burma and the yellow Robe of Siam and Ceylon is a symbol
of spiritual grandeur, and all who wear it are revered there-
for. If at times this veneration for the Robe appears excessive, this is excess of virtue, and the very respect assists the
wearer to live up to the ideals which the Robe ordains.
Poverty is a fact, for the Bhikkhu owns but his three robes,
a waist cloth, a begging-bowl, a razor, a water-strainer and
a needle. To these are often added in fact an umbrella, san-
dals, a few books and, for the writer, what may be called
his desk equipment. The monasteries, however, as distinct
from the individuals within them, own enormous areas of
land, and it is said that a third of the arable land in Ceylon
is owned by the Sangha. Yet there is no display of wealth,
and the Maha Nayaka of the richest monastery will live as
simply as the humblest novice.

Much of the year the Bhikkhus spend on pilgrimage to the
holy places, or as itinerant teachers of the Way, but the
rainy season is always spent in a communal centre or vihara,
not only for rest and meditation, but in order that the principles of the Dhamma itself may be recited and studied
collectively. Only thus, when for hundreds of years the Rules
and the Doctrine were handed down by memory, could the
importance of the one and the purity of the other be
maintained.

The Patimokkha

The Rules of the Order – 227 as they stand to-day – are
known as the Patimokkha, and this code of discipline is
accepted with slight variations by all Schools of Buddhism.
It is the most stringent code of daily observance to be found
in any extant religion, and is still formally recited twice a
month in every monastery. There are those who hold that
to-day it is too stringent, for much of the Bhikkhus' time is
consumed in keeping the letter of each observance to the
detriment of the inner development which the Rules were
designed to serve. The Rules of the Order were created for
the men who obeyed them, and it is a matter of regret that

the Council convened at the Buddha's death did not act upon
his dying permission and abolish many of the minor Rules,
the keeping of which takes up both time and energy which
might be more profitably employed. With faster and faster
means of communication the world grows daily smaller, and
Rules devised 2,500 years ago may have to be modified for
the benefit of Western Buddhists. The difficulty of applying
to the modern world a set of Rules devised for ancient India
is seen to the full when the Eastern Bhikkhu comes to the
West. Chastity is necessary to the Bhikkhu, but the Rule that
he may not live in the same building as a woman can easily
become absurd. Conversely, when the European enters the
Buddhist Sangha, and many have made the experiment, he
finds that the Rule against eating anything after noon puts
an intolerable strain on the Western body, and some have
been broken in health in making the attempt. The Japanese
and many of the Chinese monks, who live in a far colder climate, have varied the Rules to their differing modes of living,
and that about eating, for example, is modified by a 'medicine
meal' in the evening.

The Bhikkhus as Teachers

The second purpose of the Sangha was to spread the
Dhamma. 'There are two sorts of gifts, Brethren, the gift of
material things and the gift of the Dhamma. Of these two
gifts the gift of the Dhamma is pre-eminent.' But the gift as
offered by the travelling Bhikkhu is the offering of something
to be shared. The Bhikkhu has no interest in converts, and he
takes no names. He regards the Dhamma as an expression
of Truth; therefore as a message of universal application.
Striving as he does for the welfare by enlightenment of his
fellow men, he considers it his duty to place before them
such of the Dhamma as he has tested and found to be true.
In so doing he has done all that he has any right to do, for
each man's spiritual progress is no one's business but his
own.

But apart from teaching the Dhamma to adults, the Bhikkhus became in time the village schoolmasters, and as such
infused elementary education with Buddhist principles. In
this way religion became an integral part of the life of the
people, and such it has been within living memory. Now,
however, there is a tendency to secularize all education. If

this is carried to extremes, it means that the Bhikkhus will
have no necessary part in the children's lives, nor the
Dhamma in their minds. A few, no doubt, will receive the
Dhamma from their parents, and others will be sent to the
Buddhist equivalent of Sunday School. But the people as a
whole, like English children to-day, will soon be given no
sanction for morality save a fear of the criminal law, and
will dedicate their lives to 'having a good time', at whatever
expense to their fellow-men. Such is the tendency in all three
Theravada countries; if it continues, the Dhamma will die
out therefrom as it died in India.

As already described, the Buddha himself permitted the
founding of the Order of Bhikkhunis, or nuns, and for hundreds of years they lived and worked in their nunneries in
the same way as the men, but always subservient to them in
rank and observance. By the time of Asoka, however, the
female Order had declined, and to-day, though there are
still a large number of *Sila-Upasika*, lay women disciples,
in Theravada countries, there are no women members of
the Order. Yet the value of some of these, who in fact live
as Bhikkhuni, is considerable. They lead austere and useful
lives, and particularly in Burma and Ceylon are pioneers in
much that is now known in the West as social service.

Before turning to the Mahayana, it is well to note that
however the term Bhikkhu may be translated, whether as
monk, mendicant, or 'religieux', he is not a priest. He does
not belong to an apostolic succession, nor has he any power
to save or condemn, to forgive sins or to administer sacraments. As Dr Coomaraswamy puts it, 'he has no other
sanctity than attaches to his own good living.'[1] Service in a
temple, in the sense of a Christian shrine, is no part of his
duties, and he has no parish for which he is responsible. He
teaches the young, and such adults as come to the monastery
on the equivalent of Sundays and festival days to hear the
Bhikkhus preach, but there his duty to his neighbour ceases.
For the rest, he is concerned with his own deliberate enlightenment, and the general teaching of the Dhamma to his
fellow men. How the first is accomplished, and where and
when the second is carried out, is his own affair.

To the outside observer, the life of the Bhikkhu to-day in
Theravada countries may seem enviable, for though in a way

1. *Buddha and the Gospel of Buddhism*, p. 154–5.

severe it is never unduly ascetic, and in the tropics many of the worries incidental to a colder climate do not exist. But behind the façade of a dignified, slow-moving rhythm of life is a strenuous intensity of purpose which only a deeper study of the monastic life reveals. Many of the Bhikkhus are profound scholars, and meditation, though in danger of neglect, is still a regular exercise. Morality is high, and the Precepts are, generally speaking, well observed. The two main faults of the Sangha to-day are laziness, due to insufficient care in checking the motive from which young men of poor mentality enter the Order, and a tendency, grave in Burma, noticeable in Ceylon, but so far absent in Siam, to dabble in worldly politics. Nothing, it seems, so quickly alienates the affection of the people as this descent from the pedestal of concentration on eternal principles and a consequent unconcern with worldly affairs, and if the tendency goes further, it is popular disapproval which will restore the erring footsteps to the Way. There are, of course, in so large a body – and in all these countries it is, for the sake of quality, far too large – those to whom the monastic life is merely an escape from the cares of the world outside; yet on the whole it is true to say that the Sangha is to-day more worthy to enshrine its Master's Teaching than any equivalent body in the world.

The Mahayana Sangha

In the countries where the Buddhism which first arrived was of the Mahayana, notably China and Japan, the variation from the Indian Sangha was soon considerable, although the fundamental nature and purpose of the Order never changed. As already set out, the temperament of the Chinese people was inimical to the implications of monastic life, and it was a long time before permission to found a Chinese Sangha was given. The change continued in Japan, and to-day the fully ordained monk resembles the English parish priest in two particulars unknown to the Southern School. He may marry, and he is responsible for a parish, in the sense of the families who from long usage support a particular temple. Instead of the uniform yellow or orange cotton robe he wears a black kimono, and over that an abbreviated silk robe, rather like the Mason's apron, denoting his sect, but on festival occasions the robes, of the finest silk, are gorgeous in colour and quality, and the altar appointments of the humblest temple are rich and ornate compared with the flowers and the bowl of incense of the Theravada School. The bonzes do not, however, teach the village children, and they seldom preach to the people. In the monasteries of Siam, Burma, and Ceylon, congregations of both sexes and all ages will gather about a preaching Bhikkhu, and hear him tell in slow and almost chanting tones the old Jataka Tales and other moral stories from the Pali Canon, ending, maybe, with a few wise precepts of his own. Such a custom clearly forms a beloved part of the people's life. In China and Japan, however, although there are usually 'services' twice a day in the Temple or Shrine-building of each monastery, these offerings of incense and collective Sutra-readings seldom attract the people, and save on special occasions only a few exceptional lay men and women – the *upasakas* and *upasikas* of original Buddhism – attend.

The resemblance to the Christian parish priest, however, is purely superficial. The Japanese have no sacraments, nor do the bonzes baptise or marry their 'parishioners'. They do not pray to a God, nor intercede with any Power, although the Shin or Pure Land Sect moves nearer to the Church of Rome in this respect than any other Buddhist School. Like their Theravada brethren, the Mahayana Bhikkhus are individually poor. They are vegetarians who drink no liquor, and they submit to the strict discipline of the monastery in which they dwell. They go round begging in the neighbourhood of their monastery for food and money, but for the most part live on the fruits of their own labour. Nearly all monasteries contain or own elsewhere enough land to support their own population, and the foods which they cannot grow are bought with money provided by their own 'parishioners'.

Most of the monks work in the fields, and those on duty in the monastery do all the cleaning, mending, cooking and the like without regard to seniority. 'No work, no food!' said the master Hyakujo, and for a thousand years the monks of Zen have obeyed him. They receive an all-round training, physical as well as spiritual, for in Zen the two are one. Ploughing a field or peeling potatoes is to them as divine as the daily service in the Hondo or main Temple, and whether the work be of body or mind it is done with the utmost effort. 'Unless at one time perspiration has streamed down your back, you cannot see the boat sailing before the wind', said a Master of the *koan* exercise, and the same applies to a day in the fields. Whether working with his hands or his mind, the effort is high and continuous.[1]

All of the foregoing applies to the convents, for there are thousands of women monks in Japan to-day. In some cases they live in separate convent-temples; in others they share the same monastic settlement with the men, though of course living in their own quarters. They wear precisely the same clothing and as their heads are shaved it is not easy to tell young monks and nuns apart. As in Burma, many of these women are noted for their learning and piety.

As in other Buddhist lands there are many lay scholars attached to the great temples, and many of the senior bonzes are very learned as well as spiritually advanced men. In 1946 I visited more than fifty of the principal monasteries in Japan, and in every case 'took tea' with the Abbot or Abbess. In each case I was impressed with the intellect, nobility of mind, and spiritual power of the man or woman concerned, and though they differed in quality, and in the technique which they used to achieve the common Goal, their ability was undoubted, and the Buddha Sangha will long survive in the Mahayana if such is the quality of those who lead it, as the older Sangha is still led, into ways of Self-enlightenment and the enlightening of one's fellow men.

1. *Zen Buddhism.*

BIBLIOGRAPHY

FOR CHAPTER TEN

Dutt, Sukumar. *Early Buddhist Monachism.*
Hardy, Spence. *Eastern Monachism.*
Horner, I. B. *Women under Primitive Buddhism.*

Chapters or sections in the following:

Blofeld, John. *The Jewel in the Lotus* (Buddhism in China).
Coomaraswamy, Ananda. *Buddha and the Gospel of Buddhism.*
Davids, T. Rhys. *Buddhism.*
  Early Buddhism.
Eliot, Sir Charles. *Hinduism and Buddhism*, Vol. I.
Hall, H. Fielding. *The Soul of a People* (Buddhism in Burma).
Horner, Miss I. B. Introduction to *Book of the Discipline* (Vols. I–III) 'Sacred Books of the Buddhists'.
Olcott, H. S. *The Buddhist Catechism.*
Pratt, J. B. *The Pilgrimage of Buddhism.*
Saunders, Kenneth. *Epochs in Buddhist History.*
Suzuki. D. T. *The Training of the Zen Buddhist Monk* (Buddhism in Japan).
Thomas, E. J. *The Life of Buddha in Legend and History.*
Young, Ernest. *The Kingdom of the Yellow Robe* (Buddhism in Siam).

CHAPTER ELEVEN

Some Mahayana Principles

*

*The Two Schools – The Mahayana is still growing –
Some Mahayana Principles – Reality – Suchness and
Sunyata – The Pairs of Opposites – Avidya – Mind-
Only – The Trikaya – Buddhology – Nirvana*

So much for the Theravada. Before turning to the Mahayana,
it may be as well to recapitulate a few observations about
its relation to the older school.

The Two Schools

Some writers consider the two Schools as the two wings
which support the head and the heart of the Buddha's
Enlightenment. As between the two wings, the Theravada
says of the Mahayana that it is heretical and degenerate,
while the Mahayana says of the Theravada that it is right
and adequate for beginners, but inadequate for the developed mind; that it is limited in scope and object, whereas
the Mahayana includes all living things and bears them all
alike to salvation. The West, which learnt of Buddhism first
through Theravada eyes, still tends to consider the earlier
School as 'Buddhism', and the Northern School as a heterogeneous mixture of later additions and developments. To
what extent this view is the result of genuine comparison,
and how much it is due to the fact that the Theravada Canon
is tidy and complete, while the Mahayana equivalent appears
in four languages and is immensely complex, it is difficult to
say. But Dr Suzuki is obviously right in saying that 'the first
information of any event generally leaves a very strong impression and offers an almost irrational resistance to later
corrections', and in Europe the Theravada was by fifty years
the first in the field.[1]

A more accurate symbol for the Schools is two concentric
circles, the Theravada forming the compact and well-defined
inner circle, and the Mahayana a more nebulous ring about
it. For the latter is not so much a School as a Collection of

1. B. L. Suzuki, *Mahayana Buddhism*. Introduction by D. T. Suzuki, p. xii.

Schools, all of which, however, compared with the older Teaching, are adventurous, positive and boldly speculative. The Mahayana has no wish to escape from *Samsara*, the Wheel of Becoming, but claims to find salvation within it. In thought and purpose it climbs to heights unknown to the more monastic School, although on the uplands of immaterial thought it is admittedly apt to get lost in the fog.

The term Mahayana was first used to designate the Absolute Being, or 'Be-ness', as H. P. Blavatsky calls it, of which all existence is a manifestation. Only later was the term applied to a particular School, and it is important to note that it is in the former sense that it is referred to in the *Discourse on the Awakening of Faith in the Mahayana*. As a School it has three main ingredients, and he is bold who claims to tell where one begins and another ends. In the first place, it is a development from the Hinayana, for nearly all its principles have discoverable roots in the earlier School, including, for example, the deification of the Buddha Principle, the emphasis on the Bodhisattva as distinct from the Arhat ideal, the transference or sharing of 'merit', and the Sunyata doctrine as a logical expansion of the Anatta doctrine, which is, as certain Western scholars fail to understand, the very essence of the Mahayana.

The second ingredient in the Mahayana is its own unbroken tradition. This is partly exoteric and partly esoteric. The earliest Chinese Agamas, or scriptures, are translations of Sanskrit originals at least as old as the Pali Canon, and where the two teachings differ there is no reason to regard the latter as of any greater antiquity or authority for the Buddha's teaching. More important, however, is the largely unwritten tradition which came to China from India. Such is the Zen technique, to be later explained, for this famous School, the most powerful spiritual force in the Far East today, scorns the written word, and maintains, in accordance with the Indian tradition of the Guru-Chela method of teaching, that nothing worth teaching can be written down.

A third ingredient, equally difficult to define, is the additions to Buddhist doctrine which to-day are grafted on to the parent stem. Such are the Tantric teachings of Bengal; and such are the extremist teachings of the Shin sect of Japan.

The Mahayana is still growing

Yet the vast whole is enormously alive and unceasingly growing. Truth is eternal, say the Mahayanists, but our knowledge of it grows. Gotama the Buddha was a man who lived in a particular time and place and taught particular doctrines; but the Buddha-Principle of Enlightenment is utterly beyond the limitations of any one man's Teaching, and quite unaffected by the accidents of time or place. By such a standard, what does it matter when or where the Buddha taught, or whether he lived at all? Truth is immortal, and all are Buddha already. Life is a process of self-realization, of becoming what you are. Buddhism therefore includes unnumbered *upaya*, [devices, whereby the part may re-become the Whole, and 'if it should some day be demonstrated that Gotama was merely a sun myth this would be a most serious blow to the Hinayana, but the Mahayana would hardly feel it', and indeed 'the truth it presents is of such a large and philosophic nature that it would be difficult to conceive of any imaginable scientific or historical discovery which would greatly affect it.'[1]

It is difficult to summarize the principles of the Mahayana. Three great countries are involved, and as Kenneth Saunders wrote, 'if India is mystical and meta-physical, China is rationalist and humanist, and Japan is at once utilitarian and poetical.'[2] In each of these countries, as also in Tibet, Buddhism had a separate history and doctrinal development, a different language and a different cultural background. The same term is often used in different senses at different periods and in different sects at the same time. As it is fundamental to the Mahayana that life is one, and all its manifestations are but relatively 'real' and temporary manifestations of that unity, it follows that all parts of the whole are intimately related, and any attempt at clear definitive lines of analysis is vain. For the principles themselves are vainly conceived; they do not exist as such, any more than a wave of the sea.

Nor is this all. In the Mahayana, reason is used to destroy itself. The Madhyamika system propounded by Nagarjuna reduces all things to pairs of negatives and then denies them.

1. Pratt, *The Pilgrimage of Buddhism*, p. 269.
2. *A Pageant of Asia*, p. vii.

'No birth, no death; no persistence, no annihilation; no oneness, no manyness; no coming, no departing . . . this is the doctrine of the Mean.'[1] As Mrs Suzuki says, 'This is a staggering idea, but until we are thus thoroughly cleansed of all the intellectual habits contracted since our birth we cannot expect to see the Dharma itself.'[2] For we see the Dharma by the faculty of intuition and by nothing less, and it is only when the intuition is set free to function that the mind begins to move towards its own enlightenment. If the truth thus seen is to the reason non-sense so much the worse for 'sense', the limitations of which are understood for the first time. Is this mysticism? If so, Mahayana is mysticism, and it is by this quality that it became a religion. For 'mysticism is the life of religion; without it religion loses the reason of its existence; all its warm vitality is gone, and there remains nothing but the crumbling bones and the cold ashes of death.'[3] Yet the Mahayana is fiercely realistic, as will be later seen, and it is one of the paradoxes of this vast system of thought that these two facts can happily exist in harmony. Perhaps Mahayana is 'irrational realism', or 'pragmatic mysticism', yet it is truer to say that it lifts the consciousness to a plane where all these man-made labels cease to have meaning. To understand it the mind must learn to hold the opposites in living union, for the Mahayana is at once subjective and objective, concerned with eternal principles yet finding them in the here and now.

How, then, shall we summarize these principles? Analyse a flower, petal by petal, and there is no flower; hold but a handful of the river and the flow which made it a river has gone. The Mahayana is born again with every writer, and flowers in each new human experience. Its spirit is free and beyond the barriers of time. It cares but little for the passing forms it uses, and for history nothing at all. Compared with this scramble up the mountain-side of truth, the Theravada is but tram-lines on the valley floor. It is true that on the heights there are many who fall and many who lose their way, yet each man is the Way, and only he that loseth his life shall find it.

1. As translated in 'The Development of Mahayana Buddhism'. D. T. Suzuki in *The Buddhist Review*, Vol. I, p. 109.
2. *Mahayana Buddhism*, p. 13.
3. D. T. Suzuki, 'The Development of Mahayana Buddhism', p. 110.

Some Mahayana Principles

As Professor Takakusu rightly says, 'In China, when a philosopher-priest engages in philosophical studies, he does not usually take up the history of ideas, but at once goes into the speculation of whichever thought attracts his interest. Therefore there is little advantage in studying Buddhist ideas according to the historical sequence.'[1] In his famous posthumous work, therefore, he adopts an 'ideological sequence'. But again and again he has to force a fluid experience into the hard moulds of Western philosophy, and thereby loses one essential ingredient of his subject, its protean and ill-defined expressions. I propose, therefore, to mention first those principles which lie, as one needs some metaphor, at the top, and to descend, with inevitable divagations, to the market-place and the football field at the bottom. Even this is artificial. 'Buddhism in itself is not a philosophical system, although it is the most rational and intellectual religion in the world ... '[2] The very terms used in Chinese for philosophy mean 'Enlightenment', that is, direct experience, and concepts which have to be expressed in words are therefore two removes from that Bodhi which it is the purpose of philosophy to reach.

To avoid repetition, no further mention will be made of those basic principles of Theravada Buddhism which are common to nearly all sects of the Mahayana School. The three Signs of Being, the four Noble Truths, the doctrine of causation and man's responsibility for his acts, the importance of morality and the long Middle Way which leads to Enlightenment; all these and more, though raised in tone, made cosmic in scope and purpose, are of the warp and woof of the Mahayana. To these must be added, as extensions or expansions, those which follow.

Reality

It is axiomatic that Absolute Reality is inconceivable and therefore inexpressible. The finite mind can never 'know' the Infinite. Hence Buddhism acknowledges an absolute and a relative Truth. To our relative minds it follows that our first conception of the Absolute is its first manifestation, when

1. *The Essentials of Buddhist Philosophy*, p. 13.
2. Yamakami Sogen, *Systems of Buddhistic Thought*, p. 201.

the One trembles at the birth of Two. Absolute Space, bare subjectivity, 'the one thing which no human mind can either exclude from any conception, or conceive of by itself',[1] is the one limb, and one already re-discovered by modern science. The other is Absolute Motion or Life, unconditioned consciousness, that which is revealed when the illusion of 'matter' is analysed to its ultimates. 'It is only when all outward appearances are gone that there is left that one principle of life which exists independently of all external phenomena. It is the fire that burns in the eternal light, when the fuel is expended and the flame is extinguished; for that fire is neither in the flame nor in the fuel, nor yet inside either of the two, but above, beneath and everywhere.'[2] Incidentally, in this magnificent passage is the Mahayana teaching on Self, on Nirvana and, by inference, its cosmic application of the Theravada doctrine of *Anatta*.

This life, or 'Be-ness', is the highest which man can conceive of the Absolute. It manifests on a universal playground of space-time called the *Dharma-dhatu*, and all within this field of Samsara partakes of the essential nature of Be-ness, which is called, for want of another name, *Tathata*, 'Suchness'. To coalesce one's personal consciousness with the indwelling essence of Suchness is Nirvana.

Suchness and Sunyata

Suchness, the ultimate spiritual essence, or Essence of Mind (*Shinnyo* in Japanese), is beyond the Opposites, whether Nagarjuna's four pairs or any others. The term *Tathata* was first used in *The Awakening of Faith in the Mahayana*, in the fourth century A.D., and being the highest conception possible, it is, if there be such a thing, the God-head of Buddhism. But it is beyond all predicates. 'It is neither that which is existent, nor non-existent ... neither one nor many ... It is altogether beyond the conception of human intellect, and the best way of designating it seems to be to call it suchness.'[3]

In its religious aspect, *Tathata*, or *Bhutatathata* (Suchness of existence) is the *Dharmakaya* (see later), just as psycho-

---

1. H. P. Blavatsky, *The Secret Doctrine*, I, p. 14.
2. From the *Parinirvana Sutra*. From Letter CXXVII of the *Mahatma Letters to A. P. Sinnett*, p. 455.
3. From 'The Development of Mahayana Buddhism'. D. T. Suzuki, in *The Buddhist Review*, Vol. I, p. 109.

logically it equates with *Alayavijñana* (see later). But to the ordinary human mind this supreme conception is *Sunya*, void, in the sense of no-thing, which is quite different from nothing-ness. It is the absence of all predicates, for anything said about *Sunyata* is insufficient or too much. But all concepts are twofold, having a negative and positive aspect, and just as *Sunyata* is negatively the absence of particularity, it is positively the apotheosis of the Theravada doctrine of *Anicca*, change, the eternal flux of becoming. It is also the apotheosis of the doctrine of *Anatta* which, as Dr Suzuki says, 'is not the outcome of psychological analysis but is a statement of religious intuition in which no discursive reasoning whatever is employed. ... It was Buddhist philosophy which formed the theory, but that which supplied it with facts to substantiate it was Buddhist experience.'[1] For all religious experience has found the same, that when self is exhausted there remains but the Plenum-Void, however that final experience be named.

Applying this much of Mahayana thought, four tremendous principles emerge.

That the ultimate viewpoint is that of the absolute idealist, and all manifestations of the Absolute are, *qua* that Absolute, ephemeral, although 'real' to other beings in manifestation, or *Samsara*.

That this *Samsara*, the 'Wheel of Becoming', is a mode of Nirvana, and Nirvana need not be sought beyond the realm of our immediate becoming. As all things are already 'in' Nirvana, the process of becoming is one of acquiring self-consciousness of an existing state of affairs; in the end 'every blade of grass shall enter into Buddhahood'.

That an abstract principle and its manifestations are two parts of a whole; only in its application is a thought made 'true'.

That men are brothers, whether or not they know it or live as though this fact were true. All forms of life are sharing the same eternal Essence of Life. More; all is alive, and there is no death, save of the temporary form. The whole universe is one, and when the Manifest returns into the bosom of the Unmanifest all things will find their unity. The way of salvation is therefore to return to the One. The Universe is a mode of law, but love is the fulfilling of the

1. *Essays in Zen Buddhism*, Second Series, p. 269.

law, for love is the cohesive element in all illusion-separated things, and in the end the parts will know themselves as one.

The Pairs of Opposites

Meanwhile we live in a world of duality, the reality of which is falsely imagined. The major Pairs of Opposites reflect in man. 'In the one soul we may distinguish two aspects. The one is the soul as suchness, the other is the soul as birth-and-death (*Samsara*). Each in itself constitutes all things, and both are so closely interrelated that one cannot be separated from the other.'[1] Yet all these opposites exist only relatively. 'The Mahayana holds a middle position regarding the nature of the world. It is neither real nor unreal. It affirms that it actually exists, but denies its absolute reality. Waves exist but not absolutely. The world is a phenomenon, impermanent, subject to flux and change. Since the reality pervades all, everything individual is the whole potentially, or, in religious language, every individual is a potential Buddha.'[2] It follows that all phenomena exist only by virtue of their relationship, for all is motion, all is illusion, all, in the last analysis, is *Anatta*, without permanent 'self'.

> The cloud-capp'd towers, the gorgeous palaces,
> The solemn temples, the great globe itself,
> Yea, all which it inherit, shall dissolve,
> And like this insubstantial pageant faded,
> Leave not a rack behind. We are such stuff
> As dreams are made on, and our little life
> Is rounded with a sleep.[3]

Meanwhile, before that restful sleep of temporary death prepares the evolving 'Self' for fresh experience in another 'life', the tension of the opposites within grows steadily, and man's attempt to express it grows with the years. The *Tat tvam asi* of Indian thought – 'Thou art THAT' – is magnificent, but the philosophy of the Kegon School of Buddhism has reached out further, to the limits, it would seem, of the human intellect. Beyond, there lies but 'silence, and a finger pointing the Way'. The doctrine of *Jijimuge* is not simple – how could such a conception be anything but a tremendous strain upon even the highest intellect? – but in a work on Zen I have tried to express it as follows. '*Jijimuge* means the

1. *The Awakening of Faith*. Trans. D. T. Suzuki, p. 55.
2. Radhakrishnan, *Indian Philosophy*, Vol. II, p. 594.
3. *The Tempest*, Act IV, Scene 1.

unimpeded interdiffusion of all particulars. *Ji* are things, events, the concrete and particular, while *Ri* is the principle, reason, the abstract, the totality. *Ji* is discrimination; *Ri* is non-discrimination, non-distinction. *Ri* equates with *sunyata*, the Plenum-void, and *Ji* with *rupam*, form.

'The relationship of *Ri* and *Ji* is "perfect, unimpeded mutual solution" (*en-yu-muge*). $Ri = Ji$ and $Ji = Ri$. They are modes or aspects of an undivided unity. They are mutually in a perpetual state of "suchness".

'Now all *Ji* being *Ri*, if $A = x$ and $B = x$, then $A = B$, and *A* as an apple and *B* as a boat are one. This is *Rijimuge*, the interdiffusion of all *Ji* and *Ri*. But the relation between *A* and *B* is still indirect, i.e. via the common denominator, *Ri*. Thus the doctrine of *Rijimuge*, propounded by the Tendai School of Buddhism, is not even the highest conceivable, much less the highest in truth. The Kegon School went further, and insisted on direct relation between all "things", which in the Buddhist sense are seen as flowing events or minor whirlpools on the surface of becoming. *Rijimuge* seeks the Buddha (the universal) in the individual mind, the body being the devil whose limitations prison the wings of spirit; *Jijimuge*, on the other hand, the final stage of the Kegon School, with its doctrine of the *direct* interdiffusion of all *Ji*, means finding the Universal Buddha in every particular thing. The implications of this doctrine are enormous. In the words of Hindu philosophy, "Thou art THAT", and all other "thou's" are equally THAT. So far the mind can follow with ease. But according to *Jijimuge* all "thou's", or apples, or boats, are not only THAT but *directly* each other, completely and altogether. Two points on the circumference of a circle, instead of merely looking to the self-same centre, *are* at the centre all the time. This means, of course, that the circle folds up, as it were, into the Void of the Unmanifest. So it does, and why be fearful at the thought of it? But the Universe is manifest for a while on the cross of Space and Time, and meanwhile the circle (whose centre is nowhere and its circumference everywhere), is the field of the world around us. But though the intellect can just conceive that things are directly one, they never cease for a moment (still less for the Absolute Moment) to be, as Zen with a maddening grin points out, their own incomparable selves.'[1]

1. Christmas Humphreys, *Zen Buddhism*, p. 150–2.

Avidya

We know not why the Unmanifest from time to time is manifest, but even the Theravada Canon speaks of the aeonic 'unrolling and rolling up' of the world, and of 'the destruction and renewal of aeons', while the Secret Doctrine speaks of the universe as 'the playground of numberless Universes incessantly manifesting and disappearing', and again, quoting from the *Book of Dzyan*, says that 'the appearance and disappearance of Worlds is like a regular tidal ebb of flux and reflux'.[1] The Mahayana conceives the cause of this cyclic manifestation to be the presence of *Avidya*, ignorance or non-awareness, the suggestion being that manifestation is the means whereby the One becomes more and more aware of Itself. This *Avidya*, the 'Great Deep' or absolute Unconsciousness, is in one aspect the first of the twelve *Nidanas* of the Southern School, and in another the quality of imperfection in all 'things' which may be the basis elsewhere of the doctrine of original sin. Mind is conceived in its essence as a calm, unruffled pool. 'When the mind is disturbed, the multiplicity of things is produced; but when the mind is quieted the multiplicity of things disappears.'[2]

But this disturbance is the birth of action (*Karma*), and as all is one, each form of life reacts to the acts of all others. Hence the vast field of causation or interrelation in action, which, being of inconceivable complexity, is described as one of the two great 'mysteries' of Buddhism, Nirvana being the other.[3]

Mind-Only

Man, as the greatest minds have ever perceived, is a microcosm of the universal Macrocosm – 'As above so below' – and cosmic psychology, if one may so describe it, is the foundation of human psychology. In the Mahayana the doctrine of Mind-Only figures largely. All is Mind, and the stuff of the world is mind-stuff. It follows that 'all that we are is the result of what we have thought'. But not only are we the product of our thinking, but the world around us

1. *The Secret Doctrine*, Vol. I, p. 16–17.
2. *The Awakening of Faith*, trans. D. T. Suzuki, p. 78.
3. *The Mahatma Letters to A. P. Sinnett*, ed. Barker, p. 110.

has no validity for us save as the product of that Mind of which each 'mind' is a partial manifestation. The famous incident in the *Sutra of Hui-neng* (*Wei Lang*) will serve as an example. A pennant was blown in the wind, and two men argued, as to what it was which moved. One thought it was the flag which moved; the other that it was the wind. The Master rebuked them both, saying that it was the mind which moved.[1] Only when consciousness passes beyond or above the world of discrimination, which is ruled by the Opposites, does the illusion of duality fade and the suchness of things appear.

So we arrive at the difficult conception of the *Alayavijñana*. The word itself, almost a synonym for the more poetic *Tathagata-garbha*, or womb of *Tathagata-hood*, means a storage-house or 'repository-consciousness'. It is akin to the Unconscious of Western psychology, and is, so to speak, the impersonal state of awareness from which the individual draws his personal consciousness, and which, when entirely drawn into consciousness, will make the new-born Self at one with the All-Self or Plenum-Void which merges into *Bhuta-tathata*. In terms of *karma*, it is the store-house of unexpended effects created by past causes. It is therefore two-faced, being the effect of cosmic manifestation and the cause of individual effects. It is 'Mind-Only', one step down the scale of manifestation, a valve, if one may use the curious analogy, through which the Absolute passes into conditioned consciousness. Its value to the individual is therefore absolute, yet strangely enough it is also the source of the illusion by which he imagines himself to have a particular Self of his own. Only therefore when he passes back through this 'valve' is he finally freed from the illusion of *Sakkayaditthi*, the belief, which is the cause of all our sorrow, that 'I am I'. Meanwhile it 'perfumes' the lower grades of consciousness, all of which are radiations of this 'Universal Soul' or Anima Mundi.

As the personal mind slips further down into manifestation it enters the plane of *Manas*, the father of all discrimination. This is the intellect, the Western 'mind' in the sense of a thought-machine. It is that portion of *Alayavijñana* brought into consciousness by the individual, and is the measure of his greatness as mind. To the extent that he can

1. *The Sutra of Wei Lang*, ed. Christmas Humphreys, p. 24.

'perfume' his mind with the greater consciousness he reduces the value of himself as part and increases it as the
whole – he is moving to Enlightenment. Yet *Manas* is again
two-fold; it reflects its parent while enabling its parent to
manifest. But enough of personal psychology: we must
return to cosmic principles.

The Trikaya

The *Dharmakaya*, or body of the *Dharma*, is the religious
aspect of the *Bhutatathata*. It is the principle of cosmic unity
seen as the object of religious consciousness, and equates,
perhaps, with God the Father of Christianity. This religious
Absolute would not be so important but for its relation to
the Buddhist Trinity or *Trikaya*, the three-fold Body of the
Buddha, namely, *Dharmakaya*, *Sambhogakaya*, and *Nirmanakaya*, a complex group of conceptions typical of the
range and subtlety of Mahayana thought. For Buddhahood,
according to the esoteric tradition, has seven *Buddha-
kshetras* or 'vestures', of which the Trikaya represents three,
just as the Body, Soul and Spirit of St Paul is a condensed
version of the sevenfold man known to the early Gnostics.
He who wears the *Dharmakaya* is on the threshold of
Nirvana, for he is one with the *Dharma* itself. In Buddhist
mythology this principle is sometimes personified as *Adi-
Buddha*, and sometimes as *Vairocana Buddha*, the Great Sun
of Buddhahood.

The *Sambhogakaya* is best understood in relation to the
third of the Trinity, the *Nirmanakaya*. The latter is not, as
often stated, the physical body of a Buddha, but the visible
body of a Buddha whose last physical incarnation is expended. It is a Vesture which looks like a physical body yet is
made of finer matter, being used by the great ones of the
earth for the teaching of mankind when their right to enter
Nirvana, and thus to pass from the sight of men, has been
voluntarily refused. The *Sambhogakaya*, the Body of Bliss,
is the same, but of finer matter, being used for the teaching
of those sufficiently advanced to communicate with the user
upon that plane, but too fine for the student who, while
treading the Path, is not yet far upon his way.

Buddhology

As already pointed out, Gotama the Buddha became, in

Mahayana transformation, a reflection of the Supreme, and Dr Suzuki has given the reason. 'Mahayana Buddhism is a religion which developed around the life and personality of the Buddha rather than a religion based upon the words of his mouth. The person is greater and more real than his words; in fact, words gain a validity because of a person behind them . . .'[1] To the Mahayanist the Buddha *is* Supreme Wisdom. 'Other religions have made their founders into gods and sons of God; Buddhism makes its founders into the Ultimate and Only Reality, which underlies, produces, and includes all things.'[2] All of which is perfectly logical and purely mystical. Truth is one and absolute. It is expressed through advanced human beings, who express it by virtue of their identity with that Absolute, and to that extent *are* that Absolute. The Buddha had gained supreme Truth. Therefore the Buddha is supreme Truth.

Buddhology is necessarily a complex subject, being approached from many points of view. Somewhere on the way down from the inconceivable Ultimate comes Suchness, and the *Tathagata-garbha*, the *Dharmakaya* and *Adi-Buddha*, though the distinction between the meaning of these terms is subtle indeed.

In terms of the individual who becomes Buddha, he is, as set out in the chapter on Tibetan Buddhism, on various planes a *Dhyani-Buddha*, a *Dhyani-Bodhisattva* and a *manushi* or human Buddha. In the case of Gotama Buddha he was the *Dhyani-Buddha* Amitabha (Jap.: *Amida*), with Avalokiteshvara for his *Bodhisattva* and Gotama Siddhartha for his *manushi* or human body's name.

From another point of view there are grades of Buddhahood, including full Buddhas, Pratyeka Buddhas, Bodhisattvas and Arhats, though the last two terms have a very varying relationship. Below the fully developed Buddha is the Pratyeka Buddha, an 'independent' or 'private' Buddha, one who, having acquired Enlightenment by his own efforts and for the sole purpose of Nirvana, takes, as is his due, the reward of his efforts. There is great mystery about the true status of such persons, but the presumptuous contempt directed towards them may have arisen in contrast to the immense affection accorded to those Bodhisattvas who make 'the supreme

1. 'The Shin Sect of Buddhism', in *The Eastern Buddhist*, Vol. VII, p. 229.
2. J. B. Pratt, *The Pilgrimage of Buddhism*, p. 249.

sacrifice', and forgo the reward of lives of effort for the service of mankind.

Below these mighty ones is a pantheon of minor 'gods', many of them obviously borrowed from Hindu mythology; all alike are but symbols of the cosmic forces which all great beings, high or low, to some extent enshrine. They are of different rank, some being Buddhas, some Bodhisattvas (Buddhas to be), and some but distant cousins of the Buddhist family. Perhaps the most famous is Avalokiteshvara (*Avalokita-Ishvara*, 'the Lord who is seen'), the supreme SELF within, whose absorption of the individual consciousness is Buddhahood. The Chinese version of the term is better known, the male aspect being Kwan shai-yin and the later, female version, Kwan-yin (Jap.: *Kwannon*).

As J. B. Pratt says, 'The little lady Kwan-Yin is one of the loveliest forms of Buddhist mythology. She has not a trait one could wish absent or altered. In the heart of the Chinese Buddhist she holds the place which the Madonna holds in that of the pious Catholic,'[1] and the same applies to Japan. Amida is of supreme importance to the Pure Land Sects of China and Japan, and may better be considered under that heading. Maitreya, the Buddha-to-be (Chinese: *Milo Fu*), is of considerable importance in China, while Samantabhadra, representing the love aspect of the Buddha-principle, and Manjusri, representing the Wisdom aspect, are to be found on either side of a thousand 'trinities', with the Buddha in some cosmic aspect in the centre.

The remaining group of Mahayana principles centres about the Bodhisattva doctrine and its corollaries, such as the transfer of 'merit' and salvation by faith, which will be considered in the next chapter; this may be concluded with the concept of Nirvana as developed in China and Japan.

Nirvana

Nirvana (Pali: *Nibbana*) means to the Theravadin the dying out of the three fires of Greed, Anger, and Illusion. It is negatively expressed, being the extinction of undesirable qualities. In metaphysical terms this may be right, for the only statement to be made about such a state of consciousness is that it is not this and it is not that. But such a negative goal has little value as a reward for the practice of

1. *The Pilgrimage of Buddhism*, p. 297.

morality. We do not lightly strive to achieve a state which to our human minds is nothingness, and the positive Chinese mind preferred the approach already prepared by the positive thinkers of India, whereby the emphasis is laid on the Self to be attained rather than the Not-Self to be stamped out. First, therefore, they cleared the ground by developing the *anicca-anatta* doctrine to its absolute conclusion. They declared that no-thing, not even Nirvana, existed; there was therefore nothing to attain any more than a thing to attain it. But the individual man by attaining spiritual self-consciousness passes beyond the last veil of discrimination, enters the Void which is yet full and finds himself – where? In Samsara, said these strong, magnificent thinkers with an air of triumph. Nirvana, in brief, is not the goal of escapism, a refuge from the turning Wheel; it *is* the Wheel, and he who realizes himself in this discovery makes his daily life divine. For him all things are Suchness, and he sees but the Suchness of things. His *Citta*, or inmost heart and mind, is one with the Universe; he *is* Mind-Only.

On the way to such a Goal there are of course stages, and degrees of Nirvana are described. For the Way from our present blindness to our full-awareness is long and arduous. Yet in the end the self lies dead, and the Self, the expanding individual consciousness, is merged in that 'Suchness of the Heart' or *Bodhi-citta*, which is all-Love, all-Wisdom and all else. Beyond lies Parinirvana. . . .

[For Bibliography see end of Chapter Twelve.]

The Bodhisattva Ideal and the
Pure Land Schools

*

*Vicarious Salvation – the Rise of the Pure Land
School – Honen and Shinran Shonin – The Defence
of Shin Buddhism – Summary*

So important is the Bodhisattva doctrine to the Mahayana
School that the latter is sometimes called the Bodhisattva-
yana. The word itself is derived from *Bodhi* and *Sattva*, the
former term meaning wisdom or supreme intelligence and
the latter something like a state of being. Thus the word
means one whose essence has become 'Bodhi'. The term has
two principal meanings in the Mahayana, first as a being
who is only a stage, albeit a long one, short of Buddhahood,
a Buddha-to-be, and, secondly, as a stage in spiritual descent
below that of the Dhyani Buddhas yet short of incarnation as
a *manushi* or human Buddha. The two meanings are coalesced
in the esoteric doctrine of the dual movement of manifestation, 'spirit' descending into 'matter' and 'matter' ascending
to 'spirit', a teaching which alone makes sense of the complex
duality of most Eastern spiritual terms.

There are traces of the doctrine in the Pali Canon, and the
Jataka stories are the lives of a Bodhisattva who was finally
born as Gotama, to become, in that last earthly incarnation,
Buddha, a Fully Awakened One. In the Mahayana School,
the conception rose in importance until it ousted that of the
Arhat as the human ideal, and the change was perhaps inevitable. From the viewpoint of the human heart the Arhat is
cold, and wears the blinkers of a man who perceives an
unswerving path to a clearly perceivable goal. There will
always be those who demand the 'warmth' of a more emotional ideal, and there will always be those who rebel against
the unceasing and tremendous work involved in self-perfec-
tion. It was inevitable that the essentially lazy human mind
should seek to devise some means of ultimate salvation

without the effort involved in saving oneself, and if it could be cloaked in the guise of a splendid sacrifice, and still contained within the fold of Buddhism, so much the better. Quite early, therefore, the ideal of the Bodhisattva, he who saves others by his love for humanity, was created, adopted and adored. Its effect on the doctrine of Karma, essential to the older Buddhism, was, of course, immense, and indeed it is a revolt against the conception of such universal justice by those who prefer to sin without suffering its effects. It was argued by those of the new way of thought that while Karma operates in the realm of Samsara, the world of the opposites, it holds no sway in the realms beyond. Possibly, said the older School, but we are now in Samsara, and consciousness is not lifted above its sway by inventing a power to do the lifting for us; our illusion-filled and Karma-laden consciousness is raised by hard, persistent effort from self to Self and thence to Enlightenment. If that is Buddhism, said the new School, we look for something simpler, something easier. Invent it, then, the Theravadins almost snapped, but do not call it Buddhism!

Yet the Bodhisattva doctrine, as conceived in India, was not mere laziness. The Bodhisattva strove for Bodhi, universal Wisdom, which goes further in expressed intention than the Arhat ideal of 'self'-extinction. For the heart will not rest satisfied with the conclusions of the head, and the emotions cry aloud for expression. Love is a force as great as wisdom, and he who strives for his own enlightenment is in peril of forgetting his neighbour and his neighbour's needs. 'The essential nature of all Bodhisattvas is a great loving heart (*Maha-karuna-citta*), and all sentient beings constitute the object of his love.'[1] Very soon, therefore, the Mahayana was refounded upon Maha-Karuna (great compassion) as much as on Maha-Prajna (great wisdom), and the Bodhisattva, in all his grades, rapidly grew into what Kenneth Saunders rightly describes as an arresting figure: 'Charming, gentle and compassionate, full of tender and affectionate thought, unbiased, serene; he is ever zealous, and ever girded for the duties of his high calling, and has no thought that is not pure and wise. He rouses others to good deeds . . .'[2]

1. From 'A Treatise on the Transcendentality of the Bodhicitta', quoted by D. T. Suzuki in *Outlines of Mahayana Buddhism*, p. 292.
2. *Epochs in Buddhist History*, p. 90.

The Bodhisattva, moreover, is a logical conception. Life is one, say his devotees, and we live for all. It is therefore noble to work for all rather than for oneself. All deeds, whether good or ill, help or harm all other beings, and deliberate acts of good-will help all living things towards enlightenment. But the really great man grows so self-forgetful that he cares not for the self-reward of his acts of 'merit', and gladly 'turns it over' to the good of all. If, said the would-be Bodhisattva, this doctrine of *Parivarta* or *Parinamana* is contrary to the earlier teaching of Buddhism, so much the worse for the latter. For the doctrine of Karma is cold and hard and difficult; the transference of merit is filled with love and warmth and delight. We will adopt it.

Vicarious Salvation

So far the two Schools do not really clash. If the Theravada is shy about adopting in terms the principle that life is one, it readily teaches the power of thought and its influence on all who use it. The ceaseless flow of a great mind's pure benevolence helps all those about it on the road to enlightenment. But where is the limit of influence, where the dividing line between helping another in his work and doing it for him? Are not all other forms of life to some extent assisted by every thought of love, compassion, joy and equanimity, and will not he who, indifferent to the good effects on himself, offers his all to all mankind, to this extent be turning over his merit to others?

But now the summit of the pass is reached. Here are the heights and surely the limits of self-sacrifice. Beyond, the ground falls steeply into a doctrine which, though now the basis of the 'Pure Land' Schools of Buddhism, is clearly anathema to the original Teaching. How easily the argument ran down in Chinese and Japanese hands into the comfortable doctrine of vicarious salvation! If a great Bodhisattva turns his merit over to mankind, all men are blessed with a mighty store of merit which they have not, strictly speaking, earned. Magnify the merit available, and how soon will the lazy human mind permit this Mighty One to provide him with the merit which he had not the energy to earn and, basking in the sunlight of the Great One's boundless love, just wait for salvation!

Just one ingredient was required for the transformation.

In Theravada Buddhism faith is the faith of a traveller in a famous guide. The Guide has pointed the Way which he has trodden and the traveller, nothing doubting, follows in that Way. Now faith must be extended. The Guide becomes the Captain on a ship, the vessel (*yana*) of salvation for all. Faith becames faith in the power of the Bodhisattva to save the sinner from the consequences of his sins, and from the ignorance in which they were conceived. It was, thereafter, only a question of time before the necessity of all self-effort disappeared, and the devotee, the older Teaching shed, smugly awaited his faith-acquired, but otherwise unearned, salvation.

In the history of religious aspiration the meaning of faith is usually linked to that intuitive awareness of ultimate truths which is beyond the cognizance of the intellect-bound mind. In the earlier forms of the Bodhisattva Schools, faith was produced only by the practice of splendid virtues, the six *Paramitas*, which are Dana (giving in all forms), Sila (morality), Kshanti (patience), Virya (energy), Dhyana (meditation), and Prajna (supreme Wisdom), all of which themselves involve hard work. Not till the Pure Land School was settled in Japan were its doctrines pushed to the extreme. Thereafter, every conceivable form of personal effort was abolished, and salvation was left to faith and to faith alone.

The rise of the Pure Land School

The Bodhisattva doctrine was born in India, but it soon became acclimatized in China. The Pure Land School as such was founded in the fourth century, and was based on the larger and smaller *Sukhavati-vyuha Sutras* and the *Amitayur-dhyana Sutra*, all of which speak of the Western Paradise of Sukhavati, the Pure Land (Jap.: *Jodo*), in which believers will be gathered (after death, be it noted) as the reward for their faith and good works.

The Saviour of this School is Amida (Skt: *Amitabha*), whose history is curious. According to the larger *Sukhavati-vyuha Sutra*, he was a king who, moved by a sermon of the Buddha of his day, left his throne and became a wanderer dedicated to achieving Buddhahood. At some stage in his career he made a series of famous Vows (*pranidhana*), the eighteenth of which reads: 'If, after my obtaining Buddha-hood, all beings in the ten quarters should not desire in sincerity and faith to be born into my country, and if they should

T – F

not be born by only thinking of me ten times (except those who have committed the five grave offences and those who are abusive of the true Dhamma), may I not attain the highest Enlightenment.' He himself renounced the reward of his effort in order to preside over the Buddha-land of Sukhavati until all beings had arrived there. Descriptions of the Pure Land are extremely material, equating more with the Islamic Paradise than with Buddhist attempts to describe Nirvana, but at least in this Jodo School one had to work hard to achieve this state of bliss. In gratitude to Amida one strenuously strove to be worthy of his salvation, offering one's store of merit from good deeds to one's fellow men. This at its best is the Bhakti Yoga of India, a control and canalizing of the emotions into devotion to the Ideal. There is a deep sense of the unity of all parts with the whole, and a mystical sense of the Wholeness in all parts. Compassion is the deliberately cultivated power of self-abnegation and Self-fulfilment. The cry of the self is stilled in a spiritual passivity; the Buddhic principle or sense of grace within awakens as the clamour and the glamour of illusion dies away.

Honen and Shinran Shonin

Thus far the Jodo School in China. When this School reached Japan, however, Honen Shonin and his disciple, Shinran Shonin, turned a balanced discipline of faith and works into an extremist doctrine of salvation by faith alone. Honen was born in 1133, and was trained on Mount Hiei, the home of the Tendai (Chinese: *T'ien T'ai*) School. There he read in the monastic library a passage in Zendo's Commentary on the Pure Land Sutras which ran as follows: 'Only repeat the name of Amitabha with all your heart, whether walking or standing, sitting or lying; never cease the practice of it for a moment. This is the work which unfailingly issues in salvation, for it is in accordance with the original Vow of Amida Buddha.'[1] Being satisfied with this advice Honen left Mount Hiei, and founded the Japanese School of Jodo, which proved an immediate success. As Captain Brinkley somewhat drily says, 'The comforting tenet that by simple trust in Amida during life admittance to his paradise might be secured after death perfectly suited

1. Quoted in Pratt, *The Pilgrimage of Buddhism*, p. 480.

the dejected mood of the age, and would, indeed, suit the mood of men in all ages antecedent to the millennium.'[1] Especially if that trust was only manifested in the constant repetition of a formula, 'Namu Amida Butsu', which means 'Adoration to the Buddha Amida'. The faith required was child-like, but even under Honen's guidance there was still a shred of morality required, some slight co-operation between the Saviour and the saved.

Honen's disciple, Shinran, however, went all the way. 'Shinran carried the idea of Buddha's grace to extreme conclusions. A saying of Honen's runs: "Even a bad man will be received in Buddha's Land, how much more a good man!" Shinran turned this to – "Even a good man will be received in Buddha's Land, how much more a bad man!" Faith became the sole requisite to salvation; all else of the great moral-philosophy of Gotama the Buddha was swept away.'[2] Amida had acquired an inexhaustible store of merit, and he offered it to all. The sinner had but to believe in that store and his own access to it, and the Pure Land would be his. Even the incentive of improving his present lot was gone, for Sukhavati was for the after life, and not for this. Nirvana could be won, said the Theravadins, here and now, and would be achieved after as many lives as were needed to lift one's consciousness to that sublime condition. The Shin devotee, on the other hand, had to wait till physical death for his vicarious salvation, but Paradise was then as certain as the believer's faith.

The basis of all this was a theory of original sin. We men are karma-bound so deeply that it is useless for us to attempt to undo the evil done. We can but leave it to Amida to save us – and he will. True, this spiritual passivity, or negative waiting for grace 'in its highest religious connotation means breaking up the hard crust of egotism or relativism and melting itself in the infinity of the Dharmadhatu',[3] thus lifting the individual consciousness above the pairs of opposites, the realm of discrimination, into the Suchness of pure Mind. But the dangers are enormous. Why fight temptation if you will anyhow be saved? Why resist evil if you do not pay for it? These dangers were seen, and a system of strong

1. *Japan and China*, Vol. V, p. 147.
2. Anesaki, *History of Japanese Religion*, p. 182–3.
3. Suzuki, *Essays in Zen Buddhism*, Second Series, 1st Edn, p. 290.

discipline is used for the Shin devotee who is rightly, and here is the irony, not considered strong enough to use to the full the teaching which, according to theory, he adopted only because the Dhamma of the Buddha is too difficult to apply!

The Defence of Shin Buddhism

Here, then, is a form of Buddhism which on the face of it discards three-quarters of Buddhism. Compared with the Teaching of the Pali Canon it is but Buddhism and water. What is the excuse? It is that the Buddhism of self-effort (*jiriki*), of working out one's own salvation with diligence, is beyond the powers of the average man, and something easier must be devised for him. Is this thoughtful kindness, or insolence? Millions of Japanese, next-door neighbours, it may be, of the Shin practitioner, prefer and cheerfully use the 'hard' way of *jiriki*, self-effort, as distinct from *tariki*, Another's effort. Why, then, insult the remainder by saying that they cannot do the same? Both Schools, the 'self-power' and the 'other-power' School, seek the same Enlightenment, but the carrot in front of the Shin man's nose is a condition which in the esoteric tradition is known as Devachan, a state of consciousness between two lives wherein the reincarnating entity digests the best of the mind's experience and builds that noble thinking into character. This is a heaven indeed, but essentially self-won and limited in time. How much greater is that Enlightenment of which the Buddha spoke, wherein the last veil of duality has fallen, even the final distinction between the seeker and his goal? For Shin is still a dual religion; the eyes of the seeker are focused short of the final fusion of Seeker and Sought. Sukhavati is a state for the seeker to achieve; Nirvana is achievement.

What, then, is the case of those who claim that Shin is a form, albeit a 'developed' form, of Buddhism? It seems to be twofold, the frank confession that the older Buddhism is too difficult for the masses, and must therefore be 'simplified', and at the other extreme a doctrine so lofty, so subtle that only the rarest minds could understand and use it. It dwells on the heights of intuitive thought which see, with inward eyes, that the individual is nothing and the All everything; that the individual, meshed in his own ignorance, may bravely cry into the night his challenge to whatever powers may be, yet will, with his own unaided efforts, never reach the Light. Only in the knowledge, born, it may be, of faith till intuitive certainty replaces it, of the existence of the Godhead within, can he use the power of it to raise himself to the Light thus dimly seen. This is *bhakti* mysticism at its noblest, and in a nation of born mystics, such as the Indians, it is available to the humblest mind. But the Japanese are a practical, unmystical race, though steeped in a love of beauty second to none in the world. How can they use such intuitive heights of thought to rid themselves of Avidya? What they in fact do is to recite the Nembutsu by night and day and to hope, as distinct from the mystical sense of knowing, that somehow, somewhere, someone will save them from the consequences of their sins. This is an easy, simple religion, for all the work is done for one. It was therefore immediately popular, and it may be better than no religion at all. But is it Buddhism?

Summary

The Bodhisattva doctrine is a magnificent addition to the teaching of the earlier School, and the Jodo School of China and Japan, which produces a blend of faith and works, of the working of Grace within as induced by strenuous efforts in meditation, morality and good works, is an admirable addition to the vast field of Buddhism. But although pure faith may, in the exceptional mystic, produce that Enlightenment which is the common goal of all Buddhist Schools, for the people as a whole it would seem that, while they know nothing of the mystical heights of consciousness, nor do they strive by Sila (morality) and Dhyana (meditation) to achieve that Prajna (wisdom) which, when the power of Samsara is transcended, is found to make Samsara and Nirvana one. For such and no less is the Mahayana goal.

'There is no Nirvana except where is Samsara; there is no Samsara except where is Nirvana; for the condition of existence is not of a mutually-exclusive character.'[1]

1. *The Lankavatara Sutra.*

BIBLIOGRAPHY

FOR CHAPTERS ELEVEN AND TWELVE

Anesaki, Masaharu. *Religious History of the Japanese People. History of Japanese Religion.*

Barker, A. T. Ed. of *The Mahatma Letters to A. P. Sinnett.*

Beal, Samuel. *A Catena of Buddhist Scriptures from the Chinese.*

Blavatsky, H. P. *The Secret Doctrine* (1st Edition). *Theosophical Glossary.*

Cleather, Alice, and Crump, Basil. *Buddhism, The Science of Life.*

Coates, H. H., and Ishizuka, E. *Honen, The Buddhist Saint.*

Coomaraswamy, Ananda. *Buddha and the Gospel of Buddhism.*

Dayal, Har. *The Bodhisattva Doctrine in Buddhist Sanskrit Literature.*

Edkins, J. *Chinese Buddhism.*

Eliot, Sir Charles. *Japanese Buddhism.*

Johnston, R. F. *Buddhist China.*

Lloyd, Arthur. *The Creed of Half Japan.*

McGovern, W. M. *An Introduction to Mahayana Buddhism.*

Pratt, J. B. *The Pilgrimage of Buddhism.*

Radhakrishnan, S. *Indian Philosophy*, Vol. I.

Reichelt, Karl. *Truth and Tradition in Chinese Buddhism.*

Suzuki, Mrs B. L. *Mahayana Buddhism. Impressions of Mahayana Buddhism.*

Suzuki, Prof. D. T. *Acvaghosha's Discourse on the Awakening of Faith in the Mahayana.*
'The Development of Mahayana Buddhism' (*The Buddhist Review*, Vol. I).
'The Development of the Pure Land Doctrine in Buddhism' (*The Eastern Buddhist*, Vol. III).
Essays in Zen Buddhism, First, Second and Third Series.
Outlines of Mahayana Buddhism.
'The Shin Sect of Buddhism' (*Eastern Buddhist*, Vol. VII).
Studies in the Lankavatara Sutra.

Stcherbatsky, T. *The Soul Theory of the Buddhists.*

Tai Hsü, The Ven. *Lectures in Buddhism.*

Takakusu, Y. *The Essentials of Buddhist Philosophy.*

Ward, C. H. S. *Buddhism* (Vol. II), *Mahayana.*

Watts, Alan. 'The Problem of Faith and Works in Buddhism' (*The Review of Religion*, Vol. V).

Yamakami Sogen. *Systems of Buddhistic Thought.*

CHAPTER THIRTEEN

Schools of the Mahayana

*

*The Chinese Schools – The Chen-yen (Shingon)
School – The Ch'an and the Pure Land Schools –
Japanese Schools – The Five Nara Schools – Tendai
and Shingon – The Nichiren School – Shin and Zen*

THE Mahayana was formed in India, but most of the important schools of Indian Buddhism were later introduced into China and Japan. Thus the *Kusha* sect of Chinese Buddhism derived from the Sarvastivadin School; the *San Lun* (Jap.: *Sanron*) sect derived from the Madhyamika School, and the Dharmalakshana sect (Jap.: *Hosso*) was the Chinese descendant of the Indian Yogachara Sehool. But the Chinese developed new schools of their own, most of which reached Japan, where at least one new variation on the ancient theme of the Dharma was founded by Nichiren. In theory, therefore, the Schools of the Mahayana should be examined in each of these countries, but Professor Takakusu may be right in saying that the whole field of the Mahayana can best be studied in Japan, for 'in Japan the whole of Buddhism has been preserved – every doctrine of both the Hinayana and Mahayana Schools'.[1]

The following notes on Chinese Buddhism are therefore given as the basis of further consideration when the same sects or schools are examined in Japan.

The Chinese Schools

Although no active sect of the older School survives, the Hinayana or Theravada doctrines are carefully studied both in China and Japan. Two such schools were introduced into China from India, the *Lu Tsung* or *Vinaya* Sect (Tsung = school or sect) and the *Ch'eng-shih Tsung*. The latter had but little importance, but the former has been the source of the monastic discipline of most other Chinese sects.

1. *The Essentials of Buddhist Philosophy*, p. 9.

Of more importance was the *San Lun* sect, already described as deriving from the Madhyamika of India. The name means Three Shastras, for it is based, like so many of the Chinese sects, on particular scriptures. Nagarjuna is regarded as the founder, and the three treatises, each a masterpiece of logic, are still studied, particularly in Japan, where the *'Sanron'* sect, as it there became, considerably influenced Japanese Buddhism.

In the *Hua-yen Tsung* (Jap.: *Kegon*), based on the *Avatamsaka Sutra*, Buddhist philosophy reached its zenith. Thought can go no further than the doctrine, already described, of Jijimuge.

The *T'ien-'ai Tsung* (Jap.: *Tendai*) is based on the *Saddharma-Pundarika Sutra*, the 'Lotus of the Good Law'. From the first it was synthetic in purpose, and attempted to embrace all points of view. To explain the differing doctrines of various sects it divides the Buddha's Ministry into five periods in each of which he taught progressively difficult doctrines, ending, of course, with the *Saddharma-Pundarika Sutra* for those whose minds could conceive an identity of the absolute and phenomenal worlds.

The *Dharmalakshana*, or *Yogachara* School, sometimes called the Pure Consciousness Sect (Jap.: *Hosso*), was introduced into China, like so many other Indian teachings, by the great pilgrim and translator, Hiuen-Tsiang. It contains, as its name implies, the Mind-Only teaching, which is radical to the later development of the Mahayana.

The Chen-yen (*Shingon*) *School*

The three remaining Schools which need to be here considered largely moulded Chinese Buddhism. The first is the *Chen-yen Tsung*, known as the *Mantrayana*, or the Esoteric School, the name meaning 'Word of Truth' (Jap.: *Shingon*). Brought to China in the eighth century, it was the last arrival from the great field of Indian Buddhism. Its origin is compound. Traditionally, Vairocana, the Sun-deity aspect of the Buddhist pantheon, transmitted this secret wisdom to Vajrasattva, who locked up the secret in an iron tower until after seven hundred years Nagarjuna opened it and transmitted the secret by the usual line of Patriarchs. At some time the School received a large admixture from the Tantric Schools of Northern India. With this presumably came the

knowledge of *Mantras* and *Mudras*, which at its best is a
science of sound and gesture, but which, in the course of the
ages, has been inevitably debased, both in quality and user.
The western Branch of the School is known in Peking as the
Tibetan Esoteric School, while the eastern Branch, as John
Blofeld points out, having passed to Japan in the T'ang
Dynasty as the *Shingon* School, has been re-introduced into
China. There is some basis for the belief that the 'services'
used in the temples were influenced by contact with the
Nestorian Christians who flourished in China in the eighth
century.

The Ch'an and the Pure Land Schools

There remain the rival Schools of Shin and Zen. Founded
as a School in the fourth century, the *Ching-t'u* (Jap.: *Jodo*)
or Pure Land School was soon so popular that it became a
common practice for students of other Schools to add the
worship of Amida to their own religious practices. In this
School the Bodhisattva Amitabha (Amida) is elevated to a
symbol of Supreme Reality under a personal aspect. As a
School it aimed at 'simplification'. The Scriptures studied
by the intelligentsia being held to be beyond the reach of the
untrained mind, the Pure Land Scholars aimed at discarding
all such literature in favour of a simplified pure faith. It is
true that the same contempt for the written word was evinced
by the followers of the *Ch'an* School, who, however, arrived
at the same result from an opposite point of view. The *Jodo*
School stayed, as it were, below the level of the Sutras; the
Zen School rose above their usefulness. Members of the
former declared that none could understand such cold profundity; the latter stated, with logic as an unused ally, that
words are themselves but symbols, and that Truth lies even
beyond symbolic rendering.

The *Ch'an* School (Jap.: *Zen*), which will be more fully
considered in Chapter 14, was founded as a School of
Buddhism by Bodhidharma (Chinese: Tamo; Jap.: Daruma),
who reached China from South India in A.D. 520. Ch'an is
a corruption of the Sanskrit Dhyana, an untranslatable
term usually rendered as 'meditation'. It is, however, essentially dynamic, and such a passive English term in no way
describes the fierce intensity of effort used to achieve 'direct
seeing into the heart (*hsin*) of man'. Zen is therefore *par*

excellence the religion of 'self-effort' (Jiriki), just as Jodo and the later Jodo Shin became the religion of 'other-effort' (Tariki), or salvation by faith in Another's Power.

Japanese Schools

So much for the principal Schools in China. R. C. Armstrong classifies the Japanese Schools into Hinayana, quasi-Mahayana and Mahayana, and the description happens to be chronological. But the arrival of Buddhism in Japan via Korea in the sixth century was more haphazard than this clear-cut arrangement implies. Chinese scholars arrived in Japan and taught the doctrines of the School of their choosing; Japanese scholars toured in China and brought back the doctrines which excited their fancy. The utmost tolerance existed between the two national ideologies, as they would nowadays be described, and between the exponents of differing schools. Prince Shotoku, for example, chose three Scriptures for his own translation without reference to any particular School, and the mind of any one scholar was often eclectic in its patronage of widely different ideas.

The Five Nara Schools

It seems, however, that five of the Chinese sects were established in Nara, the first capital of Buddhist Japan. The purely Theravada sects were the *Kusha*, the *Jojitsu* and *Vinaya*. The word Kusha is a corruption of the title of Vasubandhu's work, the *Abhidharma-kosa-Shastra*, and derives, as already explained, from the Sarvastivadin School of North India.

Closely associated with the *Kusha* was the *Jojitsu* (Satyasiddhi) School, which derives from the Sautrantika School of India. Equally concerned with philosophic speculation, it is nihilistic to the Kusha's realism. It survives, like the Kusha philosophy, as the object of study, but has ceased to exist as a practising sect.

The *Vinaya* (Ritsu) Sect survives to-day,[1] having sprung from the *Lu Tsung* of China. As already described, it has influenced most other sects by providing them with regulations for the monkish life.

---

1. Pratt, *The Pilgrimage of Buddhism*, p. 469.

Armstrong describes the *Hosso* and *Sanron* Sects as quasi-Mahayana. The *Hosso* (Yogachara or Dharmalakshana) School, founded by Dosho, was immensely popular in China in the eighth century, when the greatest invasion of Japanese scholars was taking place, and its doctrines, based on the mystical psychology of Vasubandhu and his brother Asanga, became the scholastic theology of Japanese Buddhism. The home of the school is Horyuji, the oldest and most famous monastery in Japan to-day. It was founded by Prince Shotoku in person and completed in A.D. 607. Its frescoes were, until destroyed by fire early in 1949, the most famous east of Ajanta, and its buildings as a whole are the prototype of all Japanese Buddhist architecture.

The *Sanron* School, which derived from the Madhyamika, or Middle Path School of India, is based on three texts by Nagarjuna and his pupil, Aryadeva. Its teaching is a negative idealism, and most of its energy is consumed in refuting the wrong views of Brahmanism, the Theravada and other Mahayana Schools. It stresses Nagarjuna's Eightfold Negation.

The last of the Nara sects of Buddhism, and the first which Armstrong classifies as being pure Mahayana, is the *Kegon*, or *Avatamsaka Sutra* sect. Founded in China in the T'ang Dynasty as the *Hua-yen Tsung*, it was based on the enormous and heterogeneous *Avatamsaka* (Wreath or Garland) *Sutra*, the remaining Sanskrit portion of which is better known as the *Ganda-vyuha*. Historically it was a development from the *Hosso* sect, and was brought to Japan in 736 by Dosen, who transmitted it to Ryoben, then a priest of Todai-ji at Nara, which became its main temple and is to-day its heart and centre. This temple, the largest single wooden building in the world, houses the 50-foot bronze figure of Vairocana, or Locana (Jap.: Dainichi), the 'unveiling' of which by the Emperor of the day in 752 was a notable event in Japanese religious history.

As already set out, the Kegon philosophy of Jijimuge, of 'unimpeded interdiffusion' of Absolute Reality and each individual 'thing', is the last word in human thought. Although the School to-day is one of the smallest in Japan, its influence on Japanese Buddhism has been tremendous. Only Zen, which claims to have found a technique for passing beyond the realm of even the loftiest concepts, has had more influence. All other sects or schools but offer means to assist the mind to conceive the Ultimate. Kegon alone has stated it within the mind's periphery; Zen alone speaks certainly of the top rung of the conceptual ladder, and of the 'jump' which the mind must make, in full self-consciousness, from self-illusion to Self-Enlightenment.

Tendai and Shingon

In A.D. 784 the Emperor Kwammu moved his Court from Nara to a site nearby in the crescent of hills beside Lake Biwa. A new city was planned on the lines of Chang-an, the capital of T'ang China, and became known in time as Kyoto, 'the capital'. The move was hastened if not caused by the tiresome squabbles of the existing Buddhist schools at Nara, and the Emperor may well have felt the need for a higher synthesis of teachings and ideals. Two men arose to supply the need, Saicho, later known as Dengyo Daishi, and Kukai, later known as Kobo Daishi, the founders of Tendai and Shingon Buddhism respectively, Taking advantage of the peculiar political-religious situation, the two men united the whole of Japanese Buddhism about the new capital, and welded Church and State into a close cohesion. As Professor Anesaki says, 'the firm establishment of the central government in the eighth century had been made possible by the assistance, both moral and physical, of the Buddhist Church, while the latter's work was, in a way, a reflection of the political attainment of national unity.'[1]

The unification of the two ideals was made easier by Saicho, one of the greatest characters in Japanese Buddhist history. While still a young man he entered the Order, but, soon wearying of Nara and its then philosophy, he built himself a monastery on Mount Hiei, the highest of the hills round Kyoto, and there meditated on the Lotus Sutra, the *Saddharma-pundarika*. He attracted the Emperor's attention, and was sent by him to China for further study. There he worked in the famous T'ien-t'ai Mountains, the home of the School of that name, and returned to Japan with authority to found a Japanese sect of the school. He did so on Mount Hiei, which became the new home of Japanese Buddhism, though not without protest from the various sects at Nara.

1. *History of Japanese Religion*, p. 109.

Here was an all-embracing Middle Way designed to include all then existing schools of Buddhism, and to open the doors of the Dharma to all. On the one hand its teaching absorbed and applied the best of the *Kegon* school, and the two together, as J. B. Pratt says, 'may be called the very keel of all serious Buddhist thinking in Japan'; on the other it joined hands with the contemporaneous Shingon School created at Koya-San by Kobo Daishi. Its broadening message, to the effect that all, not merely the elect, are destined for Enlightenment, was immediately popular, and in direct refutation of the more exclusive *Hosso* School. Moreover, its very wide platform acted as a leaven of true democracy, and thereby reduced the power of the Nara Sangha which had grown overweening in its priestly demands. The Kegon's pantheistic development of the *Sanron* School, and its ingenious grading of the Scriptures, as said to have been delivered by the Buddha at different periods for the benefit of ascending levels of mind, made a very wide range of teaching possible, and to this day the *Tendai* is a Buddhism in miniature.

Kukai, later known as Kobo Daishi, was a younger contemporary of Dengyo Daishi, and an even greater man. He was immensely versatile, being a scholar, ascetic, traveller, 'business man', a very fine sculptor and a famous calligrapher. At an early age he wrote a comparative study of Confucianism, Taoism and Buddhism, and when, impressed with Saicho's visit to China, he too made the long journey, studying there for two years, he remained equally broad in his outlook, although he was principally attracted to the esoteric teachings of the True Word School. With this he returned to Japan, empowered to found a Japanese branch of it. He chose Mount Koya, some fifty miles from Kyoto, for his new headquarters, and thus avoided to a large extent the political embroilments of Mount Hiei, on the outskirts of the new capital.

The *Shingon* became the most Indian of all Japanese schools, for it imported many of the Yoga practices of Hinduism, the mantric and tantric ideas and habits of the Tantrayana of North Bengal, and a ritual which, if added to in China, was certainly further elaborated in Japan. Shingon is essentially mystical and esoteric, being divided into teachings for the common people and those which cannot be so taught. Truth is absolute, and though personified as Maha-Vairocana (the Great Illuminator) it can be known directly only through symbol. Sacraments and elaborate ritual are the only way in which the limited mind of man can know Reality; hence the complex use of *mantras*, *mudras* and *mandalas* (magic diagrams in circular form), which are found elsewhere only in the religion of Tibet.

If Tendai was of generous scope, *Shingon* went still further, for all existence was brought into its fold. All peoples and their gods were included, and this catholicity of the two great Schools made possible their common reign in Kyoto for nearly four hundred years. It is true that *Shingon* classified the Buddha's teaching under ten ascending grades, from that suitable to the lowest type of intelligence through all the other existing schools to the Shingon esoteric teaching at the top, but all other teaching was freely accepted, and this warmth of welcome largely accounted for the immediate and unintended popularity of Koya-San. This glorious group of temples, set in a forest of giant cryptomerias, is one of the holiest and one of the most beautiful places in Japan to-day, and if the magical practices of the School have been largely degraded into 'spells' for every conceivable occasion, its essentially mystical teaching, which radiates from To-Ji and Daigo-Ji in Kyoto as well as from Koya-San, is perhaps the third most powerful force in Japanese Buddhism to-day.

As several writers have pointed out, the Tendai and Shingon form a pair. They were founded at the same time, and for nearly four hundred years divided the Court favour. Both took Buddhism to the people, acting as pioneers in what is now called social service. If this had its disadvantages, tending to internal corruption through 'power politics', it also tended to spiritualize the Government of the day, and thus to make Buddhist ideals a lamp on the paths of public policy.

The Nichiren School

Before turning to the extremist Schools of *Jodo-Shin* and *Zen*, the *Nichiren School*, the most original Buddhist sect of Japan, must be briefly noticed. In the last half of the twelfth century, the Kyoto Government had so degenerated that civil war broke out. After fifty or more bloody years of strife, in which Buddhist monasteries were more than once engaged, a few of the stronger feudal lords gained power, and after fighting each other to a standstill left the Minamoto family, with the great Yorimoto at its head, in control at the new capital of Kamakura. Thereafter, until 1868, the Emperor was more or less a puppet, and Japan was ruled by hereditary Shoguns.

The civil wars had developed and perfected the cult of Bushido, the eastern equivalent of the western cult of knighthood, and the cult was ripe for spiritual guidance. The existing Buddhist sects, discredited to some extent by participation in the political wars of Kyoto, were not suited to the needs of the new capital, and the people as a whole, as well as their feudal overlords, needed new forms of Buddhism. The need produced the supply, and within a century three new schools arose, the *Jodo* of China, elaborated in Japan into *Jodo-Shin* or *Shin*, the Chinese *Ch'an*, now to be known as *Zen*, and the School of the firebrand Nichiren (1222–1282).

Nichiren ('Sun-Lotus') as this son of a fisherman later called himself, studied all Schools widely until he had decided for himself what was the true way to deliverance. He first entered the Shingon School, and then studied in the Tendai School on Mount Hiei. There he came to the conclusion that only one scripture was needed, the Lotus of the Good Law, and that the salvation of the country from its then chaos could best be achieved by a vigorous campaign of 'Back to the Lotus Sutra and the Buddha', or words to that effect.

He was a born religious demagogue, and wandered the country literally banging the drum of his beliefs at all and sundry. Because of his rudeness to all other sects he was soon in trouble with authority, and his life was a long story of persecution and all but miraculous escape. The irony of the persecution was that Nichiren considered himself the supreme patriot, teaching that religion and state should be one, but although his fervour and sanctity of life attracted many followers, his violence of method seems to have militated against his final success, and his 'new' movement was little more than an exhortation to all to apply the Tendai teachings, an attempt to transmute philosophical thought into religious action.

Shin and Zen

There remain the two extremist Japanese Schools, both
of which rose in the troublous days of Kamakura. The
Buddhism of the *Kegon-Tendai-Shingon* Schools was out of
favour in the new capital, and both the people as a whole
and the warrior cult of Bushido were left unsatisfied. The
Pure Land teaching was thereupon offered to the former,
and *Zen*, the 'spiritual cult of steel', to the latter. Each form
of teaching was and is an extreme, but extremes have a habit
of meeting, and these two Schools of thought and action –
'ways of life' is the better term – divide and unite the
attention of the greater part of Japan to-day. *Jodo*, the Pure
Land School as refounded by Honen, came early to Japan,
but Honen, the founder of the great Chion-In, the mother
temple in Kyoto, crystallized this practice into a School
which, later carried to irrational extremes by Shinran,
dominates Japanese Buddhism by sheer weight of numbers.
From the great twin monasteries of the Nishi (West) and
Higashi (East) Hongwanji Schools of Shin in Kyoto, missionaries go forth to all parts of the eastern world, from
the west coast of the U.S.A. to Singapore. Its literature is
enormous; its organization based on Western lines. As
formulated for the masses by Shinran it is the simplest religion in the world. Believe in Amida and his Original Vows
with a devoted heart, reciting the Nembutsu at all hours of
the day, and salvation in his Pure Land is a certainty. 'No
elaborate ritualism, no mystifying philosophy, no labyrinth-
ian complexity of technical terms, but a simple straight-
forward invocation of Amitabha Buddha – was this not a
wonderful leap from the Nara and Heian Buddhism?'[1]

Clearly there is a place in the religious life, and therefore
in the Buddhist life, for what Dr Suzuki calls 'passivity', for
this is the 'self-surrender' of Islam, the self-abandonment
to God of the Christian mystics, the Bhakti Yoga of India,
wherein the devotee lays all that he has and is on the altar
of the Divine Beloved. But none of these methods of rising
above the limitations of the personal, selfish self ignores the
corresponding value and necessity of 'works'. All alike assume a close co-operation between the Grace which comes
from 'God' and the personal effort which clears the way, as
it were, for the operation of Grace. *Jodo*, in brief, is a

1. D. T. Suzuki, *Japanese Buddhism*, p. 33.

balanced method of religious experience: *Shin*, by destroying that balance, thereby abandons, in the view of many,
the right to describe itself as Buddhism. If it is to be so included, it must be as one of the two attempts devised by
Buddhists to attain Enlightenment without recourse to the
usual trappings of religion. Shinran advised his followers to
give up attempting self-enlightenment, and to leave all to
Amida; Zen advises its followers to 'see directly into the
heart of man.' In either case the self, the lower, unregenerate man must die – 'Give up thy life if thou wouldst live.'
In Shin the self is abandoned to Amida; in Zen, it is first
by enormous effort of will, transcended, and then – for
Samsara and Nirvana are, at the gates of Enlightenment,
found to be one – re-integrated, as it were, into the whole
because wholly Enlightened man. The former process is well
known in religious history; let us examine Zen, the unique
flower of Buddhism.

BIBLIOGRAPHY

FOR CHAPTER THIRTEEN

Anesaki, Masaharu. *History of Japanese Religion*.
  Religious Life of the Japanese People.
Armstrong, R. C. *Buddhism and Buddhists in Japan*.
Blofeld, John. *The Jewel in the Lotus*.
Coates and Ishizuka. *Honen, The Buddhist Saint*.
Eliot, Sir Charles. *Japanese Buddhism*.
Johnston, R. F. *Buddhist China*.
Lloyd, Arthur. *The Creed of Half Japan*.
Petzold, Bruno. 'Japanese Buddhism' (in *The Young East*, for 1935).
Pratt, J. B. *The Pilgrimage of Buddhism*.
Steinilber-Oberlin. *The Buddhist Sects of Japan*.
Suzuki, Beatrice L. *Impressions of Mahayana Buddhism*.
  Koya San.
Suzuki, Daisetz Teitaro. *Japanese Buddhism* (Tourist Library, No. 21).
Takakusu, Junjiro. *The Essentials of Buddhist Philosophy*.

CHAPTER FOURTEEN

Zen Buddhism

*

*The Purpose of Zen – The History of Zen – Zen
Technique – Satori – The Effects of Satori*

ZEN is the apotheosis of Buddhism. This direct assault upon
the citadel of Truth, without reliance upon concepts (of God
or soul or salvation), or the use of scripture, ritual or vow,
is unique. It is true that the Zen School uses 'means' or
'devices' (Skt.: *Upaya*; Jap.: *Hoben*) to achieve its end, and
concepts are needed to make clear the limitations of conceptual thought. Certain of the Mahayana Scriptures, such
as the *Lankavatara Sutra* and the *Diamond Sutra*, are studied
in Zen monasteries, and 'services' of Sutra reading and
devotion are held. But no such device is necessary, and all
alike are scorned as having no essential value. So fierce, indeed, is the Zen technique, and so scornful of the usual
apparatus of religion, that it has been doubted whether Zen
is a Buddhist School at all. Certainly it forms a school of its
own, and it is difficult to place it in the field of Buddhism.
It cannot be adequately described as the Meditation School,
for in the West this term is apt to connote serene passivity,
and, as all who have worked in a Zen monastery know, each
moment of the waking day is strenuously spent on the task
in hand. This is no less than the breaking down of the bars
of the intellect that the mind may be freed for the light of
Enlightenment, and in such a task there is nothing passive
or serene. Even the hours of meditation are intensely strenuous, and the rest of the waking day is spent in the fields or
in running the monastery.

In Zen the familiar props of religion are cast away. An
image may be used for devotional purposes, but if the room
is cold it may be flung into the fire; the Scriptures are useful
on the foothills of our understanding, but as soon as they
are seen as so much paper they are better put to useful purposes; incense, chanting, and gorgeous robes may attract
the populace and calm the performer's mind, but they are

toys to be outgrown. Here is a man's religion, and he climbs best who carries the lightest load.

The Purpose of Zen

The purpose of Zen is to pass beyond the intellect. All that we know, we know but about. The expert, a wit has said, learns more and more about less and less; Zen wearies of learning about it and about, and strives to KNOW. For this a new faculty is needed, the power of im-mediate perception, the intuitive awareness which comes when the perceiver and the perceived are merged in one. All mystics use this faculty, and all alike are unable to make their knowledge known. But he who knows can only say that he knows; to communicate what he knows he has to descend to the realm of concepts, counters of agreed and common meaning. Such are words, but they are fallible means of making our knowledge known. For we can but describe our thoughts and feelings in terms of the pairs of opposites, and all description by adjectives, adverbs and verbs is a process of selection. This book itself is new, small, comprehensive, cheap; it is not old, large, specialized, expensive. It is written, according to the reviewer's opinion, well or badly; it helps or it hinders the student mind. But none shall convey to another the contents of this book, save through the medium of the selectivity of his own mind. None knows what I know, nor can I write it down. The intellect has its uses and it is an essential faculty in the human mind. But just as the emotions have their use and abuse, their range of usefulness and a limit to that range, so the intellect, by which men reach to the stars in science and philosophy, must pause and fail at the gates of spiritual knowledge. For the intellect can learn about it and about but can never, as the finest intellects discover, KNOW.

What KNOWS? The answer is *Buddhi*, the faculty of direct awareness, as present in every human mind as the intellect which all possess but few have yet developed to the full. Yet just as he who develops his intellect at the expense of his emotions ends in the consulting-room, so he who develops his intuition before the reason of the mind is well confirmed, may be a 'genius' but he will not be stable, and a tower that is built upon sand may reach to the sky but will sooner or later fall.

The intellect is itself a device or means, and Zen is the way of direct enlightenment. All must be freely abandoned before the seeker finds, even the fact of seeking and the will to find. 'What is my self?' asked a pupil. 'What would you do with a self?' asked the Master in reply. 'Am I right when I have no idea?' asked another enquirer. 'Throw away that idea of yours', was the answer. 'What idea?' asked the bewildered pupil. 'You are free, of course,' said the Master, 'to carry about that useless idea of no idea'! Truly we walk through life with a heavy burden. Two monks, returning home, came to a ford where a pretty girl was waiting, fearful to wet her clothes. One picked her up in his arms, forded the stream and, having put her down, walked on. The other was horrified, and spluttered his indignation, mile upon mile. Said the first monk, suddenly aware of the other's words, 'That girl? I put her down at the ford. Are you still carrying her?'

The History of Zen

The history of Zen is worthy of Zen. It is said that once, when the Buddha was seated with his Bhikkhus, a Brahma-Raja came to him and, offering him a golden flower, asked him to preach the Dharma. The Enlightened One accepted the flower, and holding if aloft, gazed at it in silence. After a while the Venerable Mahakasyapa smiled. Such is the origin of Zen Buddhism, for it is said that this smile was handed down by twenty-eight successive Patriarchs, the last being the Indian philosopher Bodhidharma, who arrived in China in A.D. 520. The Emperor invited him to his capital and began to boast of his devotion to Buddhism. 'I have built many temples and monasteries', he said. 'I have copied the sacred books of the Buddha. I have supported Bhikkhus and Bhikkhunis. Now what is my merit?' To which this ferocious-looking sage replied, 'None whatever, your Majesty!' The Emperor tried again. 'What is the First principle of Buddhism?' 'Vast Emptiness', replied the twenty-eighth Indian Patriarch of Zen. 'Who, then, now confronts me?' asked the Emperor, not unreasonably. 'I have no idea', said Bodhidharma. Such was the foundation in China of the School which became for a time synonymous with Chinese Buddhism, and is one of the two main schools of Japanese Buddhism to-day. The Master was equally brutal with his less exalted students. 'Pray pacify my mind', cried a pupil who had waited seven days in the snow before gaining admission to the Master's room. 'Show me your mind', said the Master. 'I cannot produce it,' said the seeker. 'So; then I have pacified your mind', said Bodhidharma. And the pupil *knew*.

It is said that Daruma, as the Japanese call him, expressed his teaching in four lines of verse:

> A special transmission outside the Scriptures;
> No dependence upon words and letters;
> Direct pointing to the soul of man;
> Seeing into one's own nature.

Thus was born the dynamic intensity of a School which allows its followers to reach such a crisis of spiritual effort as would lead, but for expert handling, to the breakdown of the health and mind. When you want Zen, said a master of Zen, as much as a man whose head is held under water wants fresh air, you are truly seeking; and nothing less is the spirit of Zen. And the power to achieve this end is within. Zen, as already explained, is Jiriki, self-effort, as distinct from Shin, or Pure Land Buddhism, which favours Tariki, salvation by Another's Power.

For five hundred years the Dhyana School, which the Chinese corrupted to Ch'an and the Japanese to Zen, grew mightily, its greatest exponent being the sixth and last of the Chinese Patriarchs, Hui-neng (in a southern dialect, Wei Lang). Thereafter its power was transferred to Japan, which it reached in the twelfth century. Two sects developed of which the Rinzai is the older and the Soto the larger, but the difference between them is only of emphasis, the former adhering to the 'sudden' technique of the Founder, and the latter adopting a gentler way in its approach to Enlightenment. A third sect appeared in the seventeenth century called Obaku, from its Chinese founder, Huang-Po, famous for the *Huang-Po Doctrine of Universal Mind*.

Zen Technique

As I have said elsewhere, 'The process of Zen is a leap from thinking to knowing, from second-hand to direct experience. For those unable to make the leap for themselves a bridge must be built which, however rickety, being built for the occasion before being flung away, will land the traveller on the "other shore" of enlightenment.'[1] The materials of this bridge are anything which will produce results, and the Zen student uses all scriptures and any philosophy which helps to make and use the bridge. The end at all times dominates the choice of means. 'If I tell you', said the sixth Patriarch, 'that I have a system of Law to transmit to others I am cheating you. What I do to my disciples is to liberate them from their own bondage with such devices as the case may need.'[2] The device is not part of Zen, for when a finger points at the moon it is foolish to confuse the finger with the moon.

Yet even Zen has produced its own technique for the 'sudden' path to Satori, the Zen name for Enlightenment. The two most famous devices of Rinzai Zen, less used in the Soto branch, are the *mondo*, a form of rapid question-answer between Master and pupil which aims at so speeding the process of thought that it is suddenly transcended, and the *koan*, a word or phrase insoluble by the intellect, which is often a compressed form of *mondo*. Neither has any meaning for the rational mind, else it would not be Zen.

First, however, there must be an intellect to be transcended, for it is where the intellect pauses, baffled and at bay, that Zen begins. The intellect is a developed instrument for the use of knowledge, but only the senses and the intuition acquire knowledge at first hand. The thought-machine, therefore, too easily becomes a cage, a workshop for the handling of second-hand material. For just as the senses acquire direct experience by touch and taste and the like, so Buddhi, the intuition, acquires direct experience, and *knows*. In the ideal process of development, this higher faculty increasingly illumines the thinking mind; in usual practice the intellect claims a final validity and closes its doors to direct experience. Hence Zen is largely a breaking into the closed doors of the mind to let the light without flood in, and any and every process which will shock the mind into such an opening is useful and may be used. A lightning answer may suffice, thrusting the question back into the questioner's

1. *Zen Buddhism*, p. 116.
2. *The Sutra of Wei Lang*, p. 95.

mind. 'How shall I escape from the wheel of birth and death?' Asked the Master in reply, 'Who puts you under restraint?' A laugh, an oath, a shout, a shaking, even a blow may do what years of 'meditation' have failed to achieve. Asked why he meditated all day long, a pupil replied that he desired to become a Buddha. The Master picked up a brick and began to rub it. Asked what he was doing, he explained that he wished to make a mirror. 'But no amount of polishing a brick will make a mirror!' 'If so, no amount of sitting cross-legged will make thee a Buddha', was the deep reply.

The *koan* is like the pebble in the mouth of a man who walks in the desert. It does not quench existing thirst, but it stimulates the means of quenching it. 'Is there Buddha-nature in a dog?' asked a monk. 'Mu', said the Master, and *mu* means No. Mu is perhaps the most famous of all koans, which are statements of spiritual fact to be intuited and not 'understood'.

Here are some more. Two hands when clapped make a sound. What is the sound of one hand clapping? What was the reason of Bodhidharma's coming from the West? If all things are reducible to the One, to what is the One reduced? There is a live goose in a bottle. How to remove the goose without hurting the goose or breaking the bottle? (The 'answer' to that one is easy. 'There, it's out!') Or, finally (but there are said to be seven hundred koans in use in Japan to-day), a man hangs over a precipice by his teeth, which are clenched in the branch of a tree. His hands are full and his feet cannot reach the face of the precipice. A friend leans over and asks him, 'What is Zen?' What answer would you make?

All these are nonsense, that is, non-sense, and so is Zen. For sense is the product of reasoning and logic, of the laws of thought; Zen roars with laughter at all of them. Zen is the joke in a joke, and cannot, like a joke, be 'explained'. It is the life within the form; it is that which reasoning strives to enshrine and frequently strangles. It is the river of life which cares not for the palaces of thought, the dictionaries and definitions, the understanding or decisions of those upon its banks. Zen technique, therefore, like the explosives used in logging, is designed to break the jam in the river, and let the waters and all which float thereon ride free. In Theravada Buddhist philosophy all is arranged in three of this and four of that with a twelve-fold Chain of Causation. Very neat, says the Zen practitioner, but, as Dr Suzuki says, 'The Buddha was not the mere discoverer of the Twelvefold Chain of Causation: he took the chain in his hands and broke it into pieces, so that it would never again bind him to slavery.'[1] In Zen the emphasis is on the breaking and not on the chain.

All objects, of thought or emotion, whether things we touch or the things which stand in our mental way, must sooner or later be smashed and removed. As the Master Rinzai himself proclaimed, 'Do not get yourselves entangled with any object, but stand above, pass on and be free.' All phrases, dogmas, formulas; all schools and codes; all systems of thought and philosophy, all 'isms', including Buddhism, all these are means to the end of KNOWING, and easily become and are not perceived as obstacles in the way. Zen technique is designed to develop the mind to the limits of thought and then to drive it to the verge of the precipice, where thought can go no further. And then? As Dr Graham Howe, the psychiatrist, often says to his patients, 'when you come to a precipice, why stop, or go round, or go back? Why not go over?' For only then can we go on, and progress is a walking on and on to the Goal. It is true that at a later stage one learns that there is no walking and no Goal, but that is Zen. . . . Meanwhile, until we achieve the goal of purposelessness, let us have this purpose: Said the Master Ummon to his monks, 'If you walk, just walk; if you sit, just sit, but don't wobble!'

Satori

What is the goal of Zen? The answer is Satori, the Zen term for Enlightenment. For as said in the Introduction to this work, the Buddha's Enlightenment is the heart and purpose of Buddhism, and Satori *is* Dhyana (Zen), Enlightenment. As Satori lies beyond the intellect, which alone can define and describe, one cannot define Satori. It is that condition of consciousness wherein the pendulum of the Opposites has come to rest, where both sides of the coin are equally valued and immediately seen. Silence alone can 'describe' it, the silence of the mystic, of the saint, of the artist in the presence of great beauty; of the lover and the poet when the fetters of time and space have for the moment

1. *Essays in Zen Buddhism*, First Series, p. 111.

fallen away. It is the plane whereon Jijimuge is reality, where
the whole is seen as such and its parts in their due proportion. It is not out of the body nor out of the world; on the
contrary, the world and all in it is seen and enjoyed more
fully than before. At first it is reached in flashes which come
and go. Later it comes in profound meditation or when the
mind, by this device or that, is raised to its highest plane,
Satori is seeing into one's own nature, and that Nature is
not one's own. The vision may come quite suddenly or
slowly arise. It is in no way to be confused with a psychic
trance or the phantasy of the schizophrenic. Nor is it concerned with morality or any man-made code. It is a foretaste
of the Absolute Moment, of Cosmic Consciousness, of the
condition in which I and my Father are one.

The Effects of Satori

The effects of Zen (and Zen means Satori) on the art and
culture of the Far East will be considered in Chapter 16.
The effects on the man are, of course, proportionate to the
degree of Satori attained. The oldest description of Satori is
contained in the Pali Canon, in the story of Assaji's summary
of the Buddha's Teaching, as told to his friend Sariputta,[1]
but in the Chinese and Japanese scriptures there are scores
of accounts of this tremendous happening. Yet attempts to
describe it are always in vain, for words are but symbols
coined by the discriminative intellect, and Satori is beyond
discrimination in the realm of Jijimuge. Sometimes the happy
man would burst into a song or an improvised poem; sometimes he merely laughed, and it is to be noted that no other
school or religion or philosophy has used, as Zen deliberately uses, laughter as a means to a spiritual end. Roars of
laughter, cleansing, healthy, ferocious laughter, are part of
the Zen monk's daily life and of those who practise Zen.
Others who have tried to describe the reward of their years
of tremendous effort speak of a sense of certainty, of serenity,
of clarity, and of unity with nature and the universe around.
Hui-neng described the serenity:

Imperturbable and serene the ideal man practises no virtue;
Self-possessed and dispassionate he commits no sin;
Calm and silent he gives up seeing and hearing;
Even and upright his mind abides nowhere.[2]

1. See chapter I I.
2. The Sutra of Wei Lang, p. 124.

With clarity of mind, whence emotion and passion have ebbed away, comes an inner certainty of purpose and the right way to achieve it, and the certainty is quite impersonal. But the mind, though aloof from the senses' attraction, is never in the clouds of an ideal world. There is a vital sense of here and this and now. Nirvana has been found within Samsara and not elsewhere, and the two are known to be and not merely conceived as one. The student achieves a sense of the Absolute Moment, and knows that all things are equally important, equally real and unreal, equally part of himself. The flower in the crannied wall is indeed the universe, and nothing exists beyond this life that is not contained within it.

These new possessions of the mind, however, are not of immediate growth; they develop anew with each experience. For a while occasional vision may have no effect on character, for the momentum of old habits of thought and thought-reaction is immensely strong. Yet slowly a new sense of values supersedes the old; truly a new man is born, and the sustained and tremendous effort to reach the new stage on the path of development was found to be worth while. As I wrote elsewhere, 'The Self has taken over, and the appetites of a pack of ill-trained animals which yelp and growl and bite at each other, and do far ruder things than that, have at least been recognized as such. If they do slip off the new lead sometimes, it is at least with the master's knowledge, if not with his consent'.[1] And that is a long stage on the way to Enlightenment.

1. *Zen Buddhism*, p. 222–6.

BIBLIOGRAPHY

FOR CHAPTER FOURTEEN

I have included an almost complete Bibliography of books in English on Zen at the end of my *Zen Buddhism* (Allen and Unwin). Here it is sufficient to draw attention to the works of Dr D. T. Suzuki, the greatest living authority on Zen Buddhism. See also Herrigel, Eugen, *Zen in the Art of Archery*; Dumoulin, Heinrich, and Sasaki, Ruth Fuller, *The Development of Chinese Zen*. For Zen in the West see my *Zen Comes West* and *Teach Yourself Zen*.

CHAPTER FIFTEEN

Tibetan Buddhism

*

*The Nature of 'Lamaism' – The History of Tibetan
Buddhism – Tantric Buddhism – Padma Sambhava –
Tsong-ka-pa – The Schools of Tibetan Buddhism –
Esoteric Buddhism – The Tibetan Pantheon – The
Dalai Lama and the Panchen Lama – Priests, Temples
and Services – The Scriptures*

THE physical conditions of Tibet lend themselves to religious
thinking. The great spaces, the height of the mountain
ranges which surround them, the rarefied air in a land which
is largely over 16,000 feet, these and the silence where men
are scarce and wild life is rarer still, all lend themselves to in-
troverted thought, to the development of abnormal ways of
thought, to the practice of the best and the worst of the
manifold powers of the mind. Nowhere save in Tibet is there
so much sorcery and 'black' magic, such degradation of the
mind to selfish, evil ends, and much of these men and their
practices has been described by travellers; nowhere, unless
the clear and almost timeless tradition of the East is of
nothing worth, are there so many men who, by becoming
masters of themselves, are the spiritual masters of mankind.
In the course of the last 2,500 years a great many men have
achieved Enlightenment, as untold numbers had achieved it
by divers 'Ways' before and since the Arhats of Theravada
Buddhism; they are the Rishis and Mahatmas of India, the
Bodhisattvas of Chinese and Japanese Buddhism, the Brothers
of many a mystical work, with equivalent titles in most of the
religions of the world. But of these the traveller in Tibet
knows nothing or, if he be of the development which will
allow such meeting, he will never mention such an experience.

The Nature of Lamaism

Lamaism, as the Buddhism of Tibet used to be called, is a
mixture of the best and worst of Buddhism, and of much
that lies between. At its best it is a noble part of the Mahayana – or a separate School within it – controlled by men of
the highest calibre; at its worst, Waddell may be right when

he says that 'Primitive Lamaism may be defined as a priestly mixture of Sivaite mysticism, magic and Indo-Tibetan demonolatry, overlaid by a thin varnish of Mahayana Buddhism.'[1]

This religion is to be found from the Caucasus to Kamchatka, and from Buryat Siberia to Ladakh ('Little Tibet'), Sikkim, Bhutan, Nepal and Yunnan. Yet in this vast area there are not more than twelve million people, an enormous proportion of whom are monks.

La-ma means the 'superior one'. It is a term which should be reserved for the heads of monasteries and the highest dignitaries, but by courtesy is given to all of the Gelong or fully ordained rank. Below the Lamas properly so called come the Gelong, and the Gestul or deacons. Below them again come the Ge-snen or lay adherents, corresponding to the Upasaka and Upasika of the Theravada. Their number in all is enormous, and in Lhasa they compose one third of the population.

The History of Tibetan Buddhism

Before the seventh century the sole religion of Tibet was the Bön. The dominating figure was the Shaman, a sorcerer working on psychic levels to produce the right weather and the other needs of an agricultural population. Sir Charles Bell points out that such a religion, a form of nature-worship with sacrifice to vaguely defined gods of the earth and sky, existed at that time over most of Siberia, and its only importance to the present study is that Buddhism, already corrupt when it arrived in Tibet, absorbed, with its usual excess of tolerance, much of the indigenous faith and practices. These Bönpas, however, must not be confused with Dugpas, who are members of the Dugpa sect, founded in Upper Tibet in the twelfth century by a spiritual descendant of Milarepa. The sect being 'Red-hats', as distinct from the 'Yellow-hats' of the later Reformation, and, having degenerated into Bön practices, have largely merged with Bönpas, and black magicians. There are, however, vast numbers of Bönpas who are not members of the Dugpa sect.

Some time in the fifth century A.D. a number of Buddhist books were brought into Tibet from India, but they seem to have been ignored, and it was not until the reign of King Srongtsen Gampo, in the middle of the seventh century, that

1. *The Buddhism of Tibet*, p. 30.

Buddhism became a force in Tibet. This powerful king, in the course of his conquests, took as his two chief wives a princess from China and another from Nepal. Both were Buddhists, and between them they converted the king to Buddhism. The king at once began to preach, and to build temples. Bön reaction was immediate, but the new religion had come to stay, and Srongtsen Gampo is revered as the founder of Tibetan Buddhism.

Tantric Buddhism

The Tantras, which are the scriptures of a Hindu school of mysticism which uses ritual of many kinds, were introduced at an early stage of Tibetan Buddhism, and all schools became deeply influenced by Tantric practices at a high or low level. For Tantric ritual, whether of the Hindu or the later Buddhist variety, has many ingredients and degrees of purity. Being highly esoteric, in that its practices are handed down only from Guru to chela, it is difficult to know how much of the ritual described in great detail is to be taken merely as symbolic and subjective and how much is objective practice. The use of *mudras*, ritual gestures, *mantras*, phrases of magical power through esoteric knowledge of sound vibrations, and *yantras*, diagrams of symbolic meaning, is clearly set out; so is an elaborate cosmology describing Adi-Buddha and the emanations from this primordial Principle of *Dhyani-Buddhas* and their *Dhyani-Bodhisattvas*. But the written scriptures contain a great deal of sexual symbolism, and what reads as the symbolic yet actual use of sexual conjugation.

As later developed, the sexual element dominated the entire system of Tantra, including its practices and iconography. It is true that one of the basic 'Pairs of Opposites' is the male-female principle, and that sex, the psychic tension between the two, is the creative principle in its dual aspect. The adherents of Tantrism, therefore, ascribed to all the gods of Buddhism, the personified abstractions of its metaphysical theology, a *Shakti*, their female counterpart, and display these couples in pictures and statues as locked in a sexual embrace. This practice met with the condemnation of nearly all early Western writers on the subject, and it seems beyond question that a great deal of immorality is practised in its name. Later writers, however, further removed from a generation which regarded all things pertaining to sex as unclean, have admitted that the earlier critics wrote through a veil of their own sex-ridden minds. The philosophy itself is neither clean nor unclean, but one of a thousand methods of enabling the mind to break the illusion of its own surroundings. Sex is a fact and a universal fact, and its force can be used to the mind's enlightenment. Its very power, however, makes it immensely difficult to handle, and no one doubts that a proportion of tantric followers merely indulge in the force which they should be learning to sublimate and harness to impersonal ends. As applied to the Buddhist Doctrine of Mind-Only of the Yoga-chara school, which, with some of the monastic Rules of the Theravada, had by this time entered Tibet from India, the doctrine of Shakti was subtly modified. The power (*shakti*) of the more passive female was sublimated into the feminine wisdom-aspect of the male power of compassion, with its countless devices (*upaya*) for helping mankind. But the Tantra remains an importation from Hinduism, and some regard it as a regrettable deviation from the main stream of Buddhist development.

Padma Sambhava

The main importer of Tantrism into Tibet was Padma Sambhava, who was summoned to Tibet by the King of the day in A.D. 747, from Nalanda, where he had acquired fame as a Tantric sorcerer. Padma Sambhava, 'the Lotus Born', also known as the Guru Rimpoche, the Precious Teacher, arrived with two wives and a chosen band of disciples, which soon included learned Tibetans. A great era of translation set in, and the fact that most of the works at first translated were from the tantric canon explains why the Tibetan Buddhist Canon has such a tantric bias. In spite of Bön opposition, the Lotus-Born's new teaching found a ready audience. It was an improvement on the prevailing Bön, but not too much in advance of it.

But the Böns, through exalted patronage, fought back successfully, and for a century or more the new faith was heavily suppressed. Not till the coming of Atisha, in the eleventh century, did the pendulum swing back in favour of Buddhism, but this famous Mahayanist monk from India, known for his wise learning and wider travels, brought with him only a further brand of tantric Buddhism. He did, however, found the reformed Kahdampa Order, and generally reformed to the best of his ability the Buddhism of Tibet. Enthusiasm was tremendous; new monasteries were built with a considerable zeal and new scriptures translated to study in them. Two of the great figures of this time are Marpa and his still more famous disciple, Milarepa (born A.D. 1038) who founded the Kargyupta School. The 'Cottonclad Mila', so called for his living on the bare hillsides in a single cotton garment, was a most remarkable 'saint'. 'First a wizard, then a saint, and always a poet, his name is a household word; his songs, as well as his biography, are universally read and often quoted.'[1] Certainly, his life as given to the West by Dr Evans-Wentz[2] is that of an almost unique figure in religious history, and few men, if any, have risen from such depths to such heights in one short life.

Tsong-ka-pa

Yet a greater figure in Tibetan Buddhism is Tsong-ka-pa (1358–1419), 'The Man from Onion Land', a district of Am-do, in north-west China. According to the exoteric writings, he carried on the reformation initiated by Atisha, collecting the scattered members of his reformed Gelugpa Order, and giving them the Vinaya rules of the Theravada, together with the distinctive yellow hat by which the whole reformed movement later came to be known. As such they were distinguished from the Red Hats of the unreformed sects, and the Black Hats of the Bön-pa. This Gelugpa ('virtuous custom') Order soon became the most powerful in Tibet, and always includes the Dalai and Panchan Lamas of the day.

Tsong-ka-pa was by all accounts a great man. 'A strong body, a rich brain, and the will to work immeasurably, all these combined to put him in the forefront of the missionary movement.'[3] As its leader he became known as Je Rimpoche, the Chief of Great Price, and his tomb in the monastery which he founded at Gan-den, about twelve miles from Lhasa, is the object of pilgrimage and veneration to this day. His religious reforms were far from complete, but though he did not abolish the tantric influences in Tibetan Buddhism, he went far to remove them. His principal work was the *Lamrin Chembo*, containing rules and instructions

---

1. Bell, *The Religion of Tibet*, p. 65.
2. *Tibet's Great Yogi Milarepa*.
3. Bell, *The Religion of Tibet*, p. 96.

T – G

in two parts, one for the ecclesiastics, and one for students of his inner or esoteric school.

For the esoteric tradition regards Tsong-ka-pa as a reformer and codifier of the inner school of Initiates as well as the creator of a reformed Church. To the higher ranks of lamas he ranks as a Dhyan Chohan, being overshadowed by the Buddha himself. This belief is confirmed by Sir Charles Bell, who says, 'Among the Yellow Hats he is known as the second Buddha.' According to the Master 'K. H.', this is no exaggeration. In his famous attempt to explain to a Westerner some of the principles of the Wisdom of which the Arhats or 'perfected ones' are the custodians for mankind, he wrote, 'When our great Buddha – the patron of all the adepts, the reformer and codifier of the occult system – reached first Nirvana on earth, he became a Planetary Spirit, i.e. his spirit could at one and the same time rove the interstellar spaces in *full consciousness*, and continue at will on earth in his original and individual body. ... That is the highest form of adeptship man can hope for on our planet. But it is as rare as the Buddhas themselves, the last Khobilgan [sometimes called 'A Living Buddha'], who reached it being Sang-Ko-Pa of Kokonor, the reformer of esoteric as well as vulgar Lamaism.'[1] It is not surprising, therefore, that the memory of this great man is venerated throughout the length and breadth of Tibet, for though his visible reform of Buddhism was enormous, his unseen work was greater still, second only to that of his Master, Gotama the Buddha.

In the thirteenth century Buddhism spread into Mongolia. An abbot of the Sakya monastery built by Marpa in the eleventh century was summoned to Peking to cure the Mongol ruler of the time, and his successor, Dro-gon, was the spiritual tutor to Kubla Khan when a boy. Later the great Emperor asked Dro-gon to introduce Buddhism into Mongolia, there supplanting the crude nature-worship which survives in Tibet as Bön. On Kubla's death the reform regressed, but was pressed to comparative completion some three centuries later. Yet the picture of Buddhism at the Mongol capital of Karakoram as given by Rubruquis, the Flemish friar, who visited the city in A.D. 1253, would serve for that city to-day, and so much do the 'services' and the like resemble those of the Catholic Church that many a later

1. *The Mahatma Letters to A. P. Sinnett*, p. 44.

writer has assumed that Tsong-ka-pa himself was influenced by the Christian mission which was established at the time in Am-do. But Sir Charles Bell points out that no one in Lhasa had even heard of this suggestion in his time, and refers to the fact that many of the details of devotion in some of the Japanese sects, established without the possibility of Christian imitation, are equally alike.

The Schools of Tibetan Buddhism

By the sixteenth century, the various Schools of Tibetan Buddhism were reasonably well defined. The Established Church, as it were, is the Gelugpa, or Yellow Hat Sect. Next comes the Kargyut-pa Sect, founded in the eleventh century by Marpa. This may be called the Semi-reformed Sect, and its members supply a large number of the 'entombed ones', monks who shut themselves in caves on the hills for a time or sometimes for life, leaving but a hole through which their disciples bring them the minimum of food and water. Another semi-reformed Sect is the Sakya, meaning tawny earth, so-called from the colour of the soil near the place of its birth. Though it claims to be an improvement on the unreformed sects, to-day it is hardly to be distinguished from them. Its members are known by the St Andrew's cross on their caps, typifying their cross-kneed posture for meditation. The Dugpas have already been mentioned.

The last of the major schools to be described, but probably the first to be founded, is the Nyingmapa or Red Hat Order, the unreformed Buddhism of Padma Sambhava. Being now on the defensive against the Reformed Schools, its members justify their practices by discovering in caves and other secret places hidden revelations (*Terma*), which they claim to be the esoteric teachings of Sambhava. These discoveries are mostly concerned with magical rites and practices, and add little to the religious worth of the sect. Beyond these Schools, reformed, partly reformed, and unreformed, lie the Bön-pa, who, though affected by Buddhism, are still the primitive nature-worshippers of pre-Buddhist days.

Esoteric Buddhism

All these Schools, however, are alike of the exoteric side of Tibetan Buddhism. But in the course of 2,500 years, a great many men have reached the stage of Arhat in the

spiritual ladder of progress. These do not die in the normal
sense, for their consciousness continues from life to life in
successive bodies. Such as make the Great Renunciation of
the bliss of Nirvana become in Tibetan eyes *Bodhisattva*,
vowed to save all humanity from the suffering which Ignorance entails before they reap the reward of their own
Enlightenment. Such men are for the most part in human
bodies, living, therefore, in some part of the world. For thousands of years these spiritual leaders and guardians of mankind, known by a score of names in various religions, have
made their home in a region as yet unsoiled with 'civilization', from which they work on the inner planes of consciousness. Not all, of course, are Buddhists, but whatever
the body and religion of the adept concerned, the task of
the Brothers is the same, to guide and influence the more
enlightened leaders of mankind into the paths of spiritual
advancement for all. Their collective wisdom is found, by
those who study the religion-philosophies of the world, in
fragmentary and often garbled form in these various schools
of thought. Two of these Masters tried to teach A. P. Sinnett,
the Editor of the *Pioneer* of India, an outline of these
principles, and the result appeared in 1883 as *Esoteric
Buddhism*. Later, the same Masters caused their pupil H. P.
Blavatsky, whom they had trained in Tibet, to give a far
fuller version in *The Secret Doctrine* (1888). In 1924 their
letters to A. P. Sinnett were published as *The Mahatma
Letters to A. P. Sinnett*, and only those who have carefully
compared the teachings contained in this great body of
literature with that of the scriptures of Mahayana Buddhism
can testify to the brilliant light which the former throws on
the latter, and to the volume of the former which the latter
contains. Difficult parables, traditional phrases and obvious
hints are suddenly seen as basic principles, which in turn
explain much else that escapes the eye of the Western scholar.
It becomes easy indeed to accept that part of the Wisdom
which speaks of Two Paths, the doctrine of the 'Eye' and
the doctrine of the 'Heart'. For 'the Dharma of the "Eye"
is the embodinent of the external, and the non-existing. The
Dharma of the "Heart" is the embodiment of Bodhi, the
Permanent and Everlasting. . . . The "Doctrine of the Eye"
is for the crowd, the "Doctrine of the Heart" for the elect.'[1]

1. *The Voice of the Silence.*

This traditional teaching applies to all sects of Tibetan Buddhism, the purest as the most corrupt, for there are adepts of the 'black' arts as well as of the 'white', the difference being merely in the purpose to which the spiritual powers obtained over the minds of others or over the powers of nature are put. All such teaching passes, as over all the East, from teacher (*Guru*) to disciple (*Chela*), by word of mouth or even, as in Zen, by a silent and even violent technique. How much, then, can the average traveller or even the would-be scholar learn of this esoteric, because unpublished, tradition, when Europeans are regarded in Tibet as persons of undeveloped minds and grossly material ideas?

The Tibetan Pantheon

Buddhism, as first conceived, knew nothing of God or gods; still less was the Buddha himself a god. Yet within a thousand years of the Teacher's passing, men who claimed to be his followers had erected and learned to worship a pantheon more complex in form and interrelation than any on earth. This complexity is due to the addition to the metaphysical Trinity and its primary Emanations of a host of minor gods and their *Shaktis*, or female counterparts, created out of the exuberance of the Indian mind.

Highest in the Tibetan mind stands Adi-Buddha, the Primordial Wisdom whose executive power, as it were, is the collective intelligence of the seven (five revealed and two unrevealed) Dhyani Buddhas. Each Dhyani Buddha inspires a Kalpa or cycle or stage of evolution, and each in turn produces or informs a number of Bodhisattvas, who are of different standing in the occult hierarchy, some being almost of the rank of a Buddha, and others but advanced men. The Dhyani Bodhisattvas in turn express themselves or manifest through a human body, which in the eyes of men becomes known as a named Buddha. Thus one of the Dhyani Buddhas or Dhyani Chohans (the fourth), reincarnated as the Dhyani Bodhisattva Avalokiteshvara, who overshadowed, as the Christ principle overshadowed the boy Jesus, the man known to history as Gautama Siddhartha, the Buddha. Thus the world of advanced, self-perfected men is not a haphazard collection of those who have preceded their fellows in spiritual development, but a descending hierarchy from the nameless Absolute to the human leaders of mankind. Some of these, says the Wisdom, have once been men, in this or in some previous planet; others have yet to be men. All alike are spiritual forces, and as such but aspects of the indivisible, eternal Unity.

The best known of these mighty beings, in the sense that their names most frequently appear in Tibetan Buddhism, are the Dhyani Buddha Amitabha (Amida in Japan, and Opame in Tibetan), Avalokiteshvara (Chenresi), who is at once a name for the collective host of the Dhyani Buddhas, and one of them, and Maitreya (in Pali, Metteyya), who will be the next human Buddha, although not for some hundreds of thousands of years. Avalokita-Ishvara, shortened to Avalokiteshvara, 'the Lord who is seen', is, universally, 'the Omnipresent Universal Spirit in the temple of nature',[1] and in man the seventh and highest of his 'principles'. He is therefore the object of supreme veneration throughout the world of the Mahayana. He is Padmapani, the 'Lotus-born', and thus the recipient of the omnipresent formula, 'Om mane padme hum.'

The lower ranks of the Tibetan pantheon are filled with a mixture of personified natural forces which range from manifestations of the above to human saints such as Tsong-ka-pa, and a host of godlings, difficult to identify, which have been erected for worship by the joint imagination of Indian *bhakti* yoga and Tibetan superstition. To the charge of the deification of the better of these Gods, J. E. Ellam, who discussed the question with various learned Lamas, puts the defence. 'The mind of man, said the Lama, is prone to superstition. If left to themselves ignorant people will invent their own superstitions, and it is better that they should find their superstitions prepared for them with a definite object in view. The deeper teachings are beyond the capacity of the majority, and if superstition helps the common people to a better life, why remove it?'[2] Before the Western reader scornfully rejects such a defence he might reconsider the observations of the best of modern psychologists, who point out that we have rid ourselves of none of our medieval superstitions but merely given them new ('psychological') names, and the demons which were once removed with bell and

1. *The Mahatma Letters to A. P. Sinnett*, p. 344.
2. *The Religion of Tibet*, p. 71.

candle now yield, or equally refuse to yield, to the technique of the psychiatrist's consulting-room.

Western travellers delight in scorning the existence of 'Living Buddhas', and if what they expect to find is men of the rank of the Buddha living as such they will continue to search in vain. But the *Chutuktus* (Tibetan) or *Khubilkans* (Mongolian) are cosmic forces of great power, and they overshadow and work through human entities. The men thus used may be fallible instruments, but the power is in them, and according to Tibetan belief at least five of the greatest Lamas of the day are thus used by these spiritual yet human forces. Thus the Dalai Lama is, to this extent, an incarnation of Chenresi (Avalokiteshvara) and the Panchen Lama of Amitabha.

The Dalai Lama and the Panchen Lama

These two are the greatest men in Tibet, the former holding the spiritual and temporal power. The relation between these two great figures – for though at a given time they may be children in years, their power is absolute – is complex. The office of Dalai Lama grew from that of the Grand Lama, first held by Tsong-ka-pa's nephew, to that of Dalai (Great Ocean) Lama, a title acquired by the 'great Fifth' Dalai Lama in the middle of the seventeenth century. He it was who built the great Potala in Lhasa which is one of the most magnificent buildings in the world. From this building, and the 'Cathedral' described in such detail by Landon,[1] this prelate-king has ruled Tibet, and the millions of Buddhists who in the outer spaces of Mongolia have looked to him as such. While the holder of this office is an infant he exercises his powers through a Regent and Council; while an adult he works through the Council of great Lamas who correspond to the cardinals of Rome. The late thirteenth Dalai Lama seems to have been a very remarkable man, as proved by Sir Charles Bell's affectionate biography[2] and the same applies to the recent holder of the office of Panchen Lama, about whom the late Mrs Alice Cleather had much to say.[3]

The Panchen Rimpoche, or Panchen Lama, has no political power outside his own province, but from his monastery of

---

1. Perceval Landon, *Lhasa*, Vol. II, p. 301.
2. Sir Charles Bell, *Portrait of the Dalai Lama*.
3. Cleather and Crump, *Buddhism, The Science of Life*.

Tashilhumpo, near Shigatse, built in 1445 to the order of
Tsong-ka-pa, he wields an authority greater for the fact that it
lacks all worldly sanction.

Much space is occupied in books about Tibet with accounts of the curious and unique method of appointing the
successor to both these offices when the holder dies. The
country is searched, sometimes for years, for a baby who
will recognize possessions of the previous holder, and thus
prove, by this and other means, that he is the new incarnation of the spiritual Principle which uses the body of this
official. The fact that each new holder of the office needs
a long regency gives great power to the Regent and his
Council, for it needs a strong-minded young man to assume
the reins of power from such a Council on attaining his
majority.

So much for the major gods of Tibet, unseen and seen.
The minor gods fill many a book of iconography. Some are
beautiful, some repulsive; many are ferocious, being the
demon counterparts of the 'good' aspects of the god concerned. To all but the least educated, however, these figures
and pictures are but symbols of higher forces, not to be
worshipped as such, still less to be propitiated. They are but
crutches for the feeble-limbed; rafts with which to cross the
river of becoming. According to Tibetan teachings, even the
Bodhisattvas are but 'supports', and when the Void is attained all such aids can be thrown away. From the artistic
point of view there are Indian, Chinese and Nepalese influences at work in these images, and the Yab-yum figures are
obscene only to those who consider that sex itself is obscene.
These coupled figures signify 'the penetration of the Material
by the Spiritual', says Heron-Allen, 'which thus become
inseparable. In and for purposes of worship, Wisdom is regarded as female, and Power and Method as Male, and they
are depicted as being in sexual union, touching at all points
of contact, denoting that Wisdom and Method, Power and
the Mind that guides and uses it, are ever in union.'[1] The
ushnisha, the protuberance on the skull, represents the
hyper-development of the supreme psychic faculty, connected with the pituitary gland, and the urna, the jewel
between the eyes, is the 'third eye', the faculty connected
with the pineal gland.

1. *Gods of the Fourth World*, p. 21–2.

Priests, Temples and Services

The three principal monasteries in Tibet are the enormous De-pung, which is said to hold nearly 10,000 men; the Sera; and the Gan-den, founded by Tsong-ka-pa, all near Lhasa. The rest are innumerable; some large, some small; some in the remote hills, difficult to find, some close to fair-sized towns. The monks at any time range from brilliant-minded, highly spiritual men to lazy, dirty wastrels, and the convents are filled with women of little less range in spiritual value. Services in these temples are elaborate, and many a traveller has commented on the amazing similarity to much of the ritual of the Church of Rome. The plays which are frequently staged in the temple courtyards are similar to the medieval mystery plays of Europe, the so-called 'devil dances' being no more than ancient folk-dances with grotesque costumes and mime.

In the temples are to be found the instruments well known in the museums of the West: the prayer-wheels, devised to hold the attention of the senses while the mind attends to its meditation, but no doubt a means by which the superstitious masses achieve, so they think, the maximum returns to their prayers with minimum effort; the *vajra* (Sanskrit – *dorje* in Tibetan), or small bronze trident, the symbol of power, and the rosaries which, in the tantric sects, are often made of human bones. Of greater value as a means of teaching the truths of Buddhism are the famous paintings of the Wheel of Life, being the twelve *nidanas*, or the 'chain of causation' pictorially described.

In this teeming world of monks and nuns and simple-minded, superstitious peasant folk, the sorcery and magic of the religion which came from India, and that of the original Bön are much in evidence. Oracles and fortune-telling abound, but much of the magical ritual has fallen from high purposes. India knows the Yoga of *mantras*, the use of sound, and *mudras*, the use of hand-postures (so-well described and illustrated in Heron-Allen's rare little work, *Gods of the Fourth World*) and it is from India, no doubt, that the use of these occult sciences has come. The Bardo Thödol, translated by Evans-Wentz as *The Tibetan Book of the Dead*, is a Nyingmapa work, though of great interest to many branches of religious enquiry, while the description in the works of Mme David-Neel of powers and practices as yet unknown to the West must be at least believed, however hard to explain, for she herself has practised some of them. Many of the meditation exercises have affinities with Indian Yoga; others are more akin to Japanese Zen.

The Scriptures

The Tibetan Canon consists of the Kanjur, in 108 volumes, and the Tanjur, an enormous commentary in 225 volumes, which Kenneth Saunders describes as 'a great encyclopedic library of ancient Indian lore on metaphysics, logic, arts, alchemy, etc.' Its contents have not yet been fully examined, but the famous Hungarian explorer, Csoma de Körös, has translated a brief analysis of the former. It is based on both the Indian and the subsequent Chinese version of the Tripitaka, but with many tantric additions. The translations from the Sanskrit in the Canon are of great value, for the original works have in many cases been lost, and it is possible from these accurate translations to recover the original.

According to the esoteric tradition, however, there is much more to the Tibetan Scriptures than even these great collections of material. The authors of the *Mahatma Letters to A. P. Sinnet*, for example, writing from Tibet, refer again and again to the *Book of Kiu-ti*. According to H. P. Blavatsky, who was trained in Tibet, thirty-five volumes of this work may be found in any Gelugpa monastery, and fourteen further volumes of commentaries contain a digest of the occult wisdom of the Arhats of all ages. It is from the text of this work that the material for much of her greatest work, *The Secret Doctrine*, has been drawn. If this be so, it explains how a work written by a Western woman contains knowledge to be corroborated only by the most careful analysis of hints and phrases scattered throughout the more esoteric because unpublished scriptures of the religions of the world.

Tibetan Buddhism, then, is a unique blend of the noblest Buddhist principles and debased sorcery, of the highest and the lowest of man's mind. It belongs, if it is not *sui generis*, to the Mahayana School, and has much in common with the interrelated principles of Chinese Buddhism. But the Tibetans claim to have many 'vehicles' or *yanas*, and it is not easy to suggest a collection of principles common to all. Yet all seem to agree that in the beginning was THAT, the

nameless Absolute which all Hindus invoke as Aum, contracted to Om, the first syllable of the Tibetan formula Om
Mani Padme Hum, the outer meaning of which is merely
'Hail to the Jewel in the Lotus', and its inward meaning
the meaning of the Universe. Within the One there stirs desire, the First Cause of which must ever remain unknown and
is not in Buddhism even the subject of speculation. The One
divides and is two, but two is inconceivable save as Three;
hence the Trikaya, the Trinity in all its forms. In manifestation there is Mind Only, and the appearance of Mind. This
relative world is subject to interrelation of causation, and
the law of Cause-Effect controls all manifested things.
Morality is the cleansing and development of the vehicles
through which the individual expresses the Absolute within;
psychology an understanding of the processes of the mind.
The Goal is Nirvana, the end of separation, the return to
the One, to THAT.

BIBLIOGRAPHY

FOR CHAPTER FIFTEEN

Bell, Sir Charles. *The Religion of Tibet.*
   Portrait of the Dalai Lama.
Combe, G. A. *A Tibetan on Tibet.*
David-Neel, Mme Alexandra. *Initiations and Initiates in Tibet.*
   With Mystics and Magicians in Tibet.
Ellam, J. E. *The Religion of Tibet.*
Evans-Wentz, W. Y. *The Tibetan Book of the Dead.*
   Tibetan Yoga and the Secret Doctrine.
Heron-Allen, E. *Gods of the Fourth World.*
Marquès-Rivière, T. *Tantrik Yoga, Hindu and Tibetan.*
Waddell, L. A. *The Buddhism of Tibet.*
Woodroffe, Sir John (Arthur Avalon). *Shakti and Shakta.*

Iconography
Bhattacharyya. *The Indian Buddhist Iconography.*
Getty. *The Gods of Northern Buddhism.*
Gordon. *The Iconography of Tibetan Lamaism.*
   Tibetan Religious Art.
Heron-Allen. *Gods of the Fourth World.*

In addition, there are many illustrated travel books on Tibet which – to some extent – describe the religion. Perhaps the best are McGovern's *To Lhasa in Disguise*, David-Neel's *My Journey to Lhasa*, Bell's *The People of Tibet*, Bernard's *Land of a Thousand Buddhas*, Pallis, *Peaks and Lamas*, Evans-Wentz, W. Y., *The Tibetan Book of the Great Liberation*, Maraini, Fosco, *Secret Tibet*, and Riencourt, Amaury de, *Lost World; Tibet, Key to Asia.*

CHAPTER SIXTEEN

The Fruits of Buddhism

*

Buddhist Art – First Beginnings – Asokan Art – Eastern and Western Art – The Art of Gandhara – Kushan Art – Sanchi and Amarāvati – Gupta Art – The Dissemination of Buddhist Art – Buddhist Art in China – Buddhist Art in Japan – Buddhist Culture.

BUDDHISM spread like a tide through Asia; what is there to show for its coming? This is a difficult question, for religion is a flower which fruits in the mind, and Buddhism in particular is a religion-philosophy of individual enlightenment. Who can say how many have attained to that Enlightenment? How many have by its means moved forward upon the Way? One can but consider the visible fruits of Buddhism in its art, its culture and its effect upon the character of those who have made it their way of life.

Buddhist Art

The West has already learnt much of Indian art, Chinese art and Japanese art, but little of Buddhist art as such. Yet as the late Professor William Cohn, one of the greatest authorities on the subject, has said, 'It is clear that the experience of Buddhist art must have a profound experience for us. In all fields – in painting, sculpture, architecture and handicraft – Buddhism has produced works of art that can be placed by the side of the highest creations of Western art'.[1]

One can go further. A careful examination of the art of Eastern countries in the light of Buddhist history enables one to say that the finest Indian art up to the sixth century A.D., and the finest of Chinese and Japanese art at any period since the introduction of Buddhism, is Buddhist art; that all great art in Ceylon, Burma and Siam is Buddhist art; that the Stupa of Borobadur is Buddhist art, and that the religious art of Tibet and Nepal is equally Buddhist. If this is

1. Berkeley Galleries Leaflet No. 2, *Buddhism in Art.*

surprising to those who still regard Buddhism as gloomy and
pessimistic, as exhorting all men to eschew the delights of
the senses and to flee from the world into annihilation, let
them study the Pali Canon itself.

Once, it is written, the venerable Ananda said to the
Exalted One, 'The half of the holy life, Lord, is friendship
with the lovely, association with the lovely, intimacy with
the lovely.' Said the Exalted One, 'Say not so, Ananda;
it is the whole, not the half of the holy life. Of a
monk who has friendship, companionship, intimacy with
the lovely, this is to be expected, that he will develop
the aryan Eightfold Path, make much of it' (*Samyutta
Nikaya*).

The Buddhist, however, distinguishes between the pursuit
of abstract beauty, as an expression of that Reality which he
seeks in Enlightenment, and the delights of its perishable
forms. The fool regards the outward form as attractive in
itself; the Buddhist controls the desires of the senses while
using the food provided by them to achieve the beauty
which those forms enshrine. As the individual pupil learns
through the senses to eschew the form in favour of the life
within, so the teacher uses the beauty of the world to teach
the way to Enlightenment. 'The Buddha himself renounced
the world and all its vanities, but the spiritual Sangha which
he founded appropriated, for the purpose of its propaganda,
the artistic heritage of the Aryan people of India.'[1] Only
thus can one explain the sensuous, not to say erotic, attraction of many of the carvings and paintings on the finest of
Buddhist creations. Many of the Ajanta frescoes, for example, breathe a spirit of: 'Such are the snares of desire, but
behold the Master's cool disdain of them. Be ye likewise
dispassionate in order that, passing beyond the forms of
beauty, ye may find itself.'

First Beginnings

Buddhist art began at the Buddha's passing, for the Scriptures say that he gave instructions as to the *Stupa*, or
reliquary mounds, to be erected over his ashes, and the four
places which should be used for pilgrimage. Whether or not
he gave any such orders, the cult of Stupa worship and pilgrimage was certainly of early origin. Soon, at the site of each

1. Havell, *Handbook of Indian Art*, p. 29.

Stupa there would be a *Chaitya* or shrine, later becoming a temple, and a railed passage about the Stupa for the perambulation of pilgrims, which later lent itself to elaborate decoration. Later again came the permanent *Vihara*, at first a Meeting Hall, but developed into a monastery gradually to replace the simple homes for the rainy season built in the Buddha's time. These finally acquired immense and beautifully carved pillars with ornate capitals.

But even when the carved reliefs about these buildings reached the dimensions and quality of memorable art, there was no attempt at iconography, and the Buddha image did not appear until at least four hundred years after the Founder's passing. His presence in the countless Jataka tales and scenes from the Scriptures, which soon adorned each foot of available space on Buddhist architecture, was shown by a Tree (the Bodhi Tree), a Wheel (the Wheel of the Law set turning at Sarnath), a Stupa (his burial mound), or else by the Footprints, or an empty saddle or throne, or even by his umbrella, for the umbrella had long been a royal symbol and is used by royalty in eastern countries to-day.

Of this earliest art no single object survives. All was of wood, and the wood has perished. Later, so sacred had the wooden models become that the stone equivalents were carved to represent the joiner's art, and the stone rails of Sanchi, for example, exhibit the joints appropriate to a wooden screen.

Asokan Art

With the reign of Asoka, all is changed. Stone and brick replaced wood, and enormous marble pillars were erected to commemorate the Emperor's conversion to Buddhism, or to place great precepts before the public eye. It is said that the capitals of these pillars are copies of Persian art; they are, however, but a stylized lotus, and the lotus was at an early date an Indian Buddhist symbol. It is just as likely that the craftsmen of Persepolis borrowed the lotus from India as that Asoka, with a wealth of symbols about him, should borrow from Persia. However this may be, all other Asokan art is purely Indian. The original Stupa at Sanchi, the rail about the site of the First Preaching at Sarnath, and the original Stupa at Amarāvati; all these are probably Asokan.

But as the Emperor's Buddhism was that of the Theravada the needs of the 'Church' were simple and Puritan in design. The Stupa-house at Karli, near Bombay, one of the first cave-temples to be built (first century B.C.) has but a nave, two aisles and, where the altar would stand in a Western chapel, a Stupa surmounted by a wooden umbrella. To the same Sunga period (180–80 B.C.) must be assigned the great Stupa at Bharhut. Here the charming if somewhat naïve reliefs are dated, making it easier to date the equivalent but finer work of Sanchi. All these great works display the love of animals and flowers which springs from a sense of the oneness of creation, and already the essential difference between Eastern and Western art is fully in evidence.

Eastern and Western Art

Generally speaking Eastern art is more subjective, symbolic, abstract and impersonal; Western art is more objective, representative, concrete, personal. Buddhism teaches that things are created by the mind rather than that the mind perceives existing things. It is therefore concerned with interpreting values rather than describing facts. It is seldom realistic or naturalistic in the Western sense. The sculptor or painter is describing a memory picture, a compound of thought and feeling based on past experience. To achieve this inner vision he strives, if need be with the aid of religious exercises, to become the object which he wishes to portray. He attempts to attune his mind to the subject, and to express the result. For the basic principle of Eastern thought is identity. 'Applied in the field of artistic activity, this is a definition of the highest form of conception, the purest kind of inspiration. The knower becomes the object of his knowledge, the artist the thing he visions or conceives, and if he possesses the proper means of exteriorization, he will transmit in symbols or shapes or signs something which contains a spark of that eternal stream of life or consciousness which abides when forms decay.'[1] As Dr Le May says, 'The Eastern artist is aware that he cannot reproduce the actual or real object either in stone or on canvas; his aim is to try and reproduce the idea behind the

1. Osvald Siren, 'Ch'an (Zen) Buddhism and its Relation to Art'. *The Theosophical Path*, October, 1934.

object. In short, he is the agent of the universal as opposed to that of the individual soul. . . .'[1]

The Buddhist artist never used a model for his portrayal of the Buddha or his Arhats. Always he strove to express the ideal man in human form, whereas the Greeks portrayed their men as gods. Nor did he consciously create a work of art. His aim was to teach, by the symbolic value of his artifact, the way to the spiritual experience of which his art was the outward and visible sign. Aesthetics had no part in his thought, and our Western valuation of a Buddhist work of art as being or not being 'beautiful' is irrelevant to its original purpose.

These complementary principles of East and West were well displayed when the so-called 'Graeco-Buddhist' School of Gandhara, spreading down into India in widening circles of influence, met the expanding waves of Mahayana thought which flowed up from the plains. For the Buddhism which mated with the Western canons of art was Mahayana Buddhism, an ethical philosophy which, with the rise of the devotional element, had newly become a religion, and was therefore ripe for iconography. Already, in the reliefs of Bharhut, Sanchi and Amarāvati, we may see the intense devotion paid to the mute symbols of Buddhahood, and Bhakti Yoga, indigenous to Indian soil, could not be long omitted from developed Buddhism. Already, it would seem, with the new-found development of sculpture in the round, images of the Buddha were being created at Mathura and in other parts of India, and the time had come for the full translation of Gotama the man into Buddha, the incarnate Principle of Enlightenment. The effect on art was tremendous, for the spirit of worship released and gave expression to the higher emotions in which the roots of all great art are found. When to this deep devotion to the spirit of Buddhahood was added the intuitive awareness that life in all its forms is one indivisible Life, and all its expressions but fleeting carriers of that Life, the way was clear for that release of spiritual energy which flowered in the greatest period of Indian art. Flowing as a tide of joy across the width of Asia, it produced the great art of China and Japan, and sings to-day in a thousand examples of the noblest art of mankind.

1. 'The Development of Buddhist Art in Burma'. From the *Journal of the Royal Society of Arts*, June, 1949.

The Art of Gandhara

The country of Gandhara lies at the foot of the North-
West Frontier of India. For centuries the cockpit of contend-
ing empires, races and ideologies, it was converted by Asoka
to Buddhism, and in the first century B.C. began to produce
a 'Graeco-Bactrian' art which influenced, through India, the
art of the whole East. The Western influence was, though
often described as Grecian, actually Roman art; the other
partner in this memorable marriage was the native art of
India. The aesthetic value of the child born of this union has
long been in dispute. Western writers on the subject early
claimed it as the greatest art of India, the product of a virile
Western father by an Indian mother, who, without the aid of
such exogamy, would never have produced such a splendid
child. To this claim an increasing number of authorities reply
that though the Western influence was wide it was never deep,
and its history is but one more example of India's genius for
absorbing such technique or ornament as it finds to its
liking, while continuing undisturbed its own development.
The latest opinion, indeed, is that the earliest Buddha images
of the Mathura School were pre-Gandharan, and that the
latter's history runs parallel to and independent of the main
current of Indian art. Nor was its effect on the latter entirely
good. As Ananda Coomaraswamy says, 'The influence of
the Western forms on all later Indian and Chinese Buddhist
art is clearly traceable; but the actual art of Gandhara gives
the impression of profound insincerity, for the complacent
expression and somewhat foppish costume of the Bodhisattvas, and the effeminate and listless gesture of the Buddha
figures but faintly express the spiritual energy of Buddhist
thought.'[1] In brief, the flower of Buddhist art in India, which
developed in the Gupta period (A.D. 300–600) is purely
Indian. 'India was not then in a state of pupillage, but the
teacher of all Asia, and she only borrowed Western suggestions to mould them to her own way of thinking.'[2]

The Buddha *rupas* or images produced in Gandhara show
to the full their Western genesis. They are personal portraits,
attempts to portray the men like gods, whereas Eastern art
attempts to show gods like men. The postures are Buddhist,

1. *Buddha and the Gospel of Buddhism*, p. 329.
2. Havell, *Indian Sculpture and Painting*, p. 105.

the full 'lotus seat' being early adopted, but the faces and robes are Hellenistic, an influence which persisted right across Asia to Japan. The *ushnisha*, a stylized expression of the flame which streams from the 'Thousand-petalled Lotus' in the brain of an All-Enlightened One, appears as a protuberance on top of the head. The hair, however, is retained, a feature which would seem to be inaccurate, for the Buddha himself cut off his hair, and Bhikkhus have always shaved their heads. The *urna*, or 'third eye' of developed wisdom, is shown as a nodule between the eyes, later jewelled, and the *mudras*, or hand postures, were soon classified into the traditional five. The nimbus, or vertical halo of glory, at first appears as a simple background to the three-dimensional figure; later it grew in size and was elaborately carved.

The Bodhisattvas were shown as kings, representing the temporal as distinct from the spiritual domain of the Buddha. Their robes are elaborate, and they are covered with jewels. More difficult to distinguish at times are the Naga kings or Devas, human forms of the manifold lines of evolution which develop parallel to man. These powerful, non-human entities play a large part in Buddhist iconography. They were early adopted as guardians of the Buddha and his Dhamma, and their lower forms, the nature-spirits of all mythology, are frequently shown at the Buddha's feet or in the sky above him. Such are the *yakshas* on the reliefs of Sanchi; such are the *nats* of Burma and the *devatas* of Ceylon. They sometimes appear in quasi-animal form, and such are the Garuda-birds which reached their full development in Siam. The Gandhara prototype of a Buddha image profoundly affected Indian iconography, but by the third century A.D. the effect of this incident in Indian art was largely spent, and even its innovations had been largely replaced by the older and more profound ideal.

Kushan Art

When the Scythians of West China overran Gandhara, and founded the Kushan kingdom of which Kanishka was the greatest king, Mathura entered its second period as a centre of Indian art. The Gandharan influence, though still appreciable, is waning, and many of the finest figures of this period are purely Indian. It was not, however, until the full flowering of the Gupta period (c. A.D. 300–600) that the

most exquisite works of Indian art were produced, although
in long-used sites like Mathura, Sanchi, Amarāvati and
Ajanta, it is difficult to date any part with strict accuracy.

Sanchi and Amarāvati

The original stupa at Sanchi, erected by Asoka, was later
enclosed in a far larger building, and this was in time sur-
rounded by an elaborate stone railing, with four magnificent
gateways which are still the glory of Buddhist art. Erected
under the patronage of the later Andhra kings (*c.* 70–60 B.C.)
they form, with Amarāvati, the high water mark of stone
relief in India. The Stupa at Amarāvati, destroyed by the
eighteenth century, and known to us to-day only by the
reliefs now in the Madras and British Museums, was probably erected in the second century A.D. Here the plastic skill
of the carvers reached even greater heights than at Sanchi.
The great railing was the largest known, and the devotional
element in the reliefs, though offered still to mere symbols
of Buddhahood, is increasingly in evidence. Contemporary
with this south Indian art is the glorious Rupa among the
trees of Anuradhapura, the original Buddhist capital of Ceylon, which is now regarded as one of the finest in the whole
range of Buddhist art.

Far better known to the West than these, however, are
the caves of Ajanta, the sculptures and frescoes of which are
in continuous development with Sanchi and Amarāvati.
Here the whole history of Buddhist art may be seen in a day,
from early reliefs of the first century B.C. to frescoes of the
seventh century or later. In the twenty-six chaityas or viharas, the art ranges from Puritan severity to a voluptuous
riot of colour and form which belongs, as Ananda Coomaraswamy says, 'to an age which could afford to permit itself
the fullest enjoyment of life, by right of innate virtue.'[1] Here
is some of the noblest art of the world, and whether created
by Buddhist Bhikkhus or Buddhist craftsmen employed by
monasteries, it is Buddhist art. Only in the Sigirya frescoes of
the fifth century A.D. in Ceylon, or in the Horyuji frescoes of
the late sixth century in Japan, has such painting survived elsewhere. But their Buddhism is that of the Mahayana; such a riot
of life and colour would never express the more Puritan School
which, by the eighth century, had virtually died in India.

1. *Introduction to Indian Art*, p. 60.

Gupta Art

The Gupta period is the golden age of Indian art. Between
the fourth and sixth centuries all alien influences were finally
reconciled, and the indigenous tendency to sensuality in
treatment and over-decoration in detail was for a time
successfully curbed. To this period belongs the Temple at
Buddha Gaya, the Damekh Stupa at Sarnath, the best of
Ajanta, and the most beautiful of the images, in stone, bronze
and gold which have survived. Thereafter Buddhism begins
to decline in India, and with it Buddhist art. In the great
cave-temples of Ellora only a part and not the best is Buddhist, and in the caves at Bagh and Aurangabad we reach the
final stage, where the frescoes and sculpture alike show a
decline in power.

Under the Pāla Dynasty of Magadhā (740–1197) a number
of very fine rupas were produced, mostly of fine black slate,
but the intensity of devotion is missing, and if the technique
is often high, the spirit of inspiration is declining to its end.

The Dissemination of Buddhist Art

The Buddhist art of India spread, with the Dhamma,
North and South and East, and even West. Buddhist art
forms crossed the northern hills into Nepal and Tibet. East-
ward the stream of influence flowed along the old silk routes
into China, and thence into Korea and Japan. From the
South of India it reached Ceylon and, by the long sea route,
South China, the two great streams uniting in China to produce that country's richest art.

How Buddhist art reached Burma and Siam, and thence
Cambodia and Java, is a complex story. The routes were as
various as the periods, styles and religious influence which
between them produced some of the greatest buildings and
images in the world. In Burma, rupas of the Pāla Dynasty
of North India abound, but by the twelfth century the Indian
influence shown in the temples of Pagan was absorbed into
a definite Burmese type which, under the influence of the
Sinhalese-Burmese rapprochement of that period, both influenced and was influenced by the earlier Sinhalese art. The
resulting Shwe Dagon pagoda at Rangoon is one of the
existing wonders of the world.

It is difficult to say that there was any truly Siamese art before the Sukot'ai period of the twelfth to the fourteenth century, and even then the architecture and sculpture alike show the influence of many lands. To-day, the Siamese *wat* or temple is characteristic in its roof design and colouring, while its rupas reveal to an unusual degree the dominance of a fluid line over physiological accuracy. Java, first influenced by Buddhist art as early as the sixth century, produced, in the Stupa of Borobadur (eighth to ninth century) the greatest Buddhist work of art extant. Its interminable galleries of Jataka stories in relief, cut with the greatest skill and taste in the difficult volcanic stone, are said to illustrate the *Lalita-Vistara*, and the fact that the sculptors chose this early Sanskrit work of the older School throws light on the migration of Buddhist principles.

The tide of Buddhist art flowed on into China, taking with it not only the sculpture and painting of India, but also its poetry and prose, both of which were destined to be translated eagerly and to affect profoundly the art and culture of China and Japan.

Buddhist Art in China

Experts have written at length on this mighty subject; here there is only room to point out that the great art of China was essentially Buddhist art. From the dawn of history the Chinese showed themselves a practical people, with a love of beauty which is almost a religion in itself. Their reaction to Indian Buddhism was therefore practical and aesthetic. On the one hand Zen Buddhism, essentially earthly and direct, was the Chinese reaction to the flowery metaphysics of Indian thought; on the other, its vital force expressed itself in some of the greatest art of the world.

In the Wei and T'ang Dynasties (fourth to ninth centuries) Buddhist sculpture was rapidly developed into a purely Chinese art, and the pictures, poetry and calligraphy, all closely allied in practice, which flowered in the Sung period (twelfth to thirteenth centuries) carried on the same high tradition, though slowly fading in inspiration as Buddhism lost its initial drive.

Though the Pure Land schools provided a stimulus to the 'devotional' figures of Kwan Yin, Amida, and the like, and the Esoteric School, better known in its Japanese form as

Shingon, was early in the field with its mandalas, or magic circles, the prime force in Chinese art was Zen, then known as Ch'an. Here was a new quality of vision. 'Here we are in a universe which is devoid of tension – not because contrarieties and conflicts have ceased to operate, but because they have somehow become intelligible. Here, in the very contemplation of transiency, we receive a measure of eternity. . . . Here the wheel turns and does not turn. Here the paradox is no longer a paradox, but rather a luminous certitude. Here we are in the very heart of peace.'[1] Being one with all, the Zen artist's mind was also one with nature. As Dr Suzuki says, 'The grandeur, the vastness, the inexhaustibility of nature are in man, and the sensitiveness and mystic impenetrability of the soul lies also in the bosom of nature.'[2] To the man of Zen, nature and man are brothers, born of the same mystery. They need not strive with one another, and when the painter paints a landscape, he expresses part of himself. Hence, with the aid of the high viewpoint of the Chinese artist, the perceiver walks about in a Chinese picture, and enters the mind of the artist. In Zen a flower is a flower, and neither a symbol of eternity nor a botanical specimen. Here is the recipe for drawing bamboos. 'Draw bamboos for ten years, become a bamboo, then forget all about bamboos when you are drawing. In possession of an infallible technique, the individual places himself at the mercy of inspiration.'[3] And the inspiration is Zen.

The use of space in Chinese art is also derived from Zen. To the Chinese mind space is a living reality, and a picture should never be bound by its frame. 'Of the formal elements of design this gift of spacing is China's greatest contribution to the world's art.'[4] For art is concerned with relations rather than with things, and the Zen sense of the unity of all things made it possible to transfer this awareness into art.

Buddhist sculpture at its best is linear, flowing and free. It is essentially rhythmic and plastic, in the sense that it is a three-dimensional projection of the artist's mind. It is neither copied, a sign of degenerate art, nor merely impressionist. It is spontaneous, however elaborate in form, and therefore exhilarating, and more than one writer has pointed out the

1. Iqbal Singh, *Gautama Buddha*, p. 303–4.
2. *Essays in Zen Buddhism*, III, p. 342.
3. Georges Duthuit, *Chinese Mysticism and Modern Painting*.
4. Roger Fry in 'Chinese Art' (*Burlington Magazine* Monograph), p. 8.

essential lightness of touch, almost a sense of gaiety, which appears in even the noblest works of Chinese art. The variety is as vast as the technique is various, and the virility of thought, the spiritual drive, it might be called, which infuses the smallest object, is a witness to the power of Zen to inform and seek expression through the human mind.

Buddhist Art in Japan

Of Buddhist art in Korea one need only say, in the words of Andreas Eckardt, 'Korea received from China her script and literature, her philosophy and her religions – Confucianism, Taoism and Buddhism – and passed them on to Japan; she forms the natural link or bridge between the Middle Kingdom and that of the Rising Sun.'[1]

Buddhist art in Japan developed from but was never a mere imitation of Chinese art. From the first introduction of Chinese influence its spirit was approved, adopted and venerated, and it is to be noted that much of the finest of Chinese art survives to-day only in Japan, as witness the works, if they are not later copies, of the greatest of Chinese painters, Wu Tao-tzu. Yet Japanese art can stand on its own feet, and some of the early wooden figures of guardians of temples, for example, belong to the finest art in the East.

Japanese art was always integral with national life; the spiritual, aesthetic and utilitarian life of the nation progressed as a whole. Its essence, as compared with China, was restraint. Opposed to the flamboyant, almost aggressive virility of Chinese art is the chastity of taste in everything Japanese, from the lines of a temple building to the knot of a girdle. Japanese art is feminine to the older civilization's masculine appeal. The Japanese have, *par excellence*, what the Scriptures of Zen in China sometimes advised in vain, a knowledge of where to stop. In their gardens, as in their architecture, in the arrangement of flowers as in their dress, the minimum is expressed and the maximum left for the beholder to supply. All this is the teaching of *Sunyata* applied to art. The elaborate and ornate, sometimes beloved of China, was to be avoided, 'as building up a wall or barrier instead of letting the thought of the artist pass free and full with the mind of the beholder. A hint, a suggestion sufficed.'[2]

1. *History of Korean Art*, p. 88.
2. Binyon, *The Spirit of Man in Asian Art*, p. 165.

The Japanese aim at *wabi*, an impossible term to translate. Dr Suzuki calls it 'aloofness in the midst of multiplicities', and it is akin to the 'poverty' of the Christian mystic. It is simplicity in all things, and the absence of visible skill. 'A solitary branch of the plum in bloom among the snow-covered woods – here is the idea of *wabi*',[1] and this, the last word in aesthetic refinement, reached its most perfect flowering in the *cha-no-yu* or 'tea ceremony'. Here is but the making and drinking of tea, but in a mood and with a quality of self-control which makes of every act a sacrament.

Yet the creators of the tea ceremony were not society women, but warriors, devotees of Bushido, the knightly cult of the Japanese Middle Ages which produced the finest swordsmen and the finest swords yet known to history. The Japanese *samurai* was beyond the fear of death, for in meditation he had faced and defeated it. Yet such a man would lay aside his swords and practise the delicate handling of a cup or the 'right' place for each stone in his garden. Here strength and gentleness combined, and the Middle Way was that of Buddhism.

Buddhist Culture

The effect of Buddhism on the culture and character of the peoples who adopted it has yet to be studied in full, and here is not the place for it. This, however, may be said, that always it fought against caste; always it fought for the freedom of women. Its love for animals and nature is proverbial, and the value placed upon the individual has always gone hand-in-hand with a remarkable tolerance. The Buddhist's purpose in life is to raise the quality of living as distinct from the standard of living, to eliminate the self which hides the light of his own Enlightenment rather than to improve the comfort of his worldly life. His proudest creation is therefore his own character, and if the average Buddhist is far from a perfect exemplar of his Master's Teaching, history has shown that the fruits of Buddhism have been not only great art and culture, but, what is greater still, great men.

1. Suzuki, *Zen Buddhism and its Influence*, p. 139.

BIBLIOGRAPHY

FOR CHAPTER SIXTEEN

Buddhist Art in General
  Foucher, A. *The Beginnings of Buddhist Art.*
  Grünwedel, A. *Buddhist Art in India.*
  Vogel, J. P. *Buddhist Art.*

Indian and Indonesian Art
  Basham, A. L. *The Wonder that was India.*
  Brodrick, Alan Houghton. *Little China. Little Vehicle.*
  Coomaraswamy, Ananda. *Introduction to Indian Art.*
    'The Origin of the Buddha Image' (from *The Art Bulletin*).
  Cunningham, Sir A. *Mahabodhi* (The Temple at Buddha Gaya).
    The Stupa of Bharhut.
  Havell, E. B. *A Handbook of Indian Art.*
    Indian Sculpture and Painting.
  India Society, The. *The Bagh Caves.*
  Kramnisch, Stella. *The Art of India Through the Ages.*
  Krom, N. J. *The Life of Buddha on the Stupa of Borobadur.*
  Mitton, G. E. *The Lost Cities of Ceylon.*
  Rowland, Benjamin. *The Art and Architecture of India.*

Burmese Art
  Le May, Reginald. 'The Development of Buddhist Art in Burma'
    (*Journal of the Royal Society of Arts*, June, 1949).

Siamese Art
  Le May, Reginald. *Buddhist Art in Siam.*
    The Culture of South-East Asia.

Chinese and Japanese Art
  Anesaki, M. *Buddhist Art.*
  Binyon, Laurence. Article on 'Painting in Chinese Art' (a
    Burlington Magazine Monograph).
  Carter, Dagny. *China Magnificent.*
  Cohn, William. *Chinese Painting.*
  Fenellosa, Ernest. *Epochs of Chinese and Japanese Art.*
  Hobson, R. L. *The Romance of Chinese Art* (Garden City Pub-
    lishing Co., New York).
  Suzuki, D. T. *Zen Buddhism and its Influence on Japanese Culture.*

Korean Art
  Eckardt, Andreas. *History of Korean Art*.

General
  Binyon, Laurence. *The Spirit of Man in Asian Art*.
  Cranmer-Byng, L. *The Vision of Asia*.
  Gordon, Antoinette. *Tibetan Religious Art*.
  Grousset, René, *The Civilisations of the East* (India, China and
    Japan).
  Humphreys, Christmas. *Via Tokyo*.
  Le May, Reginald. *The Culture of South-East Asia*.
  Mason, J. W. T. *The Creative East*.
  Saunders, Kenneth. *A Pageant of Asia*.
  Vincent, Irene Vongehr. *The Sacred Oasis*.

CHAPTER SEVENTEEN

Buddhism To-day

*

IN 1946 I visited most of the countries where Buddhism is active, and was therefore able to add personal observation to wide reading and correspondence on the condition of Buddhism in the post-war world. The result was the firm opinion that, save in China, the power of Buddhist principles has nowhere declined, and that in several countries it is steadily increasing. The unit, however, remains the country. There is little sign yet of a World Buddhism as an organized world force, although the pressure of Communist persecution in the Far East may assist in its creation. In 1950 the World Fellowship of Buddhists was founded by Dr G. P. Malalesekera in Colombo, and Congresses, largely attended, have been held every other year in Colombo, Tokyo, Rangoon, Katmandu, and Bangkok. But Buddhism does not easily lend itself to world organization, nor indeed to any organization. Its stress is on individual effort towards individual enlightenment. It has no yearning for secular power, and to the extent that members of the Sangha dabble in politics they are degrading the Robe. Buddhism has no Pope, and nowhere, save in Tibet, has the 'Church' temporal authority. International co-operation, therefore, is largely concerned with the interchange of ideas on doctrine and the best way to proclaim it. It is as a spiritual force alone that Buddhism affects and will increasingly affect the modern world.

In the individual nations, however, the Sangha and its Dhamma have much to say. In Japan, for example, Buddhism is having a remarkable revival, and this in spite of American effort to induce the Japanese to accept Christianity as the proper companion to more material blessings. The Japanese reply, it would seem, is to hand to visitors at any temple door a copy of the 'Twelve Principles of Buddhism', which the Japanese Schools of Buddhism agree to be their common ground. Indeed, the latest information goes further. As Mr Jack Brinkley, son of the famous author of *Japan and China*, writes from Japan, 'Without exaggeration they [the Twelve Principles] have been one of the most important causes of the Buddhist revival in Japan, for there is no doubt that a big awakening is taking place amongst the rank and file of Japanese Buddhists.' And as he had given over 7,000 lectures on Buddhism throughout Japan in the last ten years, his opinion is of some value.

In China alone has Buddhism, along with other religions, rapidly declined.[1] The influence of Confucius is still in evidence, but the younger generation are concerned for the most part with Western politics and what they believe to be Western ideology. What the effect of Communist control will be it is difficult yet to say but it is not likely to be favourable to a genuine revival of Buddhism.

Turning to the Theravada School, Cambodia is part of a complex of races and religions which occupy the South-East Asian peninsula, and it is difficult to form an accurate opinion when conditions are so confused. On the one hand there seems to be a decline of all religion under the pressure of civil war; on the other hand, an increasing number of Buddhist Societies are appearing all over the peninsula, presumably in answer to an increasing need.

In Thailand, or Siam, the only Buddhist kingdom, vigorous attempts are being made by the Sangha to bring themselves in touch with modern thought. The language being the obstacle to greater contact, more and more of the Bhikkhus are learning English, and an increasing number of works on Buddhism are being translated from and into Siamese. The leaders of the Sangha are using the national radio for weekly talks, and the Buddhist Association of Thailand, under royal patronage, is becoming increasingly powerful. In Burma, the threat of Communism has stimulated interest in the Buddhist way of life as the basis of national recovery. The interference in politics by members of the Sangha was fiercely resented by the laity, and Burma is still very much a Buddhist country in the sense that Buddhism is the dominating, though not always obvious, influence in the people's lives. A recent development, about the value of which there is considerable discussion, is a new system of meditation devised to reduce the time in which to obtain at least some apparent results. But there is little support to be found in Buddhist history for the belief that spiritual development can be hastened, least of all to suit the needs of the modern restless and impatient

1. See John Blofeld, *The Jewel in the Lotus*.

mind. According to tradition the Path is a long, slow road to
Enlightenment, and the effect on those of the West who sample
the new technique is, even when claimed to be good, seldom
permanent.

Ceylon, too, is showing vigorous signs of Buddhist life,
in spite of political interference which, however well-meaning,
is seldom of service in the end. The feel of the country is
still predominantly Buddhist, in spite of the Hindu element
provided by the descendants of the Tamil invaders of the
Middle Ages. With the end of foreign control, large-scale
plans were put in hand for the increase of Buddhist education
and the restoration of Buddhist monuments. The condition
of the Sangha is reasonably high. In brief, Buddhism in Ceylon
to-day is extremely virile, as is shown by the fact among others
that it has the surplus energy to send missions all over the Buddhist world, and to man and finance the ever-increasing
branches of the Maha Bodhi Society.

India, as the West does not always appreciate, ceased to
be a Buddhist country about the eleventh century A.D. The
Maha Bodhi Society, however, founded in 1891 by the late
Anagarika Dharmapala of Ceylon, is hard at work through
the length and breadth of India. Not only does it care for
pilgrims visiting Buddha Gaya and the other sacred sites of
Buddhist India, but it preaches the Dhamma far and wide,
and has provided schools and libraries, temples and book-
shops to an extent which excites the profound respect and
generous benefaction of an increasing number of Hindus.

A movement of as yet unknown importance in the return
to Buddhism in India is the mass conversion to a nominal
Buddhism by the late Dr Ambedkar of literally hundreds of
thousands of the Hindu 'untouchables'. It is easy to pass this
by as a mere political gesture, but those working to consolidate
the initial effort take a different view.

The present and future of Buddhism in Tibet are alike
unknown, but the world as a whole will suffer if the religion
and culture of this fascinating country are to be rubbed from
the face of the earth almost without protest.

East and West

The world grows daily smaller, and even as Western
thought and science is now studied throughout the East, so
Eastern thought and its older science of the mind increasingly

invades the West. Alone of the world's religions Buddhism
has nothing to fear from two activities of the modern Western mind, namely, the 'higher criticism' of previous ideas
and alleged authorities, and science, using the term in its
largest scope. As to the first, the Buddhist attitude to all
phenomena and to all teaching about it has ever been that
of the modern scientist. Let all things be examined dispassionately, objectively, assuming nothing, testing all, for
such was the Buddha's own injunction to his followers. Western science to-day is rapidly approaching the conception of
Mind-only, and a remarkable feature of the recent change in
the basis of physics is that the very terminology of its new
discoveries might be paralleled in Buddhist Scriptures compiled 2,000 years ago. Truly, Buddhism has nothing to fear
from Western science, and in the world of mind, including
that cinderella of mental science, psychology, the West has
more to learn from Buddhism than as yet it knows.

The range of Buddhism, as already observed, is enormous,
and within its vast and tolerant field all manner of human
thought has welcome, and every method of treading the Way
its honourable place. 'The ways to the Goal are as many as
the lives of men.' Buddhism embraces half the world of
geography and at least as much of thought, yet the utmost
tolerance prevails. If the central core of the Pali Canon be
'fixed', the peripheral teachings of the Mahayana are infinitely flexible and various, and even as the Dhamma
acclimatized itself in the countries of the Far East, so it has
settled down and is fast becoming at home in Western
thought and life.

Buddhism in England

No one knows when Buddhism first came West. Clement
of Alexandria wrote of 'those of the Indians that obey the
precepts of Boutta, whom through exaggeration of his dignity, they honour as God'. But apart from this and other
references to an 'Indian God' of some such name, our
knowledge begins with the first translations of Buddhist
Scriptures into Western tongues. Burnouf, Hodgson, Csoma
de Körös, Schlagintweit and Rockhill, these are the pioneers
of western Buddhism. They were followed by Oldenberg,
Beal, Childers and Fausböll, who paved the way in turn for
Max Müller, the founder and editor of the famous *Sacred*

Books of the East. Our knowledge of the Pali Canon as a whole, however, will always be coupled with the names of Professor and Mrs Rhys Davids, who, through the Pali Text Society, gave us the Pali Canon and commentaries in Roman script, and then a complete translation into English, together with numerous text-books of their own. These men and women, and others alive to-day, gave Buddhism to the Western world, and all in the West who claim to be Buddhists are paying tribute by that claim to those who made it possible.

To the close of the nineteenth century Buddhism was the concern of scholars alone, and this in spite of the enormous success of Sir Edwin Arnold's *Light of Asia*, which, with this book, is still the most potent evangelist in the literature of western Buddhism.

In 1905 the first English practising Buddhist began to lecture on Buddhism from the traditional soap-box in Regent's Park. He was R. J. Jackson, who, with J. R. Pain, an ex-soldier from Burma, opened a bookshop in Bury Street, Bloomsbury, for the sale of Buddhist literature. In 1906 these two men founded a Buddhist Society of England, and soon got in touch with an Englishman, Allan Bennett, who had taken the Robe in Burma in 1902 under the name of Ananda Metteya. With the aid of J. F. M'Kechnie, who himself took the Robe as the Bhikkhu Silacara, he founded in Rangoon a magazine called *Buddhism*, and sent this to England as advance information of his projected Mission to the West. In preparation for his coming the first Society was expanded into the Buddhist Society of Great Britain and Ireland, with Professor Rhys Davids as President, and a most distinguished Council. In April, 1908, Ananda Metteya arrived in England from Burma at the head of the first Buddhist Mission to the West, and became the heart of the new organization. The work of this Society, and its organ, *The Buddhist Review*, was a notable step in the process of converting academic study into a living religion for western people. For the first time Englishmen met Buddhist Englishmen who were proud of their new way of life, and thousands regarded with fresh eyes the Doctrine which most had considered a museum specimen.

For sixteen years the Society proclaimed the Dhamma to the British Isles, but when, in 1923, Ananda Metteya published his swan-song, *The Wisdom of the Aryas*, and thereafter died, a new impulse was required, and another English Buddhist arose to supply that need. Francis Payne, one of the first 'converts' of R. J. Jackson, and an early member of the first Society, was a true evangelist. He loved the Buddha, the Dhamma and the Sangha as with a living flame. With tremendous energy he gathered about him the remaining members of the old Society, and delivered a memorable series of thirty-six lectures on Buddhism at the (now bomb-destroyed) Essex Hall in the Strand. The increasing audience at the lectures became the founding members of a short-lived Buddhist League, and their enthusiasm was infectious.

I myself attended some of the lectures, and having been interested in Buddhism since, at the age of seventeen, I first read Ananda Coomaraswamy's *Buddha and the Gospel of Buddhism*, I formed a Buddhist Centre in the Theosophical Society, of which I was then a member. On the 19th November, 1924, the Centre became a Lodge, the Charter being handed to me by Mr C. Jinarajadasa, himself a distinguished Sinhalese Buddhist and later President of the Theosophical Society. Thus was born the Buddhist Lodge, which in 1943 became the Buddhist Society, London, with affiliated organizations and correspondents in most corners of the world.

In the twenties of this century the Buddhist element in London was strongly rationalist and ethical, and largely concerned with the negative philosophy of 'No-God, no-soul'. Yet, though at first mainly of the Theravada School, it was early affected by the interest in Buddhism shown by English Theosophists, whose forty years of teaching similar doctrines had prepared the English mind, to an extent which English Buddhists are slow to acknowledge, for the Buddha-Dhamma.

In 1925 the Anagarika Dharmapala, already mentioned, arrived in London from Ceylon to form a Branch of the Maha Bodhi Society, and was received and assisted by the Buddhist Lodge. Some years later the Mission was strengthened by three Sinhalese Bhikkhus led by the Ven. P. Vajiranana, later President of the Ceylon Branch of the Maha Bodhi Society, and by the publication of its organ, *The Wheel*. For the next fourteen years, until the opening of the Second World War, when the Mission closed down, the two Societies worked side by side with complementary activities. But whereas the Mission at all times stressed the Buddhism of the Theravada, the Buddhist Society, as it later became,

T-H

adhered to no one School, and to this day impartially studies, teaches and endeavours to apply the whole of Buddhism.

In 1926 the Lodge seceded from The Theosophical Society, and became independent. In the same year its mimeographed organ, the *Buddhist Lodge Monthly Bulletin*, edited by A. C. March, was first printed as *Buddhism in England*, a name which, in 1943, was changed to *The Middle Way*. A Buddhist Shrine was opened in Lancaster Gate, to the north of Hyde Park, and a Buddhist Library founded. Meetings were held, at first, in private houses, later at its own premises in Great Russell Street, near the British Museum, and now at 58 Eccleston Square, S.W.1. The Festival of the May Full Moon (*Wesak*), which is the Buddhist New Year and equivalent to Christmas, was jointly celebrated by all London Buddhists, for though the difference between the Schools is inevitably reflected in English Buddhism, the Society, which belongs to no one School, provides a common platform for this great occasion, and the function grows in importance in the life of London year by year.

The interest of Buddhist countries in the Western presentation of the Dhamma has always been considerable. The original Mission to England in 1908 was sponsored by Burmese effort and Burmese funds, and Burmese members have always formed a substantial proportion of the Society's membership. The King of Siam was the first Patron of the Buddhist Society in Great Britain and Ireland, and the Siamese Ambassador in London, on behalf of the Buddhist Association of Thailand, presented the present Society at its Silver Jubilee with a replica of Siam's most famous Buddha Rupa and a magnificent Shrine of lacquered teak in which to place it. Ceylon founded a London branch of the Maha Bodhi Society in 1925, and thereafter sent a succession of Bhikkhus to spread the Dhamma in the West, and it was the late Ven. Tai Hsü of China who brought about the foundation of 'Les Amis du Bouddhisme' in Paris. As for Japan, Dr D. T. Suzuki, by writing his most famous works on Zen Buddhism in English, brought a knowledge of this flower of Buddhism to the West, while the Tibetan Trade Mission to London in 1948 were as delighted to find such widespread interest in Buddhism as they were eager to assist in it by closer contact with Lhasa.

The interest between Western Buddhists and the Sangha

has always flowed both ways. Western students have entered the Sangha of both Schools, but so long as the 227 Rules of the Theravada have all to be obeyed, there will never be many at any one time who can stand the strain involved. The tendency, at present, therefore, is for those who wish to devote their lives to the study and practice of Buddhism in the East to follow the example of the Anagarika Dharma-pala and to remain on the fringe of the Sangha as an *anagarika*, or 'homeless one', keeping most of the Bhikkhus' Precepts, but retaining the right to adapt the Bhikkhus' life to Western needs. Turning to the reverse of the picture, the difficulties awaiting the Bhikkhu who visits the West are proportionate to the strictness with which he keeps the Rules. If he observes them fully he needs a constant companion for his smallest needs, for he may not even carry a bus fare. There are signs, however, that the Theras of Burma and Ceylon are beginning to face these difficulties, and they have already been grasped by the Bhikkhus, European and Oriental, resident in London. The way was paved by the Ven. U. Thittila of Burma who, in the course of his work as Honorary Lecturer for the Buddhist Society boldly adapted his life to Western conditions while in no way lowering the dignity of the Robe.

In May, 1954, a Vihara was opened by Sinhalese Buddhists at 10 Ovington Gardens, London, S.W., primarily as a home for Bhikkhus of the Theravada School. and in 1956 a house was taken at 50 Alexandra Road, St John's Wood, for a first English Vihara, in the sense of a home for English members of the Order. Already the first full ordination of a Bhikkhu has taken place on English soil, and the yellow Robe of the Sangha may in time be a commonplace of the English scene.

Modern Publications on Buddhism

Western Buddhists have as yet produced few first-class scholars, but the contrary would not be expected. A Western Buddhist is not unusual in his study of Buddhism but in his avowed attempt to live the Buddha-life towards Enlightenment. Yet some of the leading Buddhist scholars are Buddhists in this latter sense, among them Dr Edward Conze, one of the leading Buddhist scholars in the West, John Blofeld, the translator for the Buddhist Society of the teaching of Huang-Po and other Chinese classics, and Dr Carmen Blacker, a keen student of Buddhism in Japan. A. C. March, the founder of the *Middle Way*, the organ of the Buddhist Society first published in 1926, produced the first full *Analysis of the Pali Canon*, and the first separately published *Glossary of Buddhist Terms* to help the new reader cope with the terms in seven languages which would be met in normal Buddhist reading. And the *Middle Way*, now known in every corner of the Buddhist world, is one of the most important contributions of the Society to a Western knowledge of Buddhism.

In 1954 the Society achieved a long ambition in the publication of *Buddhist Texts*, edited by Dr E. Conze which, though published by Bruno Cassirer of Oxford, was inspired by a committee of the Society appointed to prepare such a compendium of extracts from the Scriptures of all schools for the use of Buddhist students. My own *Wisdom of Buddhism*, published in 1960, is an improvement on *Buddhist Texts* only in giving a fair proportion of the space to Zen Buddhism, scarcely mentioned in the earlier work. The Society's own *Buddhist Students' Manual*, published to commemorate its thirtieth anniversary, in November, 1954, should prove, with its brief History of the Buddhist movement in the West, its Glossary of Buddhist terms, its analyses of the Pali and Mahayana scriptures, and full Bibliography, the basic literature for individual study in the enormous field of Buddhism.

Buddhism in Europe

'Les Amis du Bouddhisme' was founded in Paris by Miss Constant Lounsbery, herself American born, in 1929, but whereas the movement in England has been supported mainly by the middle classes, in Paris the leaders of the Society were from the first distinguished members of famous organizations, such as the Sorbonne. Les Amis du Bouddhisme is largely of the Theravada, and makes great use of meditation. It has close links with Ceylon and French Indo-China, and like the Buddhist Society, London, has loosely affiliated bodies in various parts of Europe, and a quarterly Journal, *La Pensée Bouddhique*. The most famous French Buddhist is probably Mme Alexandra David-Neel, whose numerous works on Tibetan Buddhism, based upon first-hand knowledge and practice, have made her a world authority on the subject.

Buddhism was widely studied in Germany between the two world wars, and Dr Paul Dahlke built at Frohnau, near Berlin, the first Western Vihara. Since the recent war numerous groups and societies have come into being in German-speaking countries, and a number of conferences have been held at which attempts were made to co-ordinate these widely-spaced, spontaneous activities. In the same way groups have arisen in Holland and Belgium, Finland, Sweden, and Switzerland. Is it coincidence that such activity always seems to arise from the ashes of war? Of all the great religions Buddhism alone has faced and solved the problem of evil and suffering. Where others merely deplore man's habit of self-murder, the Buddhist explains it and points to the cause, as also to the ending of that cause, desire.

Buddhism in the U.S.A.

The Japanese population on the West Coast of the U.S.A. has for long been large, and with the immigrants came the sects of Japanese Buddhism. The Shin, or Pure Land, school predominates, with Zen, its exact antithesis, following behind. The influence on American thought has been roughly proportionate, for Zen needs fierce enthusiasm and sustained hard work, while the Pure Land doctrine calls for neither. But the American Secretary of the Society in London, specially appointed for the purpose, at one time listed more than a hundred Buddhist Societies, including those of the Japanese, in the U.S.A., and when some Pan-American Buddhist Bureau, or the like, is founded, it may be found that the genuine interest, as distinct from passing phases of no value such as 'Beat Zen', is surprisingly large.

Buddhist Influence in the West

The influence of Buddhism on Western thought is difficult to measure or define. With regard to England, hundreds of enquirers visit the Society every year and buy its literature, while thousands of the public buy its books. But Buddhism, as already indicated, does not lend itself to gregarious activities. It has no devotional 'services', and as it stresses the need of working out one's own salvation, and that with diligence, it does not encourage its members to meet for worship or prayer to a God, or for the better salvation of their 'souls'. Devotion to the Triple Gem of the Buddha, his Dhamma, and the Sangha is to the Buddhist a personal affair, and in Buddhist lands is carried out alone or with a small group of friends. Organized, collective religious activity is, generally speaking, unknown. The Western Buddhist, like his Eastern brother, works alone, and many of those, a small percentage, who do contact a Buddhist Society buy what books they require, attend a meeting or two and then return to their homes with their new discovery. Thereafter, busy with the application of these principles, they have, as they explain (though more politely) no further use for the Society.

Buddhist influence, therefore, will always be out of all proportion to the number of its declared adherents. As only a small percentage of English Buddhists join a Buddhist Society it will never be possible to state the number of Buddhists in England, nor is it easy to say what aspect of Buddhism most appeals to the Western mind. Judging by literature sold, the books most used in the Society's Library, and the questions asked at public meetings, the interest is widely spread. Strangely enough, the present English interest in Buddhism is largely in its two wings, Theravada and Zen, rather than in the solid body of principles between them. Theravada doctrines will always provide for a certain type of English mind a new and sufficient way of life, and this type will never be interested with any intensity in the rest of the vast field of Buddhism. Zen enthusiasts, on the other hand, not only find the ambit of the earlier school quite insufficient for their spiritual needs, but will not willingly study those principles of which Zen Buddhism is the final flower. Yet the English mind in search of a new Way is incurably eclectic, and in his choice the Englishman cares nothing for consistency. The rational basis for the brotherhood of man and the twin principles of karma and rebirth seem the most popular doctrines, while the puritan, rational ethics of the Theravada, the expansive, mystical philosophy of the Mahayana, and the joyous, intuitive intensity of Zen all have their devotees, though the genuine tolerance of the Eastern Buddhist for differing points of view is difficult for the more pugnacious West to acquire. Meditation is steadily increasing, but there is little demand for ritual or for the salvation by faith of the Pure Land Schools of Japan.

The West will never be 'Buddhist', and only the most unthinking zealot would strive to make it so. The Western mind will never be content with second-hand clothing, and all that Western Buddhists have the right to do is to proclaim the Dhamma to all who have 'ears to hear', and to suggest why, and in principle how, it should be applied. It may be that from the mingling streams of the Pali Canon, the compassionate splendour of the Mahayana and the astringent force of Zen will come a Navayana, a new 'vehicle' of salvation. There are many signs of it. Works by Western authors tend to ignore the differences between the two Schools, and to offer a Buddhism which has passed through the crucible of Western experience and Western spiritual needs. Brief ceremonies devised in the West for marriages and cremations are available for Buddhists in England; leading thinkers increasingly express their own discoveries in Buddhist guise. Others go further. Writes Dr Graham Howe: 'In the course of their work many psychologists have found, as the pioneer work of C. G. Jung has shown, that we are all near-Buddhists on our hidden side. ... To read a little Buddhism is to realize that the Buddhists knew, two thousand five hundred years ago, far more about our modern problems of psychology than they have yet been given credit for. They studied these problems long ago and found their answers too. We are now rediscovering the Ancient Wisdom of the East. . . .'[1]

Twelve Principles of Buddhism,[2] printed on a single sheet of paper and now translated into sixteen languages, may well be the handbook of that Navayana, for though all things are subject to change, the informing life which men call Truth moves on to its own high destiny, and where a particular 'yana' or means of self-salvation becomes unsuitable or out of date, another will be found.

It may be, on the other hand, that Buddhism can better serve the West by offering, not the ready-made cathedral of a new philosophy, but the cut and well-used stones of Buddhist principles, to be built into the temple of Western thought as the awakening mind of the West has need of them. That mind is at present eclectic, and may prefer to choose from the store of Buddhist truths the wherewithal for its patent need. The choice might include the unity of life, Mind-only, karma and rebirth to replace a personal God, the alliance of reason and compassion, the reduction of suffering by the reduction of its cause, desire, tolerance for each point of view and, above all, a tested and well-trodden Way which leads, with a trusted Guide to follow, to that peace which passeth all understanding, and which flowers when self is dead.

Peace to all Beings.

1. *Invisible Anatomy*, p. 5.
2. See chapter IV.

BIBLIOGRAPHY

FOR CHAPTER SEVENTEEN

Davids, Mrs Rhys. *A Manual of Buddhism* (Chap. I).
Ellam, John E. *Navayana or Buddhism and Modern Thought*.
Humphreys, Christmas. 'The Development of Buddhism in England' (in *A Buddhist Students' Manual*).
   Via Tokyo.
   Walk On!
Pratt, J. B. *The Pilgrimage of Buddhism*.
Saunders, Kenneth. *Buddhism in the Modern World*.
   Epochs in Buddhist History.

The Buddhist Scriptures

*

A. THE SCRIPTURES OF THE THERAVADA SCHOOL

THE Pali Canon as it stands to-day contains, as Dr E. J. Thomas points out, 'much which does not claim to be in any sense Buddha's utterance. This is recognized by the Buddhist Commentators themselves, as when they explain that certain sentences or whole verses have been added by the revisers at one of the Councils.'[1] With this proviso, it is probably true to say, with Professor Radhakrishnan, that the views set forth in these Pitakas, or Baskets of the Law, 'if not the actual doctrine taught by Buddha himself, are yet the nearest approximation to it we possess. They represent what early Indian Buddhists believed to be the sayings and doings of their master.'[2] It is not, however, legitimate for the Theravadin Buddhist to claim that this Canon contains the earliest known Teaching, for many of the Chinese Agamas are translations of Sanskrit originals at least as old as most of the Pali Canon, and it would seem that both stem from a common collection of recorded sayings. Nor is the Canon as it stands, as already explained, in any sense an authority for what is Buddhism, in the sense that the Bible is so regarded by Christian Fundamentalists. Buddhism knows no 'authority', and the Buddha's recorded words, if the Irishism be excused, are the authority for this lack of it.

The Canon was probably settled at the Third Council, but it was not until the reign of the Sinhalese King Vattagamani (29–17 B.C.) that the Bhikkhus of the day, 'since they saw that the people were falling away (from the orthodox teaching), met together, and in order that the true doctrine might endure, wrote it down in books.'[3] The very origin of Pali, the language used, is in dispute, and Dr Coomaraswamy thinks that this developed form of Magadhi, the dialect of the place of origin of early 'Buddhism', was perhaps only

1. *The Life of Buddha*, p. 249–50.
2. *Indian Philosophy*, Vol. I, p. 343.
3. *The Mahavamsa*, ch. XXXIII.

definitely fixed when the Scriptures were first written down.'[1]

How accurate was the written version, as compared with the agreed wording at the Asokan Council? The answer may lie in the Eastern power of mnemonic memory, and the retention of this wearisome repetition in the recorded version, only partly eliminated in the English translations, makes the Scriptures as they stand the very antithesis of the magnificently terse, dynamic utterance of the English Bible.

The Three Pitakas

The Tipitaka, or three Baskets of the Law, are respectively the Vinaya Pitaka, containing the Rules of the Order and commentaries thereon, the Sutta Pitaka, containing the Sermons or Teaching of the Buddha, and the Abhidhamma Pitaka, meaning 'further' or 'special' Dhamma, a heterogeneous mixture of great value for mind-training, but as an exegesis of Buddhism in no way comparable to the Sutta Pitaka.

The Vinaya Pitaka contains the Patimokkha, or Rules of life binding on all members of the Sangha. The Rules were formulated, elaborated and codified with the passage of time, probably only a few of the present 227 being declared by the Buddha.

By the third century B.C. the Sutta Pitaka had been separated into five Nikayas, known in the parallel Sarvastivadin School as Agamas. The arrangement is purely arbitrary, and for the convenience of memory. A Sutta (Skt: *Sutra*, meaning a thread) was a unit of teaching, in prose or verse, a theme of discourse on which the Master's words were strung as on a Brahman thread. The five Nikayas are the Digha Nikaya, or long Suttas, the Majjhima Nikaya, or medium long Suttas, the Samyutta Nikaya, or grouped Suttas, the curious Anguttara Nikaya, being Suttas arranged numerically, and a fifth collection into which was put all material not amenable to the above classification. This is the Khuddaka Nikaya.

Of the 34 Suttas in the Digha Nikaya, some are famous and some but little used. Their value varies considerably. As Mrs Rhys Davids was one of the first to point out, there are rare jewels embedded in unworthy clay. The most famous is the *Maha-parinibbana-Sutta*, or the Sutta of the Great

1. *Buddha and the Gospel of Buddhism*, p. 259.

Decease, which provides material both for the last three months of the Buddha's life and for some of his most famous and almost certainly authentic utterances.

The Majjhima Nikaya, containing 152 Suttas of medium length, is grouped in fifteen 'vaggas', roughly classified according to subject.

The Samyutta Nikaya contains fifty-six groups of Suttas dealing with connected subjects or persons. It contains a version of the famous Wheel-turning Sermon, the first to be taught by the Buddha after he attained Enlightenment, and various versions of the Wheel of Causation or twelve Nidanas.

The Anguttara Nikaya, or 'Adding one' Collection, contains 2,308 Suttas arranged in 11 groups, or Nipatas, from one to eleven. Thus the second group speaks of two kinds of Buddhas, two virtues of the forest life; the third of the three sorts of monks; the fourth of four ways which lead to heaven, and so on up to the eleven good and bad qualities of a Bhikkhu.

The Khuddaka ('smallish') Nikaya is the repository of all material which did not lend itself to the above treatment, and contains much of the finest material in the Scriptures. As a collection it is late, but it contains some of the oldest material in the Canon. It begins with the Khuddaka-Patha, which might be described as a Manual of the Buddhist life. In this is contained the beautiful *Metta Sutta* on the meaning and use of love, and the *Maha-Mangala Sutta* of the greatest blessings. Next comes the *Dhammapada*, the most famous of all Theravada Scriptures. This set of 423 stanzas, set in 26 vaggas or chapters, is the most perfect ethical manual extant. The aspirant to Enlightenment is given here a moral philosophy sufficient to guide him to the Goal which yet contains no reference to a Saviour, nor to an immortal individual soul which a Saviour might be invoked to save. On a basis of absolute Self-reliance, each pilgrim of the Way is here exhorted and encouraged to achieve his own deliverance from the fires of *raja*, passion, *dosa*, hatred, and *moha*, stupidity or folly, and is given a map to the Road which leads to it. It is therefore no wonder that for 2,000 years or more unnumbered millions of the world have used this guide, and that it is known and reverenced in every Buddhist land.

The *Udana* and the *Itivuttaka* are also famous. Each contains a mixture of prose and verse of ethical and philosophic value, while the *Sutta Nipata* is an immense favourite in the West as well as in the Buddhist East, for it is second only to the *Dhammapada* in the nobility of its thought and the beauty of its language.

Lower in the list come the famous *Thera-gatha* and *Theri-gatha*, the 'Psalms of the Brethren' and of the Sisters or Bhikkhunis, respectively. 'In skilful craftsmanship and beauty these songs are worthy to be set beside the hymns of the Rig Veda and the lyrical poems of Kalidasa and Jaya-deva.' Most of them are songs of joy. 'The burden of all the songs,' Dr Coomaraswamy goes on, 'is the calm delight, the peace beyond words to which they have attained who have left the world and are free from desires and from resentment; each Psalm, as it were, is a little song of triumph. . . .'[1]

Finally, in this Khuddaka Nikaya, are the famous Jataka Tales, usually described as histories of the previous lives of the Buddha. This is inadequate, for they are both less and more. Many of them are folk-lore tales far older than Buddhism, while on the other hand in this esoteric collection of animal fables, many of which found their way into later European equivalents, is an esoteric story of the evolution of human consciousness. Needless to say, this collection of myth and legend has been the inspiration of some of the greatest Buddhist art, from the caves of Ajanta to frescoes of the present day.

The Buddha's Method of Teaching

All these teachings show the repetitive method of the original teaching, or perhaps it is the repetitive form in which, for the sake of transmitting them by word of mouth, the Suttas were cast by the Bhikkhus. All show the same cool level of exposition. There is here no rhetoric, no deliberate appeal to the emotions; only the serene unfolding of a set of truths by which each man might find the way to his own Deliverance. 'Just as the mighty ocean hath but one savour, the savour of salt, even so hath the Dhamma but one savour, the savour of release.' It is for the individual to appreciate the truth of the Teaching, and to act accordingly.

The Buddha's dialectic method was always the same. 'Gautama puts himself as far as possible in the mental

1. *Buddha and the Gospel of Buddhism*, p. 283.

position of the questioner. He attacks none of his cherished convictions. He even adopts the phraseology of the questioner. And then, partly by putting a new and (from the Buddhist point of view) a higher meaning into the words; partly by an appeal to such ethical conceptions as are common ground between them, he gradually leads his opponent up to his conclusion.'[1]

A third characteristic of the Suttas is the rich use of simile and parable, and the Buddhist range of these was never excelled even by the later Christian equivalent. The Scriptures are full of them, and always they are homely, immediate and apt.

The Abhidhamma Pitaka

The Burmese Sangha sets great store upon this complex field of human thought, which is mainly concerned with the nature of consciousness and what is now called psychology. Its language is that of analytic philosophy, and though at times profound in quality it is largely arid of that spiritual insight which alone makes Scriptural 'authority' of value on the Way. Much of it is an all too human commentary on the almost superhuman beauty and insight of the Suttas, and most of it was written long after the Suttas were compiled. Nor is it the main storehouse of Buddhist psychology, for it is from the Nikayas that Mrs Rhys Davids extracted her *Buddhist Psychology*.

Of the post-canonical works, the best known is the *Milinda-Panha*, or 'Questions of King Milinda', which is actually a part of the Siamese Canon, and the *Visuddhi Magga* or 'Path of Purity' of Buddhaghosha, compiled in the fourth century A.D. in Ceylon.

For the English editions of these Scriptures, see the Bibliography to the present work.

B. THE SCRIPTURES OF THE MAHAYANA SCHOOL

The Mahayana has never reduced its Scriptures to a comprehensive system such as the Canon of the Theravada School. They have to be sought in at least four languages, Sanskrit, Tibetan, Chinese and Japanese, and many famous

1. Rhys Davids, *Dialogues of the Buddha*, p. 206.

Sutras and Sastras survive only in a translation from the language in which they were first composed. Nor is it seriously claimed that these Scriptures came from the lips of the historical Buddha, with the result that the distinction between 'authority' and 'commentary' lacks the force which it has elsewhere.

The most complete records of the Mahayana Canon which we have to-day are contained in the collections of the Chinese and Tibetan Tripitaka. Only a small percentage of the contents of these two great Canons has been translated into English, but enough has been done for a fairly accurate knowledge of their contents. Several important catalogues exist with exhaustive analyses of these collections, the most noteworthy being those of Beal, Nanjio and the Taisho Edition for the Chinese Scriptures, and of Csoma de Körös, Sakurabe and of the Tohoku Imperial University for the Tibetan version.

The Chinese and Tibetan Canons include both Hinayana and Mahayana works. The majority of the Hinayana works belong to the Sarvastivadin school, but a few works of the Theravadins, and other schools, are also found.

The Sutra Pitaka of the Chinese and Tibetan Canons consists first of a foundation of very ancient Scriptures which have been common to the various Hinayana Schools throughout the long history of their growth. They are grouped into Nikayas by the Theravadins, into Agamas by the Sarvastivadins. Upon this foundation has been built a considerable superstructure expanded from a small number of special works peculiar to the Mahayana School. Yet, although these Sutras do not exist in the Hinayana Schools as Canonical works, the roots from which they have sprung are often to be seen in the Pali and Sanskrit Sutras of the Hinayana, either in so many words or taught as the traditional implications of various passages. Large numbers of texts have clearly existed side by side for long periods of time without differing in essentials, and the mutual tolerance of the many Schools is shown by the fact that whatever the written development of a particular sect, the basic teaching has never been suppressed, discredited, or allowed to fade away.

In the same way the Vinaya Pitaka contains both Hinayana and Mahayana texts. In the Chinese Canon, the Vinaya Rules of four Hinayana Schools have been included, but in the main both the Rules and their arrangement are similar.

In the Abhidharma Pitaka of the Chinese Canon is found the same division into two main groups. The Hinayana works consist largely of translations into Chinese of the Abhidharma books of the Sarvastivadins, but some divergence exists between them and similar books in the Theravada Abhidharma. The Mahayana Section of the Abhidharma, on the other hand, is quite different in structure from that of either the Sarvastivadins or the Theravadins, and consists of commentaries and sub-commentaries on the main Mahayana Sutras. That such works should be included in the Abhidharma Pitaka is not surprising, as they are analyses of Sutra material in much the same way as the Abhidharma of the other Schools tabulates the contents of the Nikayas or Agamas. The nature of the Mahayana Sutras, however, is such that they do not easily lend themselves to tabular analysis. Thus, although their Abhidharma is still strongly analytic, it is concerned more with commentary than is that of either of the other Schools mentioned. It is noteworthy that in the case of the Theravada School commentaries have generally been preserved outside the main Canon.

In a fourth section the Chinese Tripitaka are works which belong to particular Buddhist sects of China. In this section are included, for example, the 'Sutra of Hui-neng' (T.2007, 2008), 'The Huang-Po Doctrine of Universal Mind' (T.2012), and many other works produced by writers of the Zen sect, together with various catalogues and reference works of more limited interest.

The Tibetan Kanjur and Tanjur is briefly described in the chapter on Tibet and in Dr E. Conze's *Buddhism*, at p. 32. The Scriptures composed within the fold of Japanese Buddhism are not of a standard comparable with the great works of India and China, and need no separate mention.

Pansil

*

Pansil, a contraction of Pancha Sila, the five rules of morality, is the name given to a recitation used in the Theravada for many purposes. It is 'taken' individually before a Buddhist Shrine or collectively at the beginning of a Buddhist meeting of any kind. It begins with the Praise of the Buddha, thrice repeated. This is followed by the Refuge formula, also repeated three times. Finally come five affirmations difficult to translate with an easily memorable phrase. A fuller meaning of these 'Precepts' than that given below would be: 'I undertake the rule of training in the renunciation of attachment to' – the wrong rule of conduct named.

The exact meaning is important to the Western student, who must clearly understand (*a*) that this is not a vow to God or any other Being, but a solemn undertaking to oneself, and (*b*) that it is not even an undertaking never to kill or lie as the case may be, but a vow, taken in silence or aloud, to train oneself to diminish one's attachment to the error specified. For Buddhism is at all times a reasonable Middle Way, and all that a man may usefully undertake is to wean himself with diligence from the ways of darkness (personal desire) and to set himself in the Way of light.

APPENDIX II

Namo tassa Bhagavato Arahato Samma Sambuddhassa!
(Praise to the Blessed One, the Perfect One, the fully Self-Enlightened One!)

Buddham saranam gacchami:
(I go to the Buddha for Refuge)

Dhammam saranam gacchami:
(I go to the Doctrine for Refuge)

Sangham saranam gacchami:
(I go to the Order for Refuge)

Dutiyam pi Buddham saranam gacchami
(Again I go to the Buddha for Refuge)

Dutiyam pi Dhammam saranam gacchami
(Again I go to the Doctrine for Refuge)

Dutiyam pi Sangham saranam gacchami
(Again I go to the Order for Refuge)

Tatiyam pi Buddham saranam gacchami
(A third time I go to the Buddha for Refuge)

Tatiyam pi Dhammam saranam gacchami
(A third time I go to the Doctrine for Refuge)

Tatiyam pi Sangham saranam gacchami
(A third time I go to the Order for Refuge).

Panatipata veramani sikkhapadam samadiyami
(I undertake the rule of training to refrain from injury to living things).

Adinnadana veramani sikkhapadam samadiyami
(I undertake the rule of training to refrain from taking that which is not given).

Kamesu micchachara veramani sikkhapadam samadiyami
(I undertake the rule of training to refrain from sexual immorality).

Musavada veramani sikkhapadam samadiyami
(I undertake the rule of training to refrain from falsehood).

Sura-meraya-majja-pamadatthana veramani sikkhapadam samadiyami.
(I undertake the rule of training to refrain from liquors which engender slothfulness).

A BRIEF GLOSSARY OF EASTERN TERMS
USED IN THIS WORK

Note: Ch – Chinese. Jap – Japanese. P – Pali. Skt – Sanskrit. Tib – Tibetan.

Abhidhamma (P). The 'beyond-*Dhamma*' (q.v.) Pitaka (q.v.) of the Pali Canon. It is highly philosophical and contains an entire system of mind-training.

Ahimsa (P). Non-harming or not-hurting; gentleness to all forms of life.

Amida (Jap). The Buddha viewed as the incarnation of Compassion. The spiritual principle of Buddhahood. An object of worship in the Pure Land Schools.

Anagarika (Skt). Lit: 'Homeless one'. One who enters the homeless life without formally joining the *Sangha* (q.v.).

Anatta (P) (Skt: *Anatman*). The denial of the Atman (of Hindu philosophy) conceived as a personal, immortal 'soul'. One of the Three Signs of Being.

Anicca (P). Impermanence, change. One of the Three Signs of Being.

Arhat (Skt) (P: *Arahant*). The personal ideal of Theravada Buddhism. One who has reached the end of the fourfold Way and attained *Nirvana* (q.v.).

Avidya (Skt) (P: *Avijja*). Ignorance in the sense of Nescience. The first of the Twelve *Nidanas* (q.v.) and the last of the Ten Fetters.

Bhakti (Skt). One of the three principal forms of Indian Yoga. The way of devotion and love for an ideal, usually personified, as in *Amida* (q.v.) Buddha.

Bhikkhu (P) (Skt: *Bhikshu*). A Buddhist monk of the Theravada School. Members of the female Order were called *Bhikkhunis*.

Bhutatathata. See *Tathata*.

Bodhi (Skt and P). Wisdom, Enlightenment, Awakening. Its human faculty is *Buddhi* (q.v.) intuition.

Bodhisattva (Skt) (P: *Bodhisatta*). The ideal of the Mahayana School. Cf. *Arhat* (q.v.). One whose life is dedicated to the service of mankind.

Bön (or **Pön**) (Tib). The indigenous religion of Tibet. A crude form of nature-worship which has affected Tibetan Buddhism.

Bonze (Jap). A Buddhist monk. Cp. *Bhikkhu*.

Buddhi (Skt). The faculty of *Bodhi* (q.v.). The Intuition. Esoterically, the sixth of the seven principles of man.

Chaitya (Skt) (P: *Cetiya*). A tumulus raised over a burial mound. In Buddhism almost synonymous with Dagoba, *Stupa* (q.v.), Tope or Chorten; sometimes used for a hall (for meditation).

Ch'an (Ch). A corruption of *Dhyana* (q.v.). Later further corrupted by the Japanese to *Zen* (q.v.).

Chela (Skt). The disciple or follower of a *Guru* (q.v.).

Deva (Skt). Lit: 'Shining One.' A non-human being. They range from the gods of Oriental mythology to mere nature-spirits.

Dhamma (P) (Skt: *Dharma*). A word of immensely complex meaning. Can mean Law, Norm, Duty, Teaching, Right. In the Theravada School is the Teaching of the Buddha: thus *'Buddha-Dhamma.'* One of the Three Jewels with Buddha and *Sangha* (q.v.). In the Pali plural (Dhamma) can mean things, mental states, elements of existence. In Mahayana has even more metaphysical meaning.

Dhyana (Skt) (P: *Jhana*. Ch: *Ch'an*. Jap: *Zen*). Contemplations union with Reality. The practice of attaining a high state of consciousness, often compared in Mahayana with *Prajna* (q.v.).

Dorje (Tib) (Skt: *Vajra*). The 'thunder-bolt' symbol used in art and ritual magic.

Dosa (P). Hatred, anger, ill-will. One of the 'Three Fires', which cause *Dukkha* (q.v.).

Dukkha (P). Suffering, misery, unhappiness, pain. One of the three 'Signs of Being' with *Anicca* (q.v.) and *Anatta* (q.v.).

Guru (Skt). A spiritual teacher who takes *Chelas* (q.v.) or disciples.

Hinayana (P). The earliest School of Buddhism. Lit: Small vehicle (of salvation), as compared with the large vehicle (*Maha-yana*) (q.v.). The Theravada (q.v.) is the sole surviving sect.

Hoben (Jap). See Upaya.

Jataka. The Jataka Tales or 'Birth Stories' are a collection of 550 mythological stories of former lives of the Buddha.

Jhana. See Dhyana.

Jijimuge (Jap). The doctrine of the Kegon School of the 'unimpeded interdiffusion' of all *Ji*, things. Apparently the last word in the intellectual understanding of the unity of manifestation.

Jiriki (Jap). The way of salvation by 'Self-power' or self-effort as distinguished from *Tariki* (q.v.), the way of salvation by 'Other-power' or an external Saviour.

Jodo (Jap). The Pure Land School of China as developed in Japan. 'Faith' and 'works' have an equal part. This was later developed by Honen and Shonen into the *Shin* (q.v.) School of pure faith.

Kama (Skt and P). Desire, passion, in the sense of sexual passion.

Karma (Skt) (P: *Kamma*). Lit: action, in the sense of action-reaction. The law of moral compensation. A doctrine inseverable from that of Rebirth.

Karuna (Skt and P). Pure Compassion. With *Prajna* (q.v.) one of the two pillars of the Mahayana. The second of the four *Brahma Viharas* of the Theravada.

Koan (Jap). Technical term of Zen Buddhism. A problem which cannot be solved by the intellect. An exercise for breaking its limitations and developing the intuition.

Lobha (Skt and P). Covetousness or greed. An alternative to *Rajas* (q.v.) in the 'Three Fires'.

Mahayana (Skt). Lit: 'great vehicle'. The Northern School of Buddhism, found in Tibet, Mongolia, China, Korea and Japan. It has many forms and branches.

Maitreya (Skt) (P: *Metteyya*). The name of the Buddha-to-be or next Buddha. A famous *Bodhisattva* (q.v.).

Mantra (Skt). Verbal formulas used as incantations in the magic of sound.

Metta (P). Love in the sense of loving-kindness; goodwill. The first of the four *Brahma Viharas*. The subject of the famous *Metta Sutta*.

Moha (P). One of the 'Three Fires'. Mental dullness, infatuation, stupidity. The philosophical doctrine of Maya applied to the human mind.

Mondo (Jap). A form of rapid question and answer used in Zen Buddhism to break the limitations of conceptual thought.

Mudra (Skt). The use of gesture in symbolic magic. All Buddha *Rupas* (q.v.) are shown using one of the recognized *mudras* of the hands.

Nat. The nature spirits of Burma still worshipped in village shrines. Comparable to the *Devatas* of Ceylon.

Nidana (P). The Twelve *Nidanas* are spokes on the Wheel of Becoming, links in the 'Chain of Causation' or *Paticcasamuppada*.

Nirvana (Skt) (P: *Nibbana*). The summum bonum of Buddhism. A state of supreme Enlightenment beyond the conception of the intellect. Annihilation of all we know as the personal, separative self.

Pali. The language of the Theravada Canon. May be written in many scripts. Derived from the Magadhi dialect of North India.

Pansil (P). A shortened form of Pancha Sila, the Five Precepts. A self-vow to abstain from the principal forms of immorality. *See* Appendix Two.

Paramita (Skt and P). The *Paramitas* are stages of spiritual perfection achieved by a *Bodhisattva* (q.v.) on his path to Buddhahood.

Parivarta (Skt). The Mahayana doctrine of 'turning over' acquired merit for the benefit of others.

Pitaka (P). Lit: 'basket'. The three *Pitakas* are the main divisions of the Pali Canon, the *Sutta P.* or Sermons, the *Vinaya P.* or Rules of the Order (*Sangha*, q.v.), and the *Abhidhamma* (q.v.) *P.*

Prajna (Skt) (P: *Panna*). Supreme Wisdom. Distinguished in the Mahaya from *Dhyana* (q.v.).

Puja (Skt). A gesture of worship or respect, usually that of raising the hands, palms together, the height of the hands indicating the degree of reverence.

Rajas (Skt) Restless activity. Passion as passionate anger. One of the 'Three Fires' with *Dosa* (q.v.) and *Moha* (q.v.).

Rupa (Skt. and P). Body, form. As the physical body and personality, one of the five *Skandhas* (q.v.). A Buddha *Rupa* is a Buddha image.

Samsara (Skt and P). Lit: 'faring on' or coming-to-be. The world of becoming. Existence. Life on earth. The antithesis of *Nirvana* (q.v.).

Sangha (P). The third of the Three Jewels of Buddha, Dhamma, Sangha. The Buddhist monastic Order.

Satori (Jap). The goal of Zen Buddhism. A state of consciousness which varies in quality and duration from a flash of intuitive awareness to *Nirvana* (q.v.).

Shin (Jap). The Pure Land School of Japan in its extreme form of salvation by pure faith.

Siddhi (Skt). (P: *Iddhi*). Powers of the mind not yet developed in the average man.

Skandha (Skt) (P: *Khandha*). A collection of parts forming a whole. The elements of existence. The components of the so-called 'self', being *Rupa* (q.v.), Vedana, Sanna, Sankhara and *Vinnana* (q.v.).

Stupa (Skt). A large mound usually covering a relic or relics of the Buddha.

Sunya (Skt). Emptiness, the Void. A doctrine found in the Pali Canon but fully developed in the Mahayana. Suchness (*Tathata*, q.v.) may be described as its quality.

Sutra (Skt) (P: *Sutta*). Lit: a thread, on which teachings were strung. A sermon of the Buddha.

Tanha (P) (Skt: *Trishna*). Craving, desire. The thirst for life. The cause of re-birth.

Tantra (Skt). A School of Hinduism which influenced certain schools of Mahayana Buddhism. The female aspect of nature is emphasized and sexual symbolism is used.

Tariki (Jap). The use of 'Other-Power' for salvation as distinct from Self-Power, *Jiriki* (q.v.).

Tathagata (Skt). A title of the Buddha. Derivation various. It may mean 'he who follows in the footsteps of his predecessors'.

Tathata (Skt). Suchness or Thusness. The quality of *Sunya* (q.v.).

Theravada (P). The doctrine or teaching of the *Thera*, the 'Elders' of the *Sangha* (q.v.) of the Southern School of Buddhism. The sole surviving sect of the *Hinayana* (q.v.).

Trikaya (Skt). The three 'bodies', *kaya*, or vehicles of manifestation of the Buddha; Dharma-kaya, Sambhoga-kaya and Nirmana-kaya. *See* Chapter Eleven.

Upasaka (P). A Buddhist lay disciple. Fem. form: *Upasika*.

Upaya (Skt) (Jap: *Hoben*). A device or temporary means to achieve an end.

Urna (Skt). The jewel or small protuberance between the eyes of a Buddha Rupa representing the 'third eye of spiritual vision'.

Ushnisha (Skt). The protuberance at the top of the head of a Buddha Rupa representing the flame of supreme Enlightenment.

Vihara (Skt and P). A dwelling-place for the *Sangha* (q.v.). A retreat or monastery. A state of mind. Hence the *Brahma Viharas*, the Brahma-like or divine states of mind.

Vinaya (P). One of the three *Pitakas* (q.v.) of the Pali Canon. The Rules of the *Sangha* (q.v.).

Vinnana (P) (Skt: *Vijnana*). Lit: 'without knowledge'. Consciousness. In some sense the reincarnating entity. The fifth of the *Skandhas* (q.v.). One of the Twelve *Nidanas* (q.v.)

Wabi (Jap). A mental condition or mood of serenity. The basis of all Japanese culture and art.

Wat (Siamese). A temple or monastery.

Wesak (Skt: *Vaisakha*). A lunar month corresponding to the Western April–May. The Festival at the Full Moon commemorates the Buddha's Birth, Enlightenment and Passing.

Yana (Skt). Lit: career. A way of salvation, as Maha-*yana* or Hina-*yana* or Nava(new)-*yana*.

Zen (Jap). One of the two main schools of Japanese Buddhism. The 'sudden' or direct approach to Reality, transcending the intellect.

General Bibliography

Note: As a special Bibliography is attached at the end of every Chapter, the purpose of this General Bibliography is to draw the reader's attention to certain works on the subject which, whether or not mentioned in a Chapter Bibliography, are of value in considering the whole field of Buddhism.

Arnold, Sir Edwin. *The Light of Asia.*
Beck, Mrs Adams. *The Splendour of Asia.* Reprinted as *The Life of the Buddha.*
Brown, Brian. *The Story of Buddha and Buddhism.*
Buddhist Society, London, The. *Concentration and Meditation.*
   What is Buddhism? A Buddhist Student's Manual.
Carus, Paul. *The Gospel of Buddha.*
Conze, Edward. *Buddhism, its Essence and Development.*
Coomaraswamy, Ananda. *Buddha and the Gospel of Buddhism.*
Dahlke, Paul. *Buddhism and its Place in the Mental Life of Mankind.*
Davids, T. Rhys. *Buddhism* (S.P.C.K.).
   Buddhism (American Lectures, Putnam).
   Buddhist India.
   Early Buddhism.
Davids, Mrs Rhys. *Buddhism* (Home University Library).
   Gotama the Man.
   A Manual of Buddhism.
   Sakya, or Buddhist Origins.
   What was the Original Gospel in Buddhism?
David-Neel, Mme A. *Buddhism, its Doctrine and Methods.*
Eliot, Sir Charles. *Hinduism and Buddhism.*
Ellam, John E. *Navayana, or Buddhism and Modern Thought.*
Evola, J. *The Doctrine of Awakening.*
Fussell, Ronald. *The Buddha and his Path to Self-Enlightenment.*
Goddard, Dwight. *The Buddha's Golden Path.*
Gour, Sir Hari Singh. *The Spirit of Buddhism.*
Grimm, Georg. *The Doctrine of the Buddha.*
Hackin, T., and others, *Asiatic Mythology.*
Hackmann, H. F. *Buddhism as a Religion.*
Holmes, Edmund, G. *The Creed of Buddha.*
Humphreys, Christmas. *Karma and Rebirth.*
   Studies in the Middle Way
   Thus Have I Heard.
   Walk On!
Keith, A. Berriedale. *Buddhist Philosophy in India and Ceylon.*
Lillie, Arthur. *Buddha and Buddhism.*
Metteya, Ananda, *The Wisdom of the Aryas.*

Narada, Thera. *Buddhism in a Nutshell*.
Narasu, P. Lakshmi. *The Essence of Buddhism*.
Olcott, Col. H. S. *The Buddhist Catechism*.
Power, E. E. *The Path of the Elders*.
Pratt, J. B. *The Pilgrimage of Buddhism*.
Rokotoff, Natalia. *The Foundations of Buddhism*.
Saunders, Kenneth. *The Story of Buddhism*.
Subhadra, Bhikshu. *A Buddhist Catechism*, later republished as *The Message of Buddhism*.
Tachibana, S. *The Ethics of Buddhism*.
Tai-Hsu, Shih. *Lectures in Buddhism*.
Thomas, E. J. *The History of Buddhist Thought*.
Ward, C. H. S. *Outline of Buddhism*.

*The following works
published since the first edition of the book
may also be studied with advantage.*

General
Abegg, Lily. *The Mind of East Asia*. (Thames and Hudson)
Bapat, B. V. (ed.). 2500 *Years of Buddhism*. (Government of India)
Conze, Edward. *A Short History of Buddhism*. (Chetana Ltd, Bombay)
    Buddhism. (Bruno Cassirer)
    Buddhist Thought in India. (Allen and Unwin)
Evola, J. *The Doctrine of Awakening*. (Luzac)
Fussell, Ronald. *The Buddha and his Path to Self-Enlightenment*. (Buddhist Society, London)
Humphreys, Christmas. *The Way of Action*. (Allen and Unwin)
Mehta, P. D. *Early Indian Religious Thought*. (Luzac)
Morgan, Kenneth W. *The Path of the Buddha*. (Ronald Press, New York)
Murti, T. R. V. *The Central Philosophy of Buddhism*. (Allen and Unwin)
Ross, Floyd H. *The Meaning of Life in Hinduism and Buddhism*. (Routledge and Kegan Paul)
Sangharakshita, The Bhikshu. *A Survey of Buddhism*. (Indian Institute of World Culture, Bangalore, India)
Smith, F. Harold. *The Buddhist Way of Life*. (Hutchinson)
Ward, C. H. S. *Buddhism*. Vol. 2 – *Mahayana*. (Epworth Press)
Watts, Alan W. *The Wisdom of Insecurity*. (Rider)

Theravada
Allen, G. F. *The Buddha's Philosophy*. (Allen and Unwin)
Govinda, The Lama Anagarika. *The Psychological Attitude of Early Buddhist Philosophy*. (Rider)
Rahula, Walpola. *What the Buddha Taught*. (Gordon Fraser)

Zen Buddhism and Buddhism in Japan

Benoit, Hubert. *The Supreme Doctrine*. (Routledge and Kegan Paul)

Blyth, R. H. *Zen and Zen Classics*, Vol. I. (Hokuseido Press)

Bunce, William K. *Religions in Japan*. (Tuttle)

Chang Chen-Chi. *The Practice of Zen*. (Harper, New York)

Dumoulin, Heinrich, and Sasaki, Ruth Fuller. *The Development of Chinese Zen*. (The First Zen Institute of America)
A History of Zen Buddhism. (Faber and Faber)

Gabb, W. J. *The Goose is Out*. (The Buddhist Society, London)

Fromm, Suzuki, and de Martino. *Zen Buddhism and Psycho-analysis*. (Harper, New York)

Herrigel, Eugen. *Zen in the Art of Archery*. (Routledge and Kegan Paul)
The Method of Zen. (Routledge and Kegan Paul)

Humphreys, Christmas. *Zen Comes West*. (Allen and Unwin)
Teach Yourself Zen. (E.U.P.)

Leggett, Trevor. *A First Zen Reader*. (Tuttle)

Linssen, Robert. *Living Zen*. (Allen and Unwin)

Luk, Charles. *Ch'an and Zen Teaching* (3 vols). (Rider)

Leggett, Trevor. *A First Zen Reader*. (Tuttle)

Masunaga, Reiho. *The Soto Approach to Zen*. (Layman Buddhist Society Press, Japan)

Ogata, Sohaku. *Zen for the West*. (Rider)

Reps, Paul. *Zen Flesh, Zen Bones*. (Tuttle)

Senzaki and McCandless. *Buddhism and Zen*. (Philosophical Library, New York)

Suzuki, Daisetz Teitaro. *Studies in Zen*. (Rider)
Mysticism, Christian and Buddhist. (Allen and Unwin)
Zen and Japanese Buddhism. (Japan Travel Bureau)
Zen and Japanese Culture. 2nd and Enlarged Edition. (Pantheon, New York)

Watts, Alan. *The Way of Zen*. (Thames and Hudson; Penguin Books)

'Wei Wu Wei', *Fingers Pointing Towards the Moon*. (Routledge and Kegan Paul)
Why Lazarus Laughed. (Routledge and Kegan Paul)
Ask the Awakened. (Routledge and Kegan Paul)

Tibetan Buddhism

David-Neel, Alexandra, and Lama Yongden. *The Secret Oral Teachings in Tibetan Buddhism Sects*. (Maha Bodhi Society, Calcutta)

Evans-Wentz, W. Y. *The Tibetan Book of the Great Liberation*. (Oxford)

Govinda, The Lama Anagarika. *Foundations of Tibetan Mysticism*. (Rider)

Guenther, H. V. *Sgam-po-pa. The Jewel Ornament of Liberation.* (Rider)

Harrer, Heinrich. *Seven Years in Tibet.* (Hart-Davis)

Hoffmann, Helmut. *The Religions of Tibet.* (Allen and Unwin)

Maraini, Fosco. *Secret Tibet.* (Hutchinson)

Norbu, Thubten, Jigme, and Harrer, Heinrich. *Tibet is my Country.* (Hart-Davis)

Pallis, Marco. *The Way and the Mountain.* (Peter Owen)

Riencourt, Amaury de. *Lost World: Tibet, Key to Asia.* (Victor Gollancz)

Snellgrove, David. *Buddhist Himalaya.* (Bruno Cassirer)

Tucci, Guiseppe. *To Lhasa and Beyond.* (Instituto Poligrafico Dello Stato, Rome)

Meditation

Conze, Edward. *Buddhist Meditation.* (Allen and Unwin)

Nyaponika, Thera. *The Heart of Buddhist Meditation.* (Word of the Buddha Publishing Committee, Colombo)

Buddhist Art

Gray, Basil. *Buddhist Cave Paintings at Tun-Huang.* (Faber)

Gordon, Antoinette. *Tibetan Religious Art.* (Columbia, New York)

Groslier, Bernard, and Arthaud, Jacques. *Angkor.* (Thames and Hudson)

Herrigel, Gustie L. *Zen in the Art of Flower Arrangement.* (Routledge and Kegan Paul)

Lad, Shri P. M. *The Way of the Buddha.* (Government of India)

Le May, Reginald. *The Culture of South-East Asia.* (Allen and Unwin)

Marshall, Sir John. *The Buddhist Art of Gandhara.* (Cambridge)

Saunders, E. Dale. *Mudra.* (Routledge and Kegan Paul)

Silva-Vigier, Anil de. *The Life of the Buddha.* (Phaidon)

Sis, Vladimir, and Vanis, Jan. *Tibetan Art.* (Spring Books)

Watson, William. *Sculpture of Japan.* (Studio Ltd)

Scriptures

Blofeld, John. *The Zen Teaching of Huang-Po on the Transmission of Mind.* (Rider)

Conze, Edward. *The Buddha's Law among the Birds.* (Bruno Cassirer)

Buddhist Wisdom Books. (Allen and Unwin)

Selected Sayings from the Perfection of Wisdom. (Buddhist Society, London)

Shaw, R. D. M. *The Blue Cliff Records* (Hekiganroku). (Michael Joseph)

Anthologies

Burtt, E. A. *The Teachings of the Compassionate Buddha.* (New American Library)

Conze, Edward. *Buddhist Scriptures*. (Penguin)
  Buddhist Texts. (Bruno Cassirer)
Head and Cranston. *Reincarnation*. (Julian Press, N.Y.)
Humphreys, Christmas. *A Buddhist Students' Manual*. (Buddhist Society, London)
  A Popular Buddhist Dictionary. (Arco)
  The Wisdom of Buddhism. (Michael Joseph)
Nyanatiloka, Thera. *Buddhist Dictionary*. (Frewin, Colombo)
Ross, Nancy Wilson. *The World of Zen*. (Random House, New York)

THE BUDDHIST SCRIPTURES IN ENGLISH

I have not been consistent in my reference to the Buddhist Scriptures, first because few students have a translation of the entire Canon available, as a Christian has the Bible at his elbow, and, secondly, because I have in many cases quoted a scholar's quotation from a Scripture without knowing whose translation the writer was using or whence it came. Again, it seems of more use to the ordinary reader to be given a reference to the work whence the quotation was taken, which may be obtainable from a public library, than an exact reference which not one in a thousand can verify. In the First Appendix will be found brief notes on the Buddhist Scriptures of both schools; here may at least be given some of the best-known volumes of such material.

The Theravada Canon
The Pali Text Society have now published, through the Oxford University Press (Agents: Luzac & Co.), almost the entire Pali Canon in English. Many of these 136 volumes, and the additional *Sacred Books of the Buddhist Series*, are now out of print, but reprinting is always in progress as funds are available to supply the demand. The latest information may always be obtained from the Hon. Secretary, Miss I. B. Horner, M.A., at 30 Dawson Place, W2, or from Luzac & Co., 41 Great Russell Street, WC1.
Many of the Buddhist Scriptures of both Schools will be found in the *Sacred Books of the East*, edited by the late Professor Max Müller (O.U.P.), and others, usually in extracts, in the *Wisdom of the East Series* (Murray).
A large anthology of the Pali Canon was published in 1906 by Harvard University, as *Buddhism in Translations*, by Henry Clarke Warren.
The Life of Gotama the Buddha, by E. H. Brewster, is composed of extracts from the Pali Canon.
Buddhist Scriptures, a Selection translated from the Pali by Dr E. J. Thomas, and his later version, *The Road to Nirvana*, are short

anthologies in the *Wisdom of the East Series*. *The Quest of Enlightenment* is a later selection from the Sanskrit. *Gotama the Buddha*, by Ananda Coomaraswamy and I. B. Horner, is excellent, though regrettably out of print, whilst *Some Sayings of the Buddha*, translated by the late F. L. Woodward, is still the most popular small anthology. Dr Conze's *Buddhist Texts* contain 100 pages from this School of Buddhism, translated by Miss I. B. Horner.

The Mahayana Canon

There is no such thing as a Mahayana Canon, though several small anthologies from the vast field of Mahayana works are now available. The oldest is Beal's *Catena of the Buddhist Scriptures* (1871). Dwight Goddard's *Buddhist Bible* (1932) included a résumé of the four 'favourite scriptures of the Zen sect', and was largely expanded in a second edition (1938). Dr E. J. Thomas' *The Perfection of Wisdom* is a selection of works from the Sanskrit, and *Chinese Buddhist Verse*, translated by Richard Robinson, overlaps it very little. *Buddhist Psalms*, also in the *Wisdom of the East Series*, is translated by S. Yamabe and Adams Beck from the Japanese of Shinran Shonin.

Beyond these there are but translations of individual Scriptures, such as the *Saddharmapundarika*, or Lotus of the Good Law; the *Lankavatara*; some of the Prajnaparamita group, such as the *Diamond Sutra*; the *Awakening of Faith*; the *Lalitavistaora*; the two *Sukhavati-Vyuha*; the *Sutra of Wei Lang* (*Hui-neng*); and the *Huang-Po Doctrine of Universal Mind*. There are many more, published in different parts of the world, often in small editions, quickly exhausted. Some are to be found in the *Sacred Books of the East* Series; others in the *Wisdom of the East* Series, including Kenneth Saunders' brief excerpts in *Lotuses of the Mahayana*. Mrs B. L. Suzuki has excerpts in the *Mahayana Buddhism*, and other works have the same, but a full, accurate, and usable anthology is long overdue.

Perhaps the best equivalent to a Buddhist 'Bible' is: *Buddhist Texts through the Ages*, ed. Edward Conze. This remarkable work contains, besides 100 pages from the Pali Canon, 100 pages from Sanskrit Mahayana works, a section on the Tantras, and a fourth section of extracts from the scriptures of China and Japan. See also my own anthology, *The Wisdom of Buddhism*.

Most of the books mentioned in these pages are included in the library of the Buddhist Society, 58 Eccleston Square, London, SW1 – an organization whose object is to publish and make known the principles of Buddhism and to encourage their study and practice. Full particulars may be obtained from the General Secretary.

Index